WINNING HEARTS
AND VOTES

WINNING HEARTS AND VOTES

Social Services and the Islamist Political Advantage

Steven Brooke

CORNELL UNIVERSITY PRESS   ITHACA AND LONDON

First published 2019 by Cornell University Press

Printed in the United States of America

Library of Congress Cataloging-in-Publication Data

Names: Brooke, Steven, 1980– author.
Title: Winning hearts and votes : social services and the Islamist political advantage / Steven Brooke.
Description: Ithaca [New York] : Cornell University Press, 2019. | Includes bibliographical references and index.
Identifiers: LCCN 2018026558 (print) | LCCN 2018028970 (ebook) | ISBN 9781501730634 (pdf) | ISBN 9781501730641 (epub/mobi) | ISBN 9781501730627 | ISBN 9781501730627 (cloth ; alk. paper)
Subjects: LCSH: Jamiyat al-Ikhwan al-Muslimin (Egypt) | Islam and politics—Egypt. | Faith-based human services—Political aspects—Egypt. | Social service—Political aspects—Egypt. | Egypt—Politics and government—20th century. | Egypt—Politics and government—21st century.
Classification: LCC BP10.J383 (ebook) | LCC BP10.J383 B76 2019 (print) | DDC 361.70962—dc23
LC record available at https://lccn.loc.gov/2018026558

For Melissa and Calla

Contents

Acknowledgments

Family, friends, and colleagues have supported me in various ways as I researched and wrote this book. My parents, Linda and Tom, fostered in me a sense of intellectual curiosity and provided constant encouragement over the years. My brother Danny and his wife, Liz, ensured my work trips to Boston would be both fun and productive. My in-laws, Ann and Frank Mason, have helped in ways large and small, and I am grateful for their support. My wife, Melissa, has contributed so much. She is such a happy diversion from the matters with which this book is concerned, but without her love, patience, good humor, and sympathy I am sure it could never have been written. Our daughter, Calla, is a joy, and I would like to think that her inquisitiveness and love of adventure have helped focus my work.

Jason Brownlee has seen this project develop from its earliest iterations and has unfailingly supported it at each step. His example as a mentor and social scientist is a hard one to follow, but I look forward to trying. Tarek Masoud's interest in and enthusiasm for this project has been constant, and being able to draw on his expertise and counsel has improved my work in innumerable ways. Bob Leiken died before this book was published, but I like to think that he would have been incredibly excited to read it and find his fingerprints on it. Marc Lynch of the Project on Middle East Political Science has for over a decade encouraged my development as a scholar, and I cannot thank him enough for it. Alaa Nabil was my guide to all things Egypt and is a valued friend. Josh Stacher has always been a welcome source of guidance on matters large and small.

The list of people who helped in various ways to produce this book is far too long to mention here, but I'll try. Thanks to Khalil al-Anani, Holger Albrecht, Lauren Baker, Hala Bayoumi, Dina Bishara, Josh Blank, Nathan Brown, Dave Buckley, Matt Buehler, Melani Cammett, Mary Casey, Janine Clark, Stephanie Dahle, Zachary Elkins, Kim Guiler, Jamal Haidar, Ian Hartshorn, Kamal El-Helbawy, Clement Henry, Amaney Jamal, Trevor Johnston, Kristen Kao, Neil Ketchley, Cortni Kerr, Gabe Koehler-Derrick, Vickie Langohr, Xiaobo Lü, Phoebe Luckyn-Malone, Ellen Lust, Peter Mandaville, Monica Marks, Quinn Mecham, Kate Mertes, Rob Moser, Rich Nielsen, Liz Nugent, Sarah Parkinson, Henry Pascoe, David Patel, Sumita Pahwa, Sarah Pennington, Amanda Rizkallah, Michael Robbins, Bernard Rougier, Hesham Sallam, Jillian Schwedler, Jonah Schulhofer-Wohl, Rachel Sternfeld, Tariq Thachil, and Carrie Wickham. Manu Abdo, Khaldoun almousily, Imen Ameur, Grayson Buttler, Esraa Hanafy, Abdellatif El-Husseiny

(JC), and Jess Martin all provided excellent research help over the course of this project. A very special thanks to all those I interviewed, both in Egypt and elsewhere.

A number of friends and colleagues graciously and minutely read the entire manuscript at various stages, including Julie Chernov-Hwang, Shadi Hamid, and Aaron Rock-Singer. Dan Corstange has been remarkably generous with his time and insight, and this project is much the better for his involvement. Dan McCormack has probably suffered through more of my work than anyone else, and for that alone he deserves special thanks.

A number of institutions provided research and financial support for the project, including the U.S. Institute of Peace, the Project on Middle East Political Science, the Combating Terrorism Center, the Smith Richardson Foundation, the University of Texas at Austin, and the Middle East Initiative at the Harvard Kennedy School. I particularly acknowledge Hilary Rantisi, Julia Martin, Chris Mawhorter, and Krysten Hartman for all the work they did to make my time in Cambridge so productive. Rodger Payne, Jasmine Farrier, and my home department at the University of Louisville provided a supportive environment to push this project across the finish line.

I appreciate the feedback from participants and discussants at conferences, workshops, and talks sponsored by the American Political Science Association, the Middle East Studies Association, the Midwest Political Science Association, the University of Texas–Austin Experimental and Comparative Workshops, the Institute for Qualitative and Multi-Method Research, and the Departments of Political Science at Barnard College, the University of Louisville, and the University of Nevada–Reno. An earlier version of this manuscript was presented at the Project on Middle East Political Science Junior Scholars Book Workshop, cosponsored by the Mamdouha S. Bobst Center for Peace and Justice at Princeton University, where I received a set of incredibly helpful insights. A big kudos to the team at Cornell University Press, including Roger Haydon, Susan Specter, and Jamie Fuller, for their patience and diligence throughout the production process.

Note on Transliteration

The Arabic in this book is rendered with reference to the transliteration scheme adopted by the *International Journal for Middle East Studies (IJMES)*. Diacritics (macrons and dots) are used except in personal names, place names, organizations, and titles of books and articles. As per that system, initial *hamzas* (') have been dropped, but medial and final *hamzas* (') and the letter *'ayn* (') have always been rendered. Words that appear in *Merriam-Webster's Collegiate Dictionary* (e.g., shaykh) as well as those exceptions identified by *IJMES* (e.g., Qu'ran) are rendered as they appear in those two sources. When living individuals have a preferred Anglicized spelling for their own names, I use that rather than a standard transliteration.

There is a small concession to the above general rules for the peculiarities of the Egyptian dialect. Egypt-specific names of individuals and geographic places are transliterated with a "g," representing the Egyptian pronunciation of the Arabic letter *jīm*. So Gamal 'Abd al-Nasir rather than Jamal 'Abd al-Nasir, Rod al-Farag rather than Rod al-Faraj. Official names of organizations and general concepts, however, are rendered traditionally with a "j," hence al-Jam'iyya al-Shar'iyya, or Dhū al-Ḥijja.

WINNING HEARTS AND VOTES

SOCIAL SERVICES AND POLITICAL MOBILIZATION IN NONDEMOCRATIC REGIMES

Citizens around the world rely on nonstate actors to school their children, treat their aging parents, or find themselves meaningful employment. In established democracies this type of activity is so commonplace that a prominent strain of democratic theory suggests that it is crucial to "making democracy work" (Putnam 1994). Sometimes these diffuse civic benefits take a backseat to instrumental ones, such as when providers use social services to mobilize voters or build dense organizational ties (Thachil 2014a; Cammett 2014).

Given the mobilizing potential of nonstate provision, why has this phenomenon also proliferated in autocracies? Why do regimes that so tightly monitor and control the political space allow a variety of nonstate providers, opposition organizations prominent among them, to operate social service networks that reach millions of citizens per year? Under what conditions can these organizations use social service provision to mobilize voters against the regime? In these cases, what is the nature of the "linkage" that social service provision forges between provider organization and recipient? (Kitschelt 2000).

This book builds a theory of nonstate social service provision that attempts to answer these questions. I show how nondemocratic regimes often relax constraints on these providers in order to buoy citizen welfare and navigate out of the dangerous waters of economic crisis. But this decision triggers consequences that become clear only in the years that follow. As these provider organizations become increasingly enmeshed in citizens' daily lives, the regime's ability to prevent them from politicizing their provision decreases.

Social service provision scatters the seeds of political mobilization widely, but only some fall on fertile soil. I argue that organizations who direct social services toward the poor—motivated, for example, by charity or clientelism—will generally struggle to realize political benefits from their provision. First, relying on an indigent population will restrict the reach and character of their provision, limiting its appeal to those citizens with few other options to satisfy their needs. Second, many of these poorer beneficiaries will already owe their political loyalties to proregime patrons and will be reluctant to risk that relationship by voting for the provider organization instead. In contrast, providers that target the middle class can use the stable financial flows produced by paying customers to generate consistent and quality care that broadcasts a powerful impression of honesty, professionalism, and compassion. By using the less politicized interactions that occur in the realm of social service provision, a provider organization can tangibly demonstrate that its walk matches its talk, producing reputation-based linkages with that very bloc of citizens which is most likely to support the opposition in less-than-democratic elections.

The remainder of this chapter introduces the key themes of the book, situates the argument in the current literature, and summarizes the core contribution. I begin by discussing the case that motivates my investigation: the Muslim Brotherhood in Egypt and, specifically, its largest and oldest social service affiliate: the Islamic Medical Association (IMA). Tightly focusing on a single organization consciously exchanges generalizability for specificity. But this trade-off is justifiable given that speculation about the Brotherhood's social service provision—how it relates to the regime, the ways it is run, and who it serves—has often run beyond the evidence. As it turns out, more closely assessing this evidence reveals a series of puzzles that can generate insight into areas of much broader interest. The following sections synthesize literatures on authoritarianism, party-voter linkages, and Islamist politics to identify three of these questions and ground them in larger contexts. The remaining sections preview the core argument and evidence, describe the research strategy, and outline the plan of the book.

The Mysterious Muslim Brotherhood

Egypt under Anwar al-Sadat (r. 1970–81) and Hosni Mubarak (r. 1981–2011) was a prototypical example of those regimes that combine limited electoral competition with an array of coercive strategies both heavy-handed and subtle (Brownlee 2007).[1] But under both men, nonstate social service providers, Islamist groups like the Muslim Brotherhood prominent among them, also dramatically expanded their profile. In her pioneering book *Mobilizing Islam* Carrie Wickham (2002) captured the dramatic growth of this "parallel Islamic sector" that encompassed charitable societies, cultural and social organizations, mosques, and businesses.

This seems odd. Why would any authoritarian regime countenance the existence of an opposition network with the ability to, as Sheri Berman put it, reach into "practically every nook and cranny of Egyptian life" (2003, 261)? This would be a dangerous strategy for even the most secure autocrat. As Tarek Masoud argues in his own intricate account of this era, "no authoritarian regime worthy of the name would allow such a thing" (2014a, 76). But as we will see, the Muslim Brotherhood's electoral potency stemmed in large part from its expansive social service networks.

Ideally, arguments about the Brotherhood's social service networks could be adjudicated with reference to evidence. But data on the phenomenon are frustratingly hard to come by. One cannot identify whom the Brotherhood's networks serve, how large they are, how they function, where they exist, or how they relate to the state.[2] Even those most familiar with Egypt and the Brotherhood have described the difficulties of studying this sector of the group's activism (Bibars 2001, 107; Shukr 2006, 7; Masoud 2008, 147). One author even claims that examining the subject is an "impossible task" (M. Abdelrahman 2004, 122). This is why, as Melani Cammett and Pauline Jones Luong concluded in a recent review article, critical aspects of Islamist social service efforts have been "presumed rather than demonstrated" (2014, 188).

In the face of anecdotal and conflicting evidence, it is difficult to investigate even the most basic claims about the Brotherhood's social services, let alone attempt to understand this activity in light of broader theoretical literature. Thus the purpose of this book is twofold. First, I produce a variety of new historical, qualitative, spatial, and experimental data on the largest and oldest component of the Muslim Brotherhood's social service network—the Islamic Medical Association—to add empirical weight to a subject long shrouded in speculation and presumption. Second, I use this specific and prominent case to gain theoretical insights into the broader phenomenon of nonstate social service provision, opposition activism, and political mobilization in nondemocratic regimes. The following section zooms back out, extracting from this specific case the three interrelated theoretical questions that drive this book.

Three Perspectives, Three Puzzles

Three interlinked questions structure the inquiry that follows. Scholars have begun to devote increasing attention to the political impact of nonstate service providers but have generally neglected cases in which opportunities for political mobilization are far more circumscribed. Thus the first question isolates the regime, specifically asking why the same autocrats who jealously guard political power allow a variety of opposition organizations to engage in activities that reach broad swaths of the citizenry. Operating under these regimes, however, are multiple nonstate providers, only some of whom transform their provision into political mobilization. Thus the second guiding question shifts the level of analysis to the organization to identify the conditions under which providers operating in nondemocratic contexts are able to use social service provision to amass electoral support. The final question centers on the individual: In cases where social service provision is producing political effects, what exactly is the nature of the relationship between provider and beneficiary?

Scholars have put forward various answers for each of these three questions. They have juxtaposed the opposition's civil society potency with state debility, focused on the ideological (religious) nature of certain provider groups to explain their mobilizing potential, and turned to sprawling literatures on clientelism to explain the mechanism through which this provision generates political support. While all these accounts provide important insights into the broad phenomenon, they also leave conspicuous questions unanswered and often stand at odds with key pieces of evidence drawn from perhaps the most prominent case of an organization that combined social service provision and political success, the Egyptian Muslim Brotherhood.

The Regime

Coordination between the opposition usually augurs the end of nondemocratic regimes (Van de Walle 2006; Gandhi and Reuter 2008). Autocrats understand this well, so they spend a great deal of energy and rely on a variety of strategies to keep citizens isolated and demobilized (Kuran 1991). At the extreme, the Eastern bloc–style totalitarian regimes systematically pulverized their societies, stripping citizens of even the most benign social ties that could potentially produce organized opposition (Arendt 1973; Linz 1975; Howard 2003). Even "milder" authoritarian regimes use styles of corporatist management to segment societies (Schmitter 1979; Bianchi 1989) and tinker with electoral institutions to keep opposition parties from coalescing (Lust-Okar 2005).

At the same time, scholars have noticed among Middle Eastern autocrats "a now well-entrenched trend . . . to hand over economic activities to nonstate actors" (Vandewalle 1992, 110). But nonstate social service provision could reasonably be expected to produce the very types of social capital and group solidarities that make risky collective action, up to and including insurgency and revolution, happen (McAdam 1986; Wickham 2002). More mildly, this activity also seems ideally placed to provide exactly the types of face-to-face interactions that have proven to be such a potent driver of electoral mobilization elsewhere (Gerber and Green 2000; Calvo and Murillo 2013). Regimes, assumedly, know this too: Nathan Brown explains that "social services formally provided by the state have been taken on by a welter of movements . . . but regimes become suspicious and repressive when such social activity is linked to political opposition (2012, 1). Despite these clear risks, even hegemonic single-party regimes like China (Spires 2011) and pre-Arab Spring Syria (Pierret and Selvik 2009) feature social service organizations that have managed to carve out some degree of independence. Why would any autocrat voluntarily trigger the very process that might culminate in their overthrow?

Perhaps certain providers are particularly proficient at staying off the radar of the regime. Spires (2011), in his study of unsanctioned civil society activism in China, finds that these associations manage to exist because of bureaucratic fragmentation that makes effective oversight difficult. Indeed, in her aforementioned study Carrie Wickham explains that "the flexibility and decentralization of the parallel Islamic sector were not coincidental; rather, they reflect the Islamists' efforts to evade government control" (2002, 105).[3] In his study of Mubarak-era corporatism, Robert Bianchi explains how Islamists evaded regime interference by remaining "extralegal organizations that refuse to register with the Ministry of Social Affairs" (1989, 193). Other authors often analyze Islamists' social service activism as a classic Gramscian "war of position" purposively directed toward those spaces where the state is weakest (Awadi 2004, 2005). As Quintan Wiktorowicz and Suha Taji-Farouki summarize, "rather than directly confronting the state or participating in formal politics, Islamic NGOs are engaged in social struggle at the level of cultural discourse and values" (2000, 686).

These types of explanations are attractive in that they track with a general narrative of the declining capacity of the post-1967 Arab state. Indeed, I argue that state weakness, in particular *fiscal* weakness, plays an important role in the emergence of nonstate providers in nondemocratic regimes. But what complicates the above explanations is that while certain state capacities indeed shrank during this period, the state's ability to monitor and control civil society remained quite robust. If anything, it dramatically *expanded* over the years to the point of hegemony (Wiktorowicz 2004; Tadros 2011).

During the 1960s laws designed to regulate the social and charitable sector diffused across the Arab World (Jamal 2009). Egypt was no different (Agati 2006). There, the "landmark piece of corporatist legislation" that is Law 32 of 1964 and its successor, Law 84 of 2002, gave the regime "uniform and virtually complete control over all [associations]" (Berger 1970, 96). In Denis Sullivan's study of Egyptian voluntary organizations, he tells us that "the Private Voluntary

Organization (PVO) structure and networks provide the government with direct oversight, and in many cases control, over these nongovernmental organizations" (1994, 1–2). The result, as Sami Zubaida puts it simply, is that in Egypt "civil society in the form of voluntary associations is essentially dependent on the 'law-state'" (1992, 4).

In light of this expanding monitoring capacity, we might expect that, as the authors above intuited, Islamists tried to remain informal or create shell companies to evade surveillance. But the empirical evidence suggests that the Brotherhood's social service enterprises were anything but under the radar. In fact, the Brotherhood's Islamic Medical Association was so integrated into the Egyptian state's health care infrastructure that it submitted receipts to, and received reimbursements from, the government for health care provided to the citizenry. Other examples of the Brotherhood's meticulous fidelity to regime rules are legion in the empirical record. For instance, the January 1979 issue of the official Egyptian legal gazette—*al-Waqa'i' al-Misriyya*—carried a short notification. The IMA had received as a donation a 1975 Volkswagen Microbus (motor number 823029, vehicle registration number 368642) that was being used as an ambulance/hearse. Seeking an official tax exemption for the vehicle, the IMA had submitted this information to the Egyptian government. The government granted the request and printed the material in the public record.[4] This type of minute and voluntary compliance with the regime's bureaucracy is hard to square with suggestions that "the main focus of the [Islamist] movement has been upon informal grass-roots associations, avoiding formal institutions since these tend to be controlled and monitored by the state" (M. Zaki 1995, 63). Instead, the regime was able to wrap the Brotherhood's social service activism in various layers of legal control, seemingly with full compliance from the Muslim Brotherhood itself.

The Organization

Given extensive regime oversight of its social service activism, how and why was the Brotherhood able to realize political support from these endeavors? The group's ability to make consistent electoral gains was remarkable in Egypt, where for almost forty years a froth of electoral competition lay atop a deep well of authoritarian stability (Kassem 1999; Kienle 2001; Brownlee 2007; Blaydes 2011, Masoud 2014a).

Comparative cases would suggest that particular characteristics of an organization, such as a powerful internal structure or ideologically cohesive membership, might explain how social service provision generates political support (Van Cott 2005; Anria 2013). Tariq Thachil argues that the Indian Bharatiya Janata Party (BJP) was able to draw on the "thick organizational resources" of an affiliated social movement to provide social services that proved effective at winning the support of poorer voters (2014a, 263). This "motivated cadre of . . . ideologically committed activists are willing to work for low pay," he finds, "thereby minimizing the costs of providing basic welfare" (23). Thachil even suggests that the Brotherhood might be a prime case of this argument at work beyond India (17).

Organizations able to command the support of disciplined and motivated cadres would gain a large advantage over their opponents in many spheres of activity, including political mobilization. Many authors use the Brotherhood's tight internal organization, which includes long-term programs of socialization and ideological culturing, to explain the group's social and political prowess (Trager 2011; Kandil 2014; Anani 2016). And, as I show in chapter 7, in the final months of Mohammed Morsi's turn as president, the Brotherhood began an all-out social service–based mobilization to win the support of poorer voters in a manner not dissimilar to what Thachil identified in India. The Brotherhood was one of the few Egyptian parties that could pull this off, in large part because of its ability to leverage the support of ideologically committed members willing to devote their time, talents, and treasure to further the group's political goals.

But this flurry of activity during 2013 was notable for how dissimilar it was from the Brotherhood's method of social service provision during decades of authoritarianism. For example, I began my fieldwork under the assumption that the Brotherhood's social services relied heavily on unpaid volunteers drawn from the movement. But none of those I encountered at the IMA's facilities—from the janitors to the managers—worked for free. In fact, they were paid at a rate that many conceded was quite generous relative to what they would be paid for similar work elsewhere (Clark 2004). I stubbornly persisted in my search for volunteers until one of the organization's executives told me, somewhat exasperatedly, that there was not a single volunteer worker in the IMA's network.[5] And while the employees at the headquarters as well as the management teams of individual hospitals were almost exclusively members of the Muslim Brotherhood, other employees were not. Their attitudes toward the Brotherhood ranged from sympathetic to indifferent. They worked at the IMA because they were well compensated, because the organization's approach to health care provision aligned with their own, and because it gave them opportunities for professional growth.

Networks of goods provision generally function best inside homogenous communities such as ethnic groups, where high levels of interpersonal trust and shared preferences tend to reduce transaction costs (Alesina, Baqir, and Easterly 1999; Banerjee, Iyer, and Somanathan 2005; Habyarimana et al. 2007). It may be the case, then, that the existence of dense horizontal bonds—in this case based on the perception of a shared religious mission—generates Islamist proficiency in social service provision (Hammad 1997, 187). Many of those Muslim

Brotherhood members to whom I spoke referenced their religious commitment to the idea of social service provision and justified their work specifically in those terms. Amr Darrag, a former minister in Mohammed Morsi's government, explains that the group's motivations for social service provision "are not traditionally the most expedient or the most utilitarian, but rather are principled and faith-based" (2017, 222).[6]

Emphasizing the ideological dimensions of social service provision is not simply an attractive explanation for why some groups are more effective at providing social services than others; it can also explain the mechanisms through which this activism shapes the attitudes and behaviors of recipients.[7] Salwa Ismail argues that any citizen seeking to access the resources of the Islamic charitable sector must present "herself not only as supplicant but as a deserving one in both material and moral senses" (2006, 77). Mona Atia's study of the expansion of Islamic charity in Egypt focuses on a similar process. "Direct aid," she notes, "comes with an obligation to attend religious and disciplinary lessons, inextricably linking Islamic charity to da'wa (religious outreach)" (2013, 75). Eric Trager claims that the goal of the Brotherhood is "the long-term Islamization of Egyptian society through the provision of social services" (2011, 122). Other authors note how the repeated emphasis on religion in social activism "reshap[es] the identities of the targeted people" (Eligür 2010, 27) or "chang[es] the preferences of educated youth" (Wickham 2002, 148).

There are unmistakably ideological—more specifically religious—aspects to the Brotherhood's social service provision. A key feature of the movement is precisely this sense of religious mission, what the author of the classic work on the Brotherhood described as "an idea and a personal commitment honestly felt" (Mitchell 1987, 79). But in light of the above authors' emphasis on ideological conversion and even indoctrination, one thing that stuck out fairly starkly about the Brotherhood's social service provision was the lack of an overtly religious or politicized atmosphere in the facilities. Not only were these services staffed by employees with little or no connection to the Brotherhood, but the IMA went to great lengths to dissociate itself from any political or ideological mission. The IMA's logo, displayed prominently at every facility, emphasized how the group provided care without discrimination "on the basis of religion, nationality, or social class."

This could have been just an act, obscuring the real recruitment or ideological indoctrination that was occurring away from the prying eyes of the regime and the public (or Western researchers). During the course of my fieldwork, I obtained an internal disciplinary letter sent from the IMA management in Cairo to the director of an IMA hospital in the Nile delta. This hospital director, the letter intimated, had been campaigning for the Muslim Brotherhood politician (and later Egyptian president) Mohammed Morsi while on the job. In the letter the IMA management warned the offending hospital director to cease his politicking and reminded him of the IMA's dedication to serve all Egyptians. We "do not provide any support to any party or trend or person," the letter reads. Instead "we deal respectfully with all of them."[8] Why would an organization instrumentally using its social services to generate ideological change or political support formally rebuke a member who was trying to do just that?

The Citizen

Nondemocratic regimes host extensive social service networks operated by opposition organizations, and some are quite proficient at using this activism to build political support. In these cases, what is the exact nature of the mechanism connecting provider to ordinary citizen?

Melani Cammett rightly notes that failures of governance set the conditions under which "welfare can become a terrain of political contestation" (2014, 5). Post-Nasir Egypt, where continual fiscal crises, surging urbanization, and crumbling public services created numerous cracks into which nonstate providers could flow, is a prime example. These conditions forced Egyptians to become masters at cobbling together the resources to meet their daily needs. Mariz Tadros, for example, discusses how residents of a Cairo neighborhood might secure the necessities of life: "[A] woman from [the neighborhood of] Bulaq el Dakrour might have her blood pressure taken in the nearby pharmacy; her glasses done at the Wafd [political] Party Health Centre, her blood tests taken at a private clinic, dental care sought at a government teaching hospital while sending her daughter to the female doctor at a Muslim association (a registered service-providing NGO) for gynecological treatment" (2006, 248).

We can easily see how this creates the conditions for providers to begin politicizing their provision. Tadros even mentions one provider that obviously is: the Wafd party. But this proliferation of nonstate providers of every stripe and persuasion complicates efforts to uncover the sources of the Brotherhood's advantage (Cammett and Jones Luong 2014, 193). As Lisa Anderson tells us, Islamist parties "not only effectively discredited the regimes by providing services in their stead but—and this was critical to their capacity to seize the terrain of opposition—*they also outperformed the secular political opposition*" (1997, 24, emphasis added). So instead of attempting to explain why the Brotherhood was so adept at linking social services to political mobilization, we should be examining why other political parties and social movements, such as the Wafd, failed to realize the same gains as the Brotherhood (Masoud 2014a).

It may be that the Brotherhood's social services function essentially as clientelism, the provision of material payoffs in exchange for political support

(S. Stokes 2005; Kitschelt and Wilkinson 2007b; Nichter 2008; Lust 2009). Observers often charge the Brotherhood with using their social services to "bribe" voters.[9] Perhaps when beneficiaries of the Brotherhood's social services turn out on election day, they are simply holding up their end of a clientelist bargain.

The Brotherhood is certainly not above crude vote buying, and in chapter 7 I explore how the liberalization in political competition following Mubarak's fall offered the Brotherhood the chance to do just this. But treating social service provision as a more restrained version of vote buying would need to answer why myriad other Egyptian political parties who did exactly this could not match the Brotherhood's electoral success. Consider this dispatch from the official newspaper of Egypt's opposition Wafd party (who had provided the eyeglasses for the resident of Bulaq al-Dukrur above) describing one of the party's campaign rallies in the Suez governorate: "Doctor al-Sayyid al-Badawi, head of the Wafd Party, confirmed that throughout the past years the party's social role has been no less beneficial to the people than the party's political role. He pointed to the tens of thousands of citizens who found in the party's clinics free medical exams by well-regarded professors of medicine, free surgical procedures in the best hospitals, and the distribution of numerous medicines, all free of charge."[10] Even Hosni Mubarak's son and heir apparent Gamal used targeted provision of medical services in an attempt to restore the National Democratic Party's (NDP's) shine during the waning years of the regime.[11] As these brief reports suggest, many parties tried to use social service provision instrumentally, trading things like medical care for support on election day. But if all parties did so, then what accounts for the Brotherhood's apparently singular ability to wring political rewards from this activity?

At the Wafd party rally, Dr. al-Badawi boasted (three times in one sentence, in fact) that the services his party offered to citizens were all free. This was not technically true, of course: recipients were just expected to repay the care with their votes on election day rather than with cash on the spot; if they weren't going to vote for the Wafd, they wouldn't get the care. Herbert Kitschelt and Steven Wilkinson underline how this idea of contingency and reciprocity underpins the entire clientelist transaction: "The politician's delivery of a good is *contingent upon* the actions of specific members of the electorate. . . . What makes clientelist exchange different is not simply the fact that benefits are targeted. Rather, it is the fact that politicians target a range of benefits *only* to individuals or identifiable small groups who have already delivered or who promise to deliver their electoral support to their partisan benefactor" (2007a, 10, emphasis in original).

But the details of the IMA's particular style of social service provision complicate clientelist-style analyses in one key aspect: just as there were no volunteers in the IMA, the vast majority of patients at its facilities were middle-class Egyptians who had paid, in cash, for the services received. During the course of my research I obtained almost a decade's worth of internal audit sheets from the facilities in the IMA's network, including the types of visitors broken down by whether or not they had paid for the care received. Never did the percentage of charity cases rise above 5 percent of the total patients. If the overwhelming majority of the visitors to IMA facilities were middle-class Egyptians who paid on the spot in cash for the services they received, then why should we expect them to have felt the need to pay again with their votes on election day?

All the above factors—from state weakness to organizational identity to the power of material exchange—undoubtedly help explain aspects of why the Brotherhood was so successful at connecting social service provision to political mobilization. But they also leave important theoretical questions unanswered and uncomfortably coexist with key pieces of empirical evidence. The next section builds on these approaches but ultimately departs from them to explain the relationship between social service provision and opposition electoral mobilization in nondemocratic regimes.

The Argument in Brief

Economic crisis is a particularly dangerous moment for autocrats because they are forced to choose between persevering on an unsustainable fiscal trajectory or risking an unpredictable series of reforms. In these moments, off-loading social service provision to nonstate providers—"privatization by NGO"—becomes a palatable option (Harvey 2006, 51–52). In the short term these providers, particularly in realms of health and education, can serve as shock absorbers for a vulnerable citizenry. And in these early years regimes can use a variety of bureaucratic and legal mechanisms to ensure these providers remain domesticated. This strategy allows regimes to retrench social spending to meet budgetary demands yet mitigate the risk of broad social and political upheaval often associated with the implementation of austerity measures.

Initial decisions shape long-term trajectories, generating feedback that makes it increasingly difficult to change course even as costs build (David 1985; Arthur 1989; Mahoney 2000). So while encouraging the growth of these organizations provides immediate relief for an economic pinch, as nonstate provider organizations sink their roots deeper and deeper into the society, the regime's ability to credibly threaten these organizations with sanction and closure declines. This dynamic eventually traps the regime in a situation where it must either acquiesce to a steady erosion of control over these providers or dramatically crack down and potentially provoke mass mobilization by suddenly aggrieving citizens.

Effectively, autocrats who choose to shift social welfare onto nonstate providers are bargaining away their future for their present.

The character of the authoritarian political economy structures the opportunities available to voters, and this exercises a dramatic influence over which organization will be able to successfully politicize its social service provision. Electoral authoritarian regimes often sprawl across the socioeconomic landscape unevenly, establishing strongholds in certain constituencies while bypassing others. In most cases, the key cleavage separating enclaves that staunchly support the regime from those where competition is freer is an economic one: poorer constituencies tend to yield regime electoral monopolies, while more affluent ones create the space for greater competition and, potentially, gains by the opposition (Magaloni 2006; Greene 2007; Blaydes 2011; Masoud 2014a).

The reason this is so has to do with characteristics of both the vote buyer and the vote seller. Poor voters offer the resource-maximizing political machine the possibility of mobilizing the largest number of voters for the smallest material outlay. A vote-buying dollar simply stretches further in poorer districts than in wealthier ones. For their part, poor citizens' more immediate material needs ensure that they will most readily sideline their long-term programmatic and ideological preferences for a short-term payoff (Diaz-Cayeros, Magaloni, and Weingast 2006). "The poor," Asef Bayat quips, "cannot afford to be ideological" (2007b, 588). More affluent voters, in contrast, can more easily ignore offers to buy their votes and make "ideological investments" in the opposition (Magaloni 2006, 22). Any opposition party who can appeal to these middle-class voters would possess a significant built-in advantage (Masoud 2014a). While their competitors were attempting to chisel poorer voters loose from the regime's pillars of support, these parties could rely on a constituency most able to support an opposition candidate.

This is where a social service provider's initial decisions about which audience it decides to target matters. A concentration of poor voters makes a district particularly attractive to politicians who rely largely on clientelism. And in nondemocratic contexts, the resource advantages of the regime (or proregime candidates) tend to create solid monopolies in these poorer, highly clientelist districts (Greene 2007). Thus any organization who targets social service provision to the less affluent—for instance, by providing charity—is *also* targeting those voters who are least able to translate that provision into antiregime political mobilization. In contrast, if the provider's social services disproportionately serve middle-class citizens, then they will also be targeting those who are much more free to vote for the opposition.

Better-off voters tend to be troubled by clientelism, seeing it both as morally compromised and, more instrumentally, as a signal of low-quality governance

(Weitz-Shapiro 2014). Thus provider organizations who eschew such a transactional model are quite well positioned to appeal to middle-class voters both because they are physically embedded in those neighborhoods *and* because the style of their provision speaks directly to the concerns of those voters. Specifically, when social service provision is depoliticized, technically competent, and relationally enjoyable, it can create a powerful impression about the "brand" of that provider organization (D. Stokes 1963). These visceral affiliations of the provider organization with certain characteristics held in high regard by the citizenry—traits like honesty, modesty, and competence—acquire outsized importance in the information-poor atmosphere of a less-than-democratic election. Amid a crowded field of opposition parties and candidates each claiming to be singularly honest or particularly hardworking, social service provision becomes a tangible symbol of a party's commitment to these issues (Cammett and Jones Luong 2014). In contrast to other opposition parties' nebulous claims and the regime's corruption and incompetence, a provider organization that can offer high-quality social service provision is especially well placed to convince middle-class voters that their candidates' are worthy of political support.

Specifying Social Services

Social service provision has been an integral part of the Muslim Brotherhood since Hasan al-Banna founded the organization in 1928 (Brooke and Ketchley 2018). As the movement spread, it offered social services to the population, including a variety of clinics and schools (M. S. Zaki 1980; Dasuqi and al-Abadi 2013). Yet this network did not survive the rule of Gamal 'Abd al-Nasir (r. 1954–70), who seized and shuttered these organizations as he brought the Brotherhood to heel in the 1950s and 1960s. Those Muslim Brothers whom Anwar al-Sadat began to release in the 1970s were forced to reckon with the reality that their organization—which had once claimed hundreds of thousands of members across all corners of the country—was now barely more than a clique of aging and out-of-touch ex-cons. Yet from this dispiriting realization, the Brotherhood rebuilt both its internal organization and its connections to Egyptian society, in large part as a result of its adept provision of social services.

"Social services" include school supplies, job training, child rearing and education, medical and health services, and other similar endeavors. I follow prior investigations and limit myself to the health sector (Morsy 1988; Clark 2004; Challand 2008; Cammett and Issar 2010; Cammett 2011, 2014). One benefit of medical services is that they tend toward the universal in their appeal to the population. Other types of social services usually target some specific subset (wedding services cater to younger people and schools to those with children, for example). Some of these services also imply potentially stronger background selection effects. For instance, only those with a preexisting degree of piety might attend a Qu'ranic study circle or send their children to a religious school. All of these types of activities may generate political support. But orienting the study around sickness and health—concepts to which every citizen can relate on the most basic level—maximizes its relevance.

There is a wide array of nonstate health providers in Egypt, and many assume a religious tint: mosque and church associations, family foundations, and nation-wide charity networks. One way I distinguish this book is by an explicit organizational focus on the Muslim Brotherhood. Earlier studies of Islamic social activism have yielded valuable evidence on mobilization (Wickham 2002); middle-class networks (Clark 2004); the interface of charity, religion, and neoliberalism (Harrigan and El-Said 2009; Atia 2013; Tuğal 2013; Mittermaier 2014); relations with the state (Wiktorowicz 2000; Harmsen 2008); and economic development (Sullivan 1994; Sullivan and Abed-Kotob 1999). Yet these studies have tended to examine a broad *Islamic* sector, rather than a specific organization like the Muslim Brotherhood.

Given the aforementioned difficulties that pertain to studying the Brotherhood's social service networks, I restrict focus in this book to one Brotherhood social service affiliate in particular: the Islamic Medical Association. While I lack systematic data on the overall size and apportionment of the Brotherhood's total social service portfolio, a variety of evidence points to the IMA as the most important and oldest social service affiliate of the Muslim Brotherhood. In a book published by the Brotherhood in 2011, the author referred to the IMA as "the largest medical charity initiative established by the Brotherhood to date" (Shammakh 2011, 86). As another measure of the IMA's importance, the Brotherhood's flagship Arabic-language magazine *al-Da'wa* covered the IMA prominently and consistently from the magazine's founding in 1976 until the magazine was shuttered after Egyptian President Anwar al-Sadat's assassination in 1981.[12] From 1976 to 1981, the magazine contained thirteen articles about or advertisements and announcements from the IMA.[13] The next most prominent social service initiative that *al-Da'wa* covered, the Brotherhood's al-Nassar Hospital in the city of Suez, appeared only a few times.[14] The IMA's prominence grew steadily throughout the Mubarak years and, by the summer of 2013, the association had an annual operations budget of around 100 million Egyptian pounds (EGP, roughly $14 million) and treated nearly two million Egyptians per year.[15] When Egypt's resurgent military regime confiscated the IMA's properties and other physical assets for their affiliation with the Muslim Brotherhood in January 2015, their value reportedly totaled nearly 300 million EGP (around

$42 million).[16] Given the infeasibility of tackling the entire portfolio of Muslim Brotherhood social services, I chose instead to study a large, prominent, and substantively important component of it, in the hope that it could build a theory relevant to broader phenomena (George and Bennett 2005).

I could have chosen to frame the study differently. For example, individuals affiliated with the Muslim Brotherhood operated a number of schools across Egypt, many of which were also seized by the regime after 2015 (Brooke 2017a). One reason I did not focus on these initiatives is related to the point above— I expected there to be some type of selection effect, whereby people who chose to send their children to a Brotherhood school were different in some systematic way from people who chose not to do so. While this is potentially also the case regarding health (a possibility I come back to throughout this book), I believe it to be less acute in this realm. And as the beginning of this chapter would indicate, data availability was a key concern. Owing to the near complete absence of preexisting data with which to study the question of the Muslim Brotherhood's social service provision, I made a conscious decision to study one service in detail rather than multiple services superficially. I freely admit to this trade off and hope that future scholars will turn to the other types of provision to build upon and revise my conclusions.

Even in the realm of health there were alternative ways of tackling the question of nonstate provision. In light of authors' arguments that the Brotherhood's social service networks operate informally, I began my research by focusing on that sector. There were episodes of informal assistance—for instance, when a Brotherhood member who happened to also be a doctor would open his personal clinic to district residents a few nights a week.[17] Authors in Egypt and elsewhere have conducted painstaking and valuable ethnographic research into these types of informal networks and their influence on political behavior (Singerman 1996; Auyero 2001). I chose to focus on formal, institutionalized provision because I found it puzzling that an authoritarian regime would allow an opposition *organization* to publicly operate dozens of facilities around the country. In these circumstances it would be less surprising to find evidence of various fly-by-night and clandestine initiatives.

I could also have focused on a single, stand-alone facility. For instance, the Muwasat (Compassionate) Association is centered in the Manufiyya governorate, and among its initiatives are a handful of hospitals (the IMA operates the flagship facility in Shibin al-Kum).[18] There are also "independent" Brotherhood hospitals scattered throughout Egypt, such as the Tiba Hospital in the delta governorate of Gharbiyya (B. Abdelrahman 2013). Focusing on a regional organization or single facility would have been a particularly valuable way to study the question of political effects. But I also seek to explain larger patterns of regional and local variation in service provision across Egypt, in particular why the Brotherhood's social service networks sprang up in certain areas but not others.

Finally, I could have focused on the use of public resources for political gain (Schady 2000). For instance, Brotherhood figures began to join government ministries after Mohammed Morsi was elected president in 2012, and some ministries (like the Ministry of Health) embarked on joint campaigns with the Brotherhood.[19] But this study would have been truncated, at one end by an authoritarian regime that prevented the Brotherhood from access to government ministries and at the other by a military coup that ejected the Brotherhood from power before it could embed patronage networks in the regime. And one of the most interesting facets of the Brotherhood's approach—and a key point of departure with the clientelism literature—was its ability to proliferate such extensive social service networks *without access to state resources.*

The Evidence

The aforementioned lack of material on Islamist social service networks is compounded, in the case of Egypt, by a regime that vigilantly guards even trivial information.[20] To accommodate these difficulties I draw from a variety of different types of evidence—historical, qualitative, spatial, and experimental—to mitigate inferential problems that arise when doing social science research in difficult contexts. But while much of the evidence in this book is original, none of it is perfect. However, to the extent that "truth lies at the confluence of independent streams of evidence" (a dictum often attributed to Karl Deutsch), it is my hope that triangulating across multiple sources and levels of analysis will increase the reader's confidence in the overall argument (Wilson 1999).

Given the scarcity of research on Islamist social service provision networks, this book marks an independent empirical contribution to the study of modern Egyptian politics. Following pathbreaking earlier investigations of the broad phenomenon of Islamic social and civic activism, a significant amount of the evidence in the following pages is qualitative (Wickham 2002; Clark 2004). This material distills a decade's worth of study of Egypt and the Brotherhood, including dozens of interviews, memoirs and oral histories, archival material, and over fifty years' worth of Egyptian laws, court cases, and media coverage. The fieldwork for this project encompassed close observation of multiple social service endeavors and interviews with managers and employees of multiple facilities both affiliated with the Muslim Brotherhood and not.

The above qualitative material is particularly valuable for the way that it illuminates causal mechanisms, such as how the Brotherhood decides to build facilities or the way it ensures that the care that it provides remains of high quality. But it also leaves intriguing patterns of social service provision and electoral mobilization unexamined. To investigate these questions I "scaled down" and leveraged subnational variation across Egypt's towns and cities (Snyder 2001). Thus this book includes a distinct spatial component, whereby I analyze a variety of ecological data on wealth, availability of public infrastructure, and new measures of electoral competition. Into these contexts I also nest the physical locations of hundreds of the Brotherhood's social service initiatives, allowing a precise examination of how they vary across the underlying sociopolitical terrain. Not only does this perspective help extend "the spatial revolution that is transforming the social sciences" to the Middle East (Kocher and Laitin 2006, 25), but it illustrates the utility of spatial and open-source research for tackling sociopolitical inquiry in data-poor environments.

The qualitative and spatial data provide important information about how these facilities are run and how they relate to underlying socioeconomic and political geographies. But these data cannot tell us how social service provision influences the beliefs and behaviors of the ordinary citizens who benefit from it. To systematically identify the microlevel effects of social service provision, in early 2014 I oversaw a survey of over 2,400 Egyptians.[21] In addition to collecting basic information about Egyptians' experiences with nonstate providers, this survey also contained a randomized experimental component. By subtly manipulating basic information presented to the respondents about medical services in Egypt, the survey yielded insights into how the Brotherhood's social service provision affected individual political attitudes, including how likely individuals were to support the Brotherhood in elections and what particular traits they perceived in the group's candidates for elected office.

Before concluding, I offer a note on sources. I carried out much of the fieldwork for this project during the 2012–13 academic year, roughly contiguous with the abbreviated presidential term of Mohammed Morsi. During that time I conducted dozens of interviews across a broad spectrum of society, from the classic man on the street to members of parliament, from Salafists to secularists. As befitting the topic of this book, many of those to whom I spoke were members of the Muslim Brotherhood. These included members active in their local communities, professionals, and administrators of various social service initiatives. I also encountered and spoke with those who, despite working in the Brotherhood's facilities, had no tie to the group. With only a few exceptions, those to whom I spoke agreed to be on the record at the time I spoke to them.

The situation dramatically changed following the July 3, 2013, military coup. Egypt's new military rulers turned the entire machinery of state on the Brotherhood, relying on disappearances, military trials, torture, and mass killing to bring the group to heel.[22] The campaign soon expanded beyond Islamists, to the point where few independent centers of activism still exist. In these circumstances any affiliation with the Brotherhood, no matter how tangential, could have serious consequences. In light of this I have chosen to anonymize the interviews with all except public figures.

Plan of the Book

The empirical parts of the book proceed roughly chronologically. It begins with an examination of the historical conditions surrounding the reemergence of the Muslim Brotherhood in the late 1970s. It continues through the Brotherhood's uncommon successes under the authoritarian regime of Hosni Mubarak and the country's brief democratic interlude after he stepped down in early 2011. It culminates in the July 3, 2013, military coup. At that time, the Brotherhood's celebrated network of social services was seized or shuttered by Egypt's new military regime. In addition to exploiting the dramatic institutional change over this period, at points in the book I use other Egyptian parties and organizations to illustrate key counterfactuals.

In the following chapter I more fully outline the theory, focusing on how economic crises can spur autocrats to begin devolving social service provision to nonstate providers. I then suggest how patterns of clientelism spatially segregate the electoral map, funneling competition to middle-class areas while trapping poorer ones under proregime monopolies. I trace how a provider's initial decisions about whom to target influence the subsequent development of that organization. Whereas wealthier beneficiaries provide financial independence for an organization and put them in contact with mobilizable voters, catering to the poor saps the quality of the enterprise while prioritizing those citizens highly unlikely to reciprocate with political support. I close by emphasizing how social service provision can speak to "valence" issues, in particular honesty, competence, and modesty, helping middle-class citizens make inferences about whom to support in nondemocratic elections.

I introduce the empirical evidence in chapter 3, examining the circumstances surrounding the founding of the Islamic Medical Association in 1977. I first show how Anwar al-Sadat encouraged the emergence of new social service providers—the Brotherhood but one among them—to help mitigate the consequences of his cuts to Egypt's social safety net. Then, using a variety of material drawn from memoirs, government documents, and contemporaneous coverage in Islamist periodicals, I tell the story of how the Brotherhood built up its social services with the financial and symbolic support of the regime. The chapter's final sections trace the escalation of the regime-Brotherhood conflict through the end of the Mubarak era. This shows how the regime steadily lost the ability to restrain the Brotherhood's social service activism even as the group lodged increasingly successful electoral challenges that were built on this provision.

Chapter 4 sketches out the internal characteristics of the Brotherhood's social service provision. After charting the collapse of public-sector facilities, I draw on multiple site visits and interviews to illustrate how the IMA envisioned and operated its social service networks effectively as businesses, targeting middle-class citizens caught between collapsing public facilities and out-of-reach private ones. This decision gave the group a steady income stream, which in turn allowed it to emphasize consistency and quality, fusing technical proficiency with bedside manner. These factors became self-reinforcing, helping the Brotherhood generate consistently high quality and compassionate care that were especially amenable to middle-class citizens upon whom the group would come to rely. The final parts of the chapter compare the Brotherhood's style of service provision with that of other parties and organizations in order to isolate how and why different styles of provision often struggle to generate political effects.

Chapter 5 begins to connect social service provision to larger dynamics of electoral mobilization. Using new subnational data on district-by-district electoral competition from 1990 to 2010 I show that Egypt's authoritarian political economy squeezed electoral competition—including the Muslim Brotherhood's candidates—toward middle-class areas and away from those locales with a predominance of less affluent voters. I then return to an implication from the historical and qualitative evidence, which suggests that the Brotherhood's "brick-and-mortar" (Cammett and Issar 2010) facilities should *also* be physically located in Egypt's wealthier areas. To drive home the connection, I show how Brotherhood candidates consistently appeared in middle-class districts with social services and, furthermore, that many of those candidates were intimately tied to those facilities as founder, funder, or manager. I close the chapter by matching a geo-located data set of precinct-level results for the 2012 Egyptian presidential elections with the locations of IMA facilities throughout Cairo to isolate the effect of proximity on pro-Brotherhood voting.

Chapter 6 examines at the individual level the connection between social service provision and electoral mobilization. The first half of the chapter uses a variety of administrative materials and information culled from site visits to highlight, from the patient's perspective, the atmosphere at the IMA's facilities. The second half introduces a 2,400-person survey experiment that allows a more systematic examination of the powerful reputational linkages the Brotherhood's social services generated with citizens. Not only does this show how social service provision can produce electoral support, but hundreds of descriptive terms about the Brotherhood's facilities drawn from survey respondents, as well as a causal mediation analysis, show how Egyptians use the high-quality and compassionate care prevalent in the Muslim Brotherhood's social service facilities to make political judgments about the group's candidates for elected office.

Although this book considers elections in less-than-democratic settings, it generates a number of empirical implications about how patterns of social service provision would be different if the institutional context were to change. Chapter 7 exploits over-time variation inside the Egyptian case—namely, Mubarak's resignation in early 2011 and the subsequent liberalization of political competition through the July 3, 2013, military coup—to examine how the *style* of the Brotherhood's social service provision shifted. A spatial data set of nearly five hundred mobile "medical caravans" dispatched by the Muslim Brotherhood in anticipation of parliamentary elections during the first half of 2013 shows that, as the NDP's monopoly over the poor disintegrated, the Brotherhood began a large-scale, and effectively clientelist, outreach strategy to mobilize exactly those constituencies. Not only does this provide a new perspective on the Islamist advantage, but it confirms the theoretical importance of considering the ways that the institutional context shapes styles of social service provision.

The conclusion sums up the findings of the prior chapters and provides a brief narrative of the Brotherhood's social service networks after the July 3, 2013, military coup. I then discuss the book's implications for how we think about authoritarian durability, opposition mobilization, Islamist electoral potency, party-movement interactions, and implications for democratic competition. I close by identifying outstanding areas of research.

MIDDLE-CLASS PROVISION, REPUTATION, AND ELECTORAL SUCCESS

Nondemocratic regimes the world over have granted to nonstate actors various degrees of freedom to operate local, regional, and national networks of goods provision. This phenomenon is particularly prevalent in the Middle East, where Islamist groups provide social services to millions of citizens per year. Why do autocrats allow this? Of all the organizations involved in social service provision, why are only some able to use this activism to generate political mobilization? And finally, what are the ways in which this social service provision affects the beliefs and behaviors of those who rely upon it?

Answering these questions requires appreciating how critical decisions, usually made in a moment of crisis, establish long-term trajectories whose consequences are neither known nor appreciated until later. For the regime, devolving power to nonstate providers helps alleviate short-term distributive burdens while minimizing the risk that aggrieved citizens will revolt. In the long term, however, this strategy makes it more and more difficult for the regime to constrain those providers' activism. Provider targeting is the other side of the coin. Organizations that focus on providing social services to less affluent populations will find their ability to generate political mobilization limited because these citizens tend to owe their loyalties to proregime patrons. In contrast, providers that focus on middle-class audiences will interact with those voters most likely to vote their preferences. The particular middle-class character of the social services helps explain the nature of the linkage connecting provider to citizen. Instead of generating clientelist ties or furnishing information about programmatic or ideological stances, social service provision can signal politically valuable traits of honesty, competence, and approachability.

Economic Crisis and Regime Survival

Economic crisis can destabilize even the most robust authoritarian regime (Pepinsky 2009). "Next to war," Henri Barkey tells us, "stabilization measures are possibly some of the most difficult sets of policies a government has to institute" (1992, 4). They take a particularly acute form in populist regimes that have used the state to drive economic growth. In their first stages of development these states experience rapid industrialization and, quite often, the extension of social safety nets to the citizenry. Yet upon exhausting the initial stages, they must reckon simultaneously with seriously contracting revenues and expanding social and economic obligations. The ensuing crisis often entails a difficult choice as regimes "find it extremely difficult to continue simultaneously with their twin developmentalist and welfarist roles" (Ayubi 1996, 336). The expansion of social safety nets, undertaken in times of plenty, now become a millstone around the neck.

These crises—and particularly the shuffling of economic winners and losers both inside the ruling coalition and in the population at large—pose a significant threat to autocrats (Svolik 2012). From the bottom, anodyne terms of "stabilization" and "adjustment" obscure often jarring changes in citizen welfare, the types of pain that can provoke exactly the kinds of mass mobilizations able to topple even the most secure autocrats (Seddon 1993; Walton and Seddon 2008; Wallace 2013). Yet allowing the status quo to persist raises the specter of economic collapse and loss of capacity, potentially threatening the autocracy from the top down (Skocpol 1979). With default looming and the possibility of regime-shaking protests prompted by spending cuts growing, a leader's incentives to adopt otherwise risky strategies that *might* stabilize the regime grow (Chiozza and Goemans 2004).

Regimes can navigate between default and revolt by devolving social provisioning to a variety of nongovernmental providers, including charities, family associations, mutual aid societies, and social organizations. Becoming what Geoff Wood (1997) calls a "franchise state" is not a panacea; for citizens, the state's withdrawal—especially from such realms as health and education—often produces notable inequalities (Huber, Mustillo, and Stephens 2008). This is particularly evident for those citizens who must rely more and more upon their limited discretionary income to access services, such as health, that they once obtained from the public sector (Stork 1989). This strategy also raises deeper questions of citizenship and accountability (Cammett 2014). But for a regime facing imminent threats of mass street protests, these are decidedly second-order concerns.

Many of those empowered by the regime's withdrawal from the social arena—including the private sector, charitable organizations, and kin-based mutual help societies—are unlikely to politicize their newfound visibility (Baylouny 2006). Yet other actors, including social movements and political parties, can also seize this opportunity to engage in new types of activism, expand existing repertoires, and make claims against the state (Kitschelt 1986; Tarrow 2011). The challenge for regimes, then, is to shift the distributive burden onto these actors' social service networks yet ensure that their ability to use that newfound social power to threaten the political order remains limited.

A strategy of "contingent symbiosis" between regime and nonstate providers allows a regime to buoy public welfare under conditions of resource scarcity (Spires 2011). But while the regime may be financially weak, it still has the ability to bring bureaucratic and legal powers to bear on those it begins to rely on. And if these more subtle strategies fail, co-optation and coercion are always an option (Bellin 2000; Heydemann 2004; Hibou 2006; Buehler 2015). So while the regimes facilitate the emergence of these nonstate provider organizations with one hand, they fetter them with the other. Invasive laws and regulations governing the civic and social sector make the provider organization's entire operation visible to the state apparatus and therefore easily manageable (Wiktorowicz 2000). And submitting to these onerous laws allows the provider organizations to make a costly signal to the regime, simultaneously assuaging concerns that they seek to alter the existing distribution of power and giving the regime an eye into their operations (Fearon 1997; Simmons and Hopkins 2005).

Enmeshing nonstate providers in a web of bureaucratic and legal monitoring mechanisms provides the regime short-term assurance that these organizations will not leverage their newfound freedom to rock the political boat. But this initial decision instantiates longer-term trajectories that are difficult to reverse. This is because the longer nonstate providers are left to take up social responsibilities—providing health, education, and other vital daily services—the less credible the regime's threats to rein these providers back in for politicizing their services become. Restricting the operation of a provider that has been at work for only a few months causes superficial trauma; shuttering a network that has been at work for years can prompt the very type of public unrest this strategy was designed to prevent in the first place. This establishes a set of perverse consequences for the regime: the better the nonstate actor is at providing social services to the citizenry, the more difficult it is to curtail its operations if it begins to threaten the political order.

The Geography of Authoritarianism

Many nondemocratic regimes generate political support by extending clientelist networks throughout the country (Magaloni 2006; Greene 2007; Blaydes 2011). By leveraging their resource advantage and ability to dole out rewards and punishments, these types of regimes produce durable majorities at the ballot box, generate impressive public spectacles, and tamp down the public display of dissatisfaction. But they are not able to do so universally. These actors cannot escape a basic resource dilemma, and so they must target their spending to those constituencies that offer the highest returns (Dixit and Londregan 1996; Calvo and Murillo 2004). Particularly in developing countries, this dynamic often means that poorer citizens make up the bulk of regime support.

Not only do the poor offer the lower marginal cost for the resource-maximizing vote buyer, but they are also that constituency most dependent on the provision of short-term material benefits (Stokes et al. 2013, 152–71). Like their more affluent counterparts, poorer citizens have a variety of ideological and programmatic commitments. However, their immediate material needs ensure that their ability to vote on these decidedly longer-term commitments remains weak. This dynamic ends up locking the poor into supporting the regime not because they prefer it but because they stand to suffer the most if the regime revokes their material benefits for supporting someone else (Diaz-Cayeros, Magaloni, and Weingast 2006). "When one's livelihood and one's political activism collide," Kelly McMann concludes, "the latter suffers" (2006, 1).

Wealthier voters are better able to ignore offers to buy their ballot and instead vote for parties and candidates on ideological or programmatic bases (Magaloni 2006, 22). The key, as Herbert Kitschelt and Steven Wilkinson tell us, is that these wealthier voters "have enough assets (especially human capital endowments) to become entirely indifferent to clientelistic-targeted goods and therefore incur zero opportunity cost when their favorite programmatic party loses to a clientelist contender" (2007a, 25). In technical terms, the satisfaction these wealthier voters gain from voting for parties or candidates whose ideology, program, or reputation aligns with their own preferences outweighs the value of losing the economic benefits that could be realized from selling their vote to the highest bidder.

John Sidel tells us that "local economic conditions are determinant of local political outcomes" (2014, 165). Building on this insight, scholars working in a variety of contexts have found that the above logic often manifests spatially, as patterns of electoral competition closely map onto underlying socioeconomic cleavages. Ethan Scheiner, for example, relates how clientelism in Japanese elections created an essentially "parallel party system" of competitive middle-class districts coexisting alongside clientelist-dominated poor ones (2006, 5).

Jacqueline Behrend (2011) found that, in Argentina, weak local economies tended to produce "closed games," constituencies where small cliques of individuals were able to use their control over resources to establish long-term monopolies over politics. Relying on an examination of local electoral outcomes in Russia and Kyrgyzstan, Kelly McMann (2006) found that in locales where individuals lacked "economic autonomy" (because of higher levels of state control of the economy) opposition political activism was effectively quashed. And Edward Banfield and James Wilson (1966) captured the interaction between socioeconomic context and electoral competition in their classic distinction between "river wards" and "newspaper wards" in American politics. The river wards were poorer neighborhoods where political machines reliably delivered the vote through clientelism, while the newspaper wards were more well-to-do locales where residents tended to vote on substantive and programmatic issues—those types of issues highlighted in the newspapers they supposedly read.

Many electoral authoritarian regimes are subdivided in the same ways. Constituencies composed largely of poorer voters will disproportionately host electoral monopolies dominated by proregime parties and politicians. In districts where more affluent citizens are predominant, the opposition will find it much easier to mount an electoral challenge because the electoral arena is much more capacious.

This dynamic produces counterintuitive expectations for the ways that social service provision and political mobilization interact. Social service providers can enter the market driven by a wide variety of motivations. They can operate as religious providers who seek to provide charity to the poor, as family associations or co-ops dedicated to privileging members over outsiders, as political parties seeking to explicitly trade social services for political support, or effectively as businesses targeting a base of paying customers. But the key point is that opposition social service providers who target the poor are effectively asking their beneficiaries to abandon their proregime patrons and support the provider organization at the polls. More often than not, this approach will fail. In contrast, providers who target the middle class can avoid asking their beneficiaries to make such a heroic sacrifice. Instead, they confront a different question: how to distinguish themselves from their opponents *and* offer something that makes citizens go through the trouble of voting for the opposition rather than simply staying at home.

Middle-Class Care

Providing social services costs money, and organizations have a number of strategies at hand to support their endeavors: they can use their internal movement resources to finance the provision directly, they can indirectly finance it by lever-aging the free labor of committed cadres, they can rely on financial support from an outside patron or donations, or they can establish a pay-for-service model targeted at more affluent citizens. A key argument of this book is that an organi-zation's decision about *how* to fund this activity shapes the subsequent *quality* of that provision and establishes a particular trajectory that determines whether or not it will be able to turn this activism into political mobilization.

A powerful predictor of an opposition organization's ability to use social ser-vices to generate political mobilization is whether or not they target a middle-class, paying audience. Organizations may make this decision for a variety of reasons, from instrumental ones based on an objective assessment of their own capabilities to an intrinsic commitment to privileging this social class over others. But the decision to provide for a more affluent audience triggers four mechanisms—relating to competition, consistency, depoliticization, and independence—that produce the type of care that so powerfully speaks to the concerns of middle-class voters.

Organizations that provide services for free or minimal costs often lack both the incentive and the means to provide more than a basic level of care. This is because those citizens who might be appreciative of this provision generally suf-fer from fewer alternative options. For poorer citizens, in other words, *any* service is critical and appreciated. In his detailed study of the Indian Bharatiya Janata Party's (BJP's) social service outreach, Tariq Thachil found that the "very basic standard of services offered by the [BJP's movement affiliate] is such that services are appealing only in areas where even basic public provisioning is absent, and even then only to those voters who cannot pay to obtain these services privately" (2011, 446). And even if a provider *wanted* to offer higher-quality or more tech-nologically advanced services, it would be inevitably constrained by the fact that better services require more resources.

To be wealthy is to have options. In contrast to those providers who target the poor, organizations aiming at the middle-class market must attract the support of those who have some ability to choose another provider if they are dissatisfied: to send their daughter to another private elementary school or have their son's broken arm mended at another private hospital. It is difficult for organizations to compete in this market without recourse to a consistent—and considerable—stream of funding. Not only does maintaining an edge in the market require fiscal sovereignty, but competition establishes incentives for these facilities to develop beyond the minimal standards that lower-priced or free services could offer. Their audience is less captive and, potentially, could take its business elsewhere.

A dependable revenue stream triggers a second dynamic that shapes the *qual-ity* of care a facility can provide. Authors generally assume that parties who are able to uniquely access the resources of affiliated social movements gain a valuable (and free) edge over their competitors. In her study of indigenous organizations in Latin America, Donna Lee Van Cott found that "successful candidates could depend on free labor and loyalty of members of these affiliated organizations to serve as counterweight to their competitors' greater access to financial resources for campaigning, advertising, and patronage" (2005, 218). Tariq Thachil's aforementioned study of the Indian BJP reports the same (2014a, 23).

As these authors note, under certain conditions, anchoring social service provision in volunteer labor and movement resources can produce powerful electoral rewards. But this strategy can also seriously hamper an organization's ability to provide the type of care attractive to more affluent citizens. First, reliance on volunteers or in-house resources often precludes the possibility of offering the types of services that are *needed*. Instead, organizations tend to end up providing only those services that are *available*. An organization composed largely of teachers, for example, will struggle to sustain a network of medical providers. Second, relying on volunteer labor limits an organization's ability to institute and enforce consistent standards. If a manager knows that disciplining a volunteer who is sloppy with patients or brusque in the classroom might cause the volunteer to quit and leave that initiative short-staffed, then he or she will be much more likely to indulge rather than correct poor behavior.

Organizations that function on a pay-for-service model, however, can surmount these obstacles. Not only does it allow the provider organization to react to specific niches in the market, but it also allows supervisors to exercise a much greater degree of control over employees. This ability to monitor quality, consistently enforce standards, and quickly fix mistakes is an important factor in creating and sustaining the type of care that can speak to middle-class voters. Hints of why this might be so comes from Robert Michels's classic work *Political Parties* ([1915] 1966). In that work, Michels noticed a particularly vexing difference among European socialist parties in the years leading up to World War I. Why, he wondered, were the German socialists so effective in party work, while defections, poor management, and infighting plagued their continental colleagues? After a brief examination he found that "the German [socialists'] practice is to pay for all services to the party, from the most trifling notice contributed to a newspaper to the lengthiest public discourse . . . [This] gives to the organization a remarkable cohesion, and an authority over the personnel . . . [constituting] one of the most important and indispensable bases of the party life" (137). Essentially, the more a party relied on free labor from committed ideologues, the less reliable and effective that party became. This counterintuitive finding suggests why any organization that manages these facilities essentially as *businesses*, in which staff are paid, duties are well defined, and managers are allowed to actively monitor the employees, can gain an edge in organization and consistency. In contrast, organizations who treat their social service provision as charity or clientelism—in which staff volunteer their time and patients are treated for free—have much less ability, or even need, to attend to the quality of that provision.

The ways in which a paying audience triggers mechanisms related to competition and consistency are general. Tackling the question of political mobilization in an authoritarian context raises two specific salutary dynamics that flow from a steady, customer-based revenue stream. In traditional clientelist exchanges, organizations that rely on material exchange to mobilize political support must be wary that clients may take the benefit but defect in the privacy of the voting booth. This incentivizes providers to politicize the exchange (to make sure the recipients know what is expected of them) *and* to closely monitor the beneficiaries (to ensure that they can revoke provision if beneficiaries do not provide political support) (S. Stokes 2005). Effectively, because citizens receive a good for which they do not pay, they are either coerced by a political boss or nagged by their own intrinsic sense of fair play to accommodate the provider when election day rolls around.

When citizens pay on the spot in cash for the services they receive, politicization assumes much lower importance. First, social services delivered on a professional, pay-for-service basis allow the provider to maintain a division (conceptually if not always concretely) from the "dirty river" of politics (Thachil 2011, 437). Because they do not need to justify an immediate political return on their investment, providers can instead step back from so baldly instrumentalizing their interaction with beneficiaries, avoiding the "public stigma attached to clientelist methods" (Hale 2007, 231). This is important for the question of audiences and, in particular, for the way such politicization would alienate blocs of middle-class supporters. As Rebecca Weitz-Shapiro (2014) shows, not only do more affluent voters interpret a politician's recourse to clientelism instrumentally, as a signal of low-quality governance, but they are also put off by the ethical implications of the transaction.[1] Instead of alienating more affluent citizens by browbeating sick patients with party propaganda or expelling the child of a political opponent from school, the provider organization can generate powerful perceptions of honesty and competency by plausibly claiming to divorce provision from politics.

Second, and in more practical terms, this means that pay-for-service providers do not need to monitor recipient behavior to threaten that if recipients do not reciprocate with political support, "they would be cut off from the flow of minor payoffs in the future" (Brusco, Nazareno, and Stokes 2004, 76). In fact, just the opposite is true: a social service provider that can effectively tie its own hands—to credibly commit *not* to revoke provision if political support wanes—can reap powerful rewards. As Melani Cammett and Sukriti Issar summarize, "high-fixed-cost projects, embodied in physical structures, equipment, and regular personnel, show a party's willingness to invest in a community, rendering out-group service provision all the more surprising and meaningful" (2010, 390). Operating on a pay-for-service basis not only allows a provider organization to appear unconcerned with politics but incentivizes it to do so.

Depoliticizing service provision is especially critical in nondemocratic environments. As described above, regimes fret that provider organizations will use their social service provision to generate political support, and they tend to set rather hard constraints against such explicit politicization. Any organization that gets too close to this red line—for instance, by canvassing for votes among beneficiaries—risks triggering consequences, up to and including closure. Yet an organization that operates on a pay-for-service basis can passively amass goodwill, more safely navigating the legal architecture designed to prevent the politicization of the social and civic sector.

The authoritarian environment also dictates the style of provision in another important way. These regimes can use forced closures and bureaucratic manipulation to deter or divert potential challengers. But if these tools do not work, regimes can also target funding. In these conditions, organizations without independent financial support—for instance, those that rely on the deep pockets of donors or the labor of committed cadres—are thus vulnerable to co-optation or targeted repression. In contrast, a base of paying customers provides opposition organizations a measure of independence from regime manipulation and, potentially, a way to resist more subtle regime efforts to disrupt the enterprise.

Finally, the way pay-for-service facilitates independence suggests revising the above-discussed arguments about the beneficial effects of social movement–party interaction (McAdam and Tarrow 2010). In many democratic contexts, being able to leverage the resources of "party substitutes" to boost one's mobilizing capacities can be a key difference between political success and failure (Hale 2007, 227). But in nondemocratic situations, oppositions that proliferate linkages between their political and social activities—for example, by letting activists freely cross over between the realms or drawing financial resources from movement coffers—will be inviting a regime crackdown. Instead, smart providers should make every effort to prevent their social and electoral realms from bleeding together—a separation that the pay-for-service model facilitates.

A Reputation for Good

Targeting a paying customer base incentivizes an organization to provide high-quality, consistent, and depoliticized social services. In these situations, what is the precise nature of the "linkage" that this type of social service activism generates between provider and recipient (Kitschelt 2000)? What is the causal mechanism that connects an individual's receipt of services to political mobilization?

Citizens in nondemocratic regimes often struggle to figure out what exactly opposition parties stand for. This is not particularly surprising, given how these regimes tilt the playing field by barring opposition campaign rallies, shuttering opposition media outlets, and arresting politicians and organizers (Levitsky and Way 2010). And of course, by their very nature they rob opposition parties of an opportunity to use performance in government to signal competence, further depriving voters of valuable cues they would otherwise use when deciding how to apportion electoral support. "Opposition parties," as Beatriz Magaloni puts it when speaking of the Partido Revolucionario Institucional's (PRI's) dominance of the Mexican electorate, "are highly uncertain entities to voters because they have never governed" (2006, 19).

As we have seen, this problem of low (and low-quality) information is mostly unimportant for less affluent voters, whose interaction with politicians and parties tends to be centered on material exchange rather than programmatic or ideological assessments. But for more affluent voters social service provision—particularly the high-quality and relationally enjoyable type highlighted above—may boost an organization's electoral fortunes by providing a tangible demonstration of what a party or politician stands for (Cammett and Jones Luong 2014). Susan Stokes and her coauthors suggest that "by generating goodwill among constituents who receive assistance, and by allowing the politician to build a reputation for fairness and competence, constituency service is probably an effective electoral strategy" (2013, 16).[2] Other studies of party voter linkages in Taiwan (Wang 1994, 183) and Argentina (Levitsky 2003, 213–15) have also found instances of this type of relatively depoliticized, "constituency service" behavior but have not explored its influence over voter perceptions or relationship to political outcomes in any depth.

Constricting the scope of the examination to Islamist parties provides more guidance for theorizing how social activism, voter heuristics, and electoral mobilization coincide. Thomas Pepinsky, William Liddle, and Saiful Mujani show that when individuals are unsure about policy—in particular economic—issues, a party's "Islamic" identity helps citizens quickly figure out what that party stands for. "Uncertainty," they go on to summarize, "plays a critical role in shaping the electoral fortunes of Islamic parties" (2012, 585). Tarek Masoud's (2014b) survey evidence suggests that Islamic social institutions contribute to Islamist electoral success by signaling to voters that Islamist parties will pursue pro-poor (redistributionist) policies once in office. In contrast to these rationalist and programmatic-type linkages, Melani Cammett and Pauline Jones Luong (2014) hypothesize that a reputation for honesty bred by social service provision, along with their public embrace of religious identity and tight-knit organizational structures, might contribute to the "political advantage" Islamist groups supposedly enjoy over their non-Islamist competitors.

Social service provision influences vote choice not by revealing information about specific policies but rather by more viscerally communicating a valuable reputation for competency, trustworthiness, and approachability. By associating an organization "with some goal or state or symbol that is positively or negatively valued (by the electorate)," social service provision helps a party establish its brand (D. Stokes 1963, 373). These types of linkages, based on impressions and traits rather than explicit politicization or programmatic commitments, can exercise a disproportionately large influence over an individual's vote choice (Huddy and Terkildsen 1993; Funk 1996; Bartels 2002; Fiske, Cuddy, and Glick 2007; Fridkin and Kenney 2011). As Daniel Butler and Eleanor Powell argue, these "valence issues" have "an impact on constituents' vote choice that is comparable or even bigger than other important factors (such as economic and ideological factors) and at the same time is easier to influence" (2014, 492).

These associations are particularly helpful to middle-class voters struggling to navigate the uncertainty about parties and politicians that is a foundational feature of elections in nondemocratic regimes. By offering a physical space where "parties meet voters," social service–based interactions can help citizens obtain valuable first-hand information about the provider organization (Calvo and Murillo 2013). As Pradeep Chhibber argues in his study of politico-religious mobilization in India, depoliticized and coequal spatial interactions help citizens identify with politicians on a personal, visceral level: "If voters can share spaces with an elected representative, they will be more likely to see their representative as sharing their vision than if they experience their relationship with the representative as defined by the constraints of a social hierarchy" (2014, 20–21). Talk is one thing, but being able to use social services to demonstrate the "observable qualities" that form the basis of inferences about party and candidate can be a potent source of political information and thus political support for a provider organization (McGraw 2003, 399).

A provider's fair, consistent, and interpersonally enjoyable care traverses the "fuzzy and permeable boundary" between social and partisan activism, helping citizens use the information generated by the former to make inferences about the latter (Goldstone 2003, 2). This type of information is particularly valuable to more affluent voters because the particular characteristics of many electoral authoritarian regimes mean that these citizens are the most likely to use this type of information when making a decision about how to allocate their support on election day.

Accounting for Contingency

Prior investigations of nonstate social service provision make it clear that organizations devote a great deal of time and energy designing these efforts for maximum political effect. Thachil, for instance, explains that the Indian BJP's politicization of social service provision was "painstaking" (2014b, 14). Kikue Hamayotsu explains how the PKS in Indonesia has "strategically" crafted its own social service–based outreach strategy (2015, 158–59). Herbert Kitschelt and Daniel M. Kselman explain that clientelist networks "are generally the result of long, hard organizing efforts" (2013, 1458).

Not coincidentally, these observations all spring from democratic contexts in which the regime is relatively uninvolved in the story. Switching the institutional environment to nondemocracies immediately highlights the limits of these purposive and calculated accounts. In such a context, any organization that deployed such a clearly instrumental strategy of mobilizing political support through social service provision would not get very far, even in situations where economic crises force the regime to relax controls in order to gain short-term stability. This disjuncture should prod us to consider the extent to which any connection between social service provision and political mobilization in these cases is produced by considered actions, and how much is the result of "contingent events [that] set into motion institutional patterns or event chains that have deterministic properties" (Mahoney 2000, 507–8).

Reforms often have dramatic and counterintuitive implications for politics that often become visible only in retrospect (Bates [1981] 2005). This book fits firmly into that tradition, in particular its recourse to a congruence of historical circumstances to explain the puzzling reality of an authoritarian regime that allows its opponents to operate a sprawling network of social service provision that benefits millions of citizens per year. This assumption of contingency shapes the research design, in particular by highlighting the importance of key and contingent junctures where different choices would have produced different long-term results.

The first switch point is the emergence of an economic crisis. Absent the pressing need to reform, autocrats would be able to limit the ability of providers to emerge and amass support through three mechanisms. First, they can simply prevent them from operating, using bureaucratic and coercive power to nip nascent efforts in the bud. Second, they can allow providers to operate but use their control over state resources to function as a patron, co-opting and shaping the behavior of potentially oppositional providers. Third, absent economic crisis and subsequent reduction in public safety nets, the efforts of a social service provider simply lose their appeal for large swathes of the population (Pepinsky 2014).[3]

The onset of economic crisis creates the space for nonstate providers to enter the market by causing regimes to grudgingly relax constraints on opposition organizations. But political mobilization is still not a foregone conclusion, largely because of factors relating to how provider organizations conceptualize targeting. The most obvious (and cost-effective) route for an organization seeking to translate social service provision into political mobilization is to target the poor (Thachil 2014b; Szwarcberg 2015). But in contrast to instances of democratic competition, this decision would actually limit that party's ability to build broad political support in nondemocratic contexts. Not only would it put it in direct competition with the largest provider (the regime) for the support of the poor, but this style of provision would alienate the middle class. While an organization that targets the poor can, under certain circumstances, use this provision to make political gains, these will be sporadic rather than widespread. In contrast, focusing on the middle class sets a provider organization on a trajectory that intersects with those voters most able to support the opposition. Further, it triggers the internal mechanisms necessary to produce the type of care that appeals to those citizens. Thus the second switch point is the provider's initial decision to target its social services at the middle class rather than the poor.

This reliance on timing, contingency, and feedback mechanisms imposes specific demands on the research design. In particular, it highlights the need for an in-depth and longer-term perspective that sees outcomes as the result of processes rooted in specific historical contexts as much as actors' calculated and strategic behavior (Pierson and Skocpol 2002; Thelen and Steinmo 1992). Over the coming chapters I exploit two comparisons in order to trace out the effects produced by states and organizations that head in different directions. First, at key points I contrast *organizations*. I show how, for instance, other providers' choices to rely on different funding models constrained their long-term ability to use social service provision to make electoral inroads against the regime. Second, I make use of within-case variation by carrying the investigation through the democratic but abbreviated term of Mohammed Morsi, who was removed by military coup in the summer of 2013. Exploiting shifts in institutions, specifically from authoritarianism to more liberalized political competition, provides additional explanatory leverage over how the political context does, and does not, structure styles of social service provision.

Provision, Probity, and Politics

Autocrats grant leeway to nonstate providers to help compensate citizens for the loss of public services. For regimes, strategically divesting social welfare to nonstate actors provides short-term benefits while imposing long-term costs.

While the influx of new providers mitigates the immediate social consequences of destabilizing austerity measures, it empowers those who may, in the future, lodge a considerable political challenge. Under conditions of state retrenchment, organizations that target their social service provision at the poor are only weakly able to translate their activism into political mobilization. While they may provide services widely, those citizens who consume the benefits are also least likely to defect from the regime and support the opposition at the ballot box. Organizations that target the middle class, by comparison, are well positioned to make political gains. Not only are they most likely to be in daily, face-to-face contact with those voters most likely to support the opposition, but they are able to generate the *type* of care that appeals to these voters. On technical as well as relational dimensions these organizations' provision will distinguish them from both the regime and their counterparts in the opposition by helping more affluent voters make inferences about the honesty, competence, and modesty of their candidates for elected office.

The remainder of this book turns to the empirical evidence, using the history of Egypt and the Muslim Brotherhood from the 1970s until 2013 to test key empirical implications of the theory. The next chapter delves into Anwar al-Sadat's presidency (r. 1970–81), describing the initial confluence of circumstances that resulted in the formation of the Islamic Medical Association. This organization would grow from its 1977 founding, amid the Muslim Brotherhood's return to prominence after the repression of the Nasir years, to become the Muslim Brotherhood's largest social service provider.

REBUILDING THE BROTHERHOOD BRAND

The ability of the Brotherhood to use social services to generate political support had its roots in a particular configuration of events from Egypt's (relatively) recent past. Assuming power after Gamal 'Abd al-Nasir's death in 1970, Anwar al-Sadat faced an economic crisis that threatened to bankrupt the country. After a maladroit attempt to cut subsidies provoked regime-shaking "bread riots" in 1977, Sadat turned to a variety of nonstate social service providers in an attempt to relieve the pressure on the state budget. Among those organizations was the Muslim Brotherhood, which had emerged from decades of repression and was attempting to rebuild its presence in Egyptian society. But Sadat did more than simply tolerate the growth of the Brotherhood's service provision network; he actively supported it. Months after the bread riots, Sadat's government gave the Brotherhood official permission to form a social service association—the Islamic Medical Association (IMA)—which would grow into the largest organized sector of the Muslim Brotherhood's social service network.

This chapter isolates a number of critical early choices, made by both the regime and the Brotherhood. The regime's initial decision to allow nonstate providers more room to operate alleviated the immediate economic crisis. But over the longer term it complicated efforts to keep these providers—the Muslim Brotherhood among them—from using their activities to mount a political challenge against the regime. Indeed, as the Brotherhood began to take a more and more prominent role in opposition politics in the 1990s and into the 2000s, the regime was forced to choose between allowing the Brotherhood's potent social service networks to continue fueling the group's political rise or risking social upheaval by suddenly shuttering their facilities.

The Costs of Economic Reform

One of Gamal 'Abd al-Nasir's most noteworthy domestic achievements was to extend to Egyptians a social safety net that included a substantial public health component (Nasir 1954, 208; Gallagher 1990; Bayat 2006, 136). Yet during the second half of the 1960s internal and external developments combined to frustrate his strategy of aggressive state-led growth. Domestically, his industrialization policy had stalled and further growth required a potentially dangerous reshuffling of the social and political coalition on which the regime rested (Ayubi 1996, 336). In the realm of foreign policy, misadventures in Yemen and Israel's dramatic victory in the 1967 war forced Nasir to devote more and more resources to the task of rebuilding Egypt's decimated military (Ferris 2012). By the time of his 1970 death Egypt was in dire financial straits.

Facing growing debt, lagging domestic productivity, and a debilitating military stalemate, Nasir's successor, Anwar al-Sadat, inherited an economy that had, as he put it, "fallen below zero" (1981, 214–15). To navigate out of the crisis Sadat proposed to fight on two fronts. First, he hoped his limited military campaign in 1973 would force Israel to the negotiating table, allowing him to claim a peace dividend by carving away the defense expenditures that were monopolizing Egypt's budget (Brownlee 2012, 20–23). Then, in the 1974 October working paper and in the accompanying Law 43 of 1974 Sadat outlined a long-term plan to revitalize Egypt's moribund economy by reducing currency controls and establishing the tax incentives he believed would spur Arab and Western investment. The hope, as one observer quipped, was that "Egyptian potential plus Arab capital plus Western technology equals development and progress" (Cooper 1982, 89).

Nasir's aggressive state-led development, the breakup of large rural estates, and expansion of the Egyptian state had sparked a new Egyptian middle class. Made up of graduates flowing from Egypt's expanding state university system and increasingly ensconced in the lower levels of the state's new bureaucracy, this class formed a backbone of Nasir's potent appeal (Amin 2001; Moore 1980; Binder 1978). But Sadat's policy of *infitāḥ* (opening) marked a potentially dangerous change in course. The gains of this new policy would mainly accrue to a rising bourgeoisie composed of opportunistic businessmen and canny bureaucrats (Naggar 2009; Ayubi 1991; Waterbury 1985).

Yet while the door was opening for the *munfatiḥūn* (those who benefited from the infitāḥ), it was closing on the rest. By the time Sadat took the helm, Nasir's safety net had grown to the point where a large portion of the state budget was devoted to artificially supporting the prices of basic items, what Mark Cooper calls a "mass subsidization of subsistence" (1982, 35). In the October paper Sadat hinted at the pain to come, pointing to a "growing awareness of the need to call to account the public sector, public utilities, and public services" (1974, 32). So while Nasir's policies had stimulated the expansion of the middle class, Sadat's subsidy cuts, rising inflation, and reduction in state services threatened to knock them back down the socioeconomic ladder.

The year of the October paper witnessed hundreds of minor strikes and work stoppages as Egypt's society began to pull apart, exposing often macabre gaps between the haves and have-nots. Crowds chanting *"Yā baṭal al-ubūr, fayn al-fuṭūr?* [O hero of the (Suez Canal) crossing, where's breakfast?]" rang in the 1975 New Year as they rampaged outside international hotels and flashy nightclubs where a year of their wages would be insufficient to pay the cover charge for the parties inside. Three months later the military had to break up a strike of tens of thousands of workers in the restive delta industrial city of al-Mahalla al-Kubra, and further strikes followed in August and September (Hirst and Beeson 1981, 230–35).

Sadat spurred his program forward even as the discontent became palpable. As one dispatch from the British ambassador to Egypt warned the Foreign Office in early 1976, "Social discontent is at its worst not in the lower levels, protected to some extent by the subsidies of the basic essentials by which they live, but in the class immediately above–the ranks of minor public officials, teachers, students, who have been hard hit by the inflation in rents and prices of non-subsistence consumer goods that they have been used to enjoying and which are important to them as symbols of status."[1] That same year the nominally pro-infitāḥ publication *al-Iqtisadi* similarly condemned Sadat's liberalization policies, noting particularly the way that the infitāḥ pinched those who had so recently benefited from Nasir's reforms. The country, the magazine editorialized, "has now become composed of a destitute class and a rich class, while the middle class has been transformed into a treadmill, straining on the path to maintain a minimum standard of living" (Cooper 1982, 107).

Sadat forged ahead in hopes that economic reforms and diplomatic movement would soon begin to deliver tangible gains to those frustrated by the specter of social dislocation, but time ran out in early January 1977. Amid a near tripling of foreign debt and steadily increasing domestic subsidies, Egypt was forced to accept a standby agreement from the International Monetary Fund (IMF) mandating that Egypt reform its economy and trim domestic expenditures. While the IMF offered general advice on how to cut spending, it was the Egyptians who determined the final form the cuts would take. A key early target, Sadat's team decided, would be the subsidies. And while cuts seemed insignificant—in many cases amounting to only a few cents—they did cause acute financial pain by targeting everyday items: food, cooking oil, sugar, gas. The effect was compounded by poor communication, as the government made little effort to prepare Egyptians for the change and had even reassured them the day prior that there would be no price increases. But on January 18 newspapers carried word that prices on some thirty basic commodities would increase (Beattie 2000, 206–8).

The first riots erupted in the industrial Cairo suburbs of Hilwan, following which crowds spread to the city center and then quickly to the rest of the country. Demonstrators tore up railway lines and trashed government buildings, chanting "We are dying of hunger now, so go ahead and shoot us, Sadat" (Seddon 1993, 106) and "No liberalization without food!"[2] The crowds quickly overwhelmed the police, and the country teetered on the edge of revolution. As one Cairo-based observer put it, "Political order had broken down completely" (Cooper 1982, 236).

Sadat, who had retired to a villa in Aswan to prepare for a meeting with the Yugoslavian leader Josef Tito, was caught unawares. He first learned of the uprisings, according to Mohammed Haykal, while filming a television interview. Spotting smoke rising from the city center in the distance, he speculated about the source. "Perhaps the rioting has spread here," responded the reporter, to which the astonished president replied, "What rioting?" As the disturbances grew, Sadat's bodyguards advised him to get to the airport before the swelling crowds blocked the roads. Leaving behind both personal and official possessions in Aswan, he fled ignominiously, according to one report disguised as a *fellah* in a cab to escape detection by the crowds (Haykal 1983, 91; Hirst and Beeson 1981, 245).

Once he was in the air, the situation was judged so serious that Sadat's aircraft was forced to loiter for two hours as his staff worked to determine if the airports in Alexandria and Cairo were safe (Shukri 1981, 323–24). Even after he landed, a plane stood by at Abu Suwayr airport on the Suez Canal waiting to take him and family to Iran if the need arose (a few years later, of course, Egypt would serve as a haven for the fleeing shah of Iran) (Haykal 1983, 92). However, after a few tense days the Egyptian army was able to regain control of the country's streets and squares, aided by a nationwide curfew and shoot-on-sight orders for people outside without permits (Seddon 1993, 100). As the dust settled, one newspaper surveyed the wreckage and indicted a system of "economic apartheid" that juxtaposed a nation struggling to meet basic needs against a small clique of citizens with "dreadful buying power, dismembering and destroying Egyptian society with it" (Cooper 1982, 238).

The riots not only drove home the risks of the infitāḥ policy but also called the viability of the regime itself into question. A CIA report assessed that the whole episode, culminating in the need to deploy the army to restore order, was a "severe setback" to Sadat.[3] British diplomats in Cairo worried that the events "put in doubt the lengths to which the armed forces would go in suppressing future popular disturbances stemming from economic grievances" and warned that "the docility of the Egyptian masses can no longer be depended on."[4] Sadat was shaken. In the aforementioned 1974 October paper he had also authorized parliamentary elections under the umbrella of three official political platforms—left, right, and center—in the hope that *political* liberalization would compensate for *economic* hardship (Brumberg 1992). Yet the strategy had backfired; instead of dampening popular mobilization, the political liberalization had sparked it (Beattie 2000, 222). Although in the October paper Sadat confidently proclaimed that "we do not fear difference of opinion, nor are we perturbed by free debate and expression" (1974, 39), in a speech following the 1977 riots he indicted democracy for having "fangs one hundred times sharper than the extraordinary measures of dictatorship" (Brownlee 2012, 25).

Subcontracting Social Welfare

The proximate cause of the bread riots was the sudden and unexpected rise in the costs of basic consumer goods. These events also tapped into broad, cross-class frustration with an economy based on "austerity and cuts in consumption for those at the bottom and growing consumption and enrichment for those at the top" (Hinnebusch 1988, 71). Yet while the uprising of 1977 vividly highlighted the risks inherent in any austerity program, it did little to change Egypt's financial realities.

Faced with an unpalatable choice between waiting out economic default or provoking a social revolution, Sadat settled on a third option: he would shift the state's social welfare responsibilities onto a revitalized civic and associational sector. Months after the bread riots, Sadat called on social service providers to take up new "national duties" by integrating their work into a national economic plan designed to back the public sector out of its commitments (1978, 362). At the centerpiece of this plan was the empowerment of the country's ecology of Christian and Muslim religious associations.

Putting aside the growing tension with the Coptic community, in October 1977 Sadat and the Coptic patriarch, Pope Shenouda, jointly laid the foundation stone for the St. Mark's Charity Hospital in Cairo (Sadat 1977). Sadat had also devoted 50,000 Egyptian pounds (LE) from the state budget to get the endeavor started.[5] Government support for the project was visible: beside Sadat at the ceremony was the then-vice president, Hosni Mubarak, as well as the prime minister, Mamduh Salim.[6]

Sadat also sought to revive Egypt's traditional Islamic charities (*waqf*, pl. *awqāf*), which Nasir had sidelined as part of his drive to consolidate power and grow the power of the Egyptian state (Pioppi 2004, 4). Some of these charities included integrated medical centers, kindergartens, and associations integrated into the mosque. Sadat made a special push to enroll Egypt's vast ecosystem of mosques in his new strategy, framing it as a return to the idea of the "comprehensive mosque" that supposedly recalled the traditional role of the mosque as a provider of basic social and community services in early Islam. Not only would this model of mosque-based private welfare provision burnish his Islamic credentials, but it would unlock a potentially vast—and privately funded—social service network onto which he could unload the state's unsustainable distributive burden.

Coverage of the regime's efforts to make social service provision a "basic goal" of religious practice began to pepper the pages of state newspapers, and prominent regime figures repeatedly praised the plans.[7] For example, in 1981 the state-owned religious daily *al-Liwa' al-Islami* told readers that "President Sadat has given the Minister of Religious Endowments directives stressing the need to give attention to mosques and their mission and the need to establish new comprehensive mosques in every district of Egypt containing hospitals, outpatient clinics, nurseries and libraries."[8] One government official quoted in the report admitted that the goal was to get these organizations—including but not limited to the mosques—to assume the social welfare obligations that the government was no longer able to meet. "There are numerous projects to provide popular service, to avoid casting the entire burden for services on the government. Among these services is the establishment of the national committee for comprehensive mosque services, which has the goal of making the mosque a center of cultural advancement in the environment in which it is located."[9]

As more and more of these "comprehensive mosques" began to spring up across Egypt, some citizens began to question whether or not there was a religious basis for tacking such an array of services onto a house of worship. One Ahmed 'Abd al-Mun'im wrote into the religious magazine *al-Itisam* in early 1980 and requested a fatwa (religious opinion). Was it legitimate, he asked, to use "hospitals, religious institutes, workshops, classes . . . libraries and laboratories" to attract people to the mosque? The president of al-Azhar's Fatwa Council (rather than the editor of the magazine, who usually handled these requests) replied that these additional features were indeed legitimate, endowing the venture with a prominent stamp of religious approval.[10]

An oft-cited model of this new comprehensive mosque was the Rightly Guided Caliphs' Association in Heliopolis, "a complete religious and social institution [housed] in the mosque of Abu Bakr al-Siddiq with a clinic, senior living facility, library, and hall."[11] This particular association made frequent appearances in the government press for its commitment to mosque-based social service provision. In March 1979 *October* had profiled the organization, which the reporter praised for being "undoubtedly among the best efforts ever exerted." He specifically highlighted its self-financed nature: "The works are carried out by donations and are completely supervised by its people." The goal of the article, the author went on to note, was to "present these examples to the society so that the citizens can follow the same path."[12] Another article in *October* reviewing the growth of the mosque-based associations again used the Rightly Guided Caliphs Association to emphasize the concept of the comprehensive mosque. "This is how the era of the Prophet was," the writer explained. "The mosque was a place of praying, religious lessons, medical treatment activities and a place to receive people on a charity basis." The article quoted the Minister of Religious Endowments, 'Abd al-Rahman al-Naggar, who explained that it was the goal of the Ministry of Religious Endowments to "choose the largest mosque in each popular neighborhood and annex to it a medical clinic," while encouraging Egyptians to take the lead in establishing their own community mosques: "Every work of charity based on the involvement of the community shall be successful."[13]

The Rightly Guided Caliphs Association was but one example of a larger process by which the regime encouraged nonstate providers to assume social service functions that had once been the near-exclusive preserve of the state. By doing so, Sadat hoped to navigate between popular protest and economic default. This effort was broad-based, encompassing Christian initiatives such as the St. Mark's Coptic Hospital, Islamic organizations such as the Rightly Guided Caliphs Association, and Egypt's thousands of neighborhood mosques. But this effort would reverberate longest for the way that it eventually helped the Muslim Brotherhood use social services to establish a powerful connection with Egyptian voters.

Ahmed al-Malt and the Brotherhood's Return

The absence of basic information that has hampered study of the Brotherhood's social service networks is particularly evident when it comes to their historical development. Information on the conditions under which these organizations formed, the goals of their founders, and their relationships with the regime is exceedingly sparse (Wickham 2002, 97; Masoud 2014a, 75). This absence of detail makes it particularly difficult to assess a key argument of this book: that early junctures exercise a significant influence on an organization's ability to transform social service provision into political mobilization. The remainder of this chapter refocuses the historical investigation away from the socioeconomic and political pressures that buffeted Anwar al-Sadat and the general expansion of nonstate provision and toward the specific motivations of those Brotherhood figures who played key roles in establishing the Islamic Medical Association during this time, most prominently its founder, Ahmad al-Malt.

Early in his term Sadat turned to religion as a bulwark against Nasirist remnants and an assertive leftist student movement. Rhetorically, he styled himself as "the believer president" (al-ra'is al-mu'min) presiding over an Egypt of "science and faith" (al-'ilm wa-l-iman) (Arian 2014, 86). He also released many Muslim Brothers from their Nasir-era prison sentences and allowed them to resume their activities, including publishing their monthly magazine al-Da'wa ('Isa 1977; Baker 1990).[14] As they reentered Egyptian society, not only did the Brothers have to rebuild their shattered organization, but they had to figure out how to reconnect with a society saturated by decades of Nasir's anti-Brotherhood propaganda (Habib 2012, 67–68; Futuh 2012, 24–25).

One of the most consequential Muslim Brothers whom Sadat released in those early waves was Dr. Ahmad al-Malt (1917–95).[15] Trained as a surgeon, Malt had overseen the Brotherhood's medical efforts in the front lines of the 1948 Palestine War. He had also been a member of the Brotherhood's clandestine "special section" (al-niẓām al-khāṣṣ), where his duties involved physical examination of potential recruits, including the steadiness of their nerves and strength. Malt had been arrested in 1948–49 for fomenting revolt against the British and was briefly jailed. In 1954 he was arrested again as part of Nasir's crackdown on the Brotherhood and sent to prison for nearly twenty years, where his steadfastness and devotion to the Brotherhood helped other incarcerated members preserve the organization.[16] Malt would go on to become one of the most important figures in the Brotherhood's history, serving as the deputy general guide (second in command) to three post-Nasir leaders of the Muslim Brotherhood: 'Umar Tilmisani, Hamid Abu Nasr, and Mustafa Mashhur.[17] In the Brotherhood's internal bureaucracy, Malt was also responsible for the group's "Egypt Office," a position that effectively gave him day-to-day control over all Muslim Brotherhood activity in Egypt (Maligi 2009, 249; Habib 2012, 439).

Malt spent the early years of his release pondering how to reestablish the Brotherhood's connections to Egyptian society.[18] A Friday sermon from the Islamist scholar Muhammad al-Ghazali crystallized these ideas. Afterwards, Malt approached Ghazali and asked him how to transform the zeal he felt while in the mosque into broader social activism. Ghazali replied, "Our power as preachers is through the spoken word. As for those of you who work in the practical fields of medicine, engineering, education, and the professions . . . you turn the word into action, the idea into the project, and the dream into reality."[19] For Malt, himself a surgeon, medicine was a natural field on which to focus. "Without a doubt medicine is among the most favorable fields in which a Muslim can serve his faith," he observed. "The difference between serving Islam in this field and serving it in another field is huge."[20] Medical work also offered another benefit because it would viscerally affect people who might be unswayed by lofty rhetoric. "A high-performing Muslim doctor and his behavior in serving the sick and ill can promote the religion and set an example which the tongue [alone] cannot do," noted an announcement in the November 1977 issue of al-Da'wa (likely written by Malt).[21] And so, shortly after the discussion with Ghazali, Malt and three fellow Muslim Brothers formed a "medical committee" to explore organized work in that sector (Malt 1993, 175–76).

Medical work would serve at least one organizational purpose by giving the Brotherhood an avenue through which to build connections to the nascent Islamic student movement (Arian 2014). The IMA fit into this strategy, Malt envisioned, because it would provide a forum for new medical students and doctors to challenge themselves, learn, and continue to improve their knowledge of medicine and skills as a doctor (1993, 176).[22] As Malt noted when he introduced the IMA in the pages of al-Da'wa, two objectives of the association were "to help those students in medical school with their studies" and "to help [existing] doctors continue in their studies and specialize in the different medical branches."[23] The emphasis on continuing education was very important because at that time, according to the former Muslim Brother and past president of the IMA 'Abd al-Mu'nim Abu al-Futuh, there was no incentive or reason to develop one's skills. As he recalled, "Doctors lacked the requirement to better themselves through training or education. Nothing was forcing him to be reaccredited or study, other than his own interests or a decision to get another degree, but there's nothing obligatory. He could stay a general doctor all his life, and there is nothing forcing him to do more. . . . What will have been added to his knowledge or experience in 40 years?"[24]

The association set up a variety of practical mechanisms in order to entice this nascent middle class of medical students and recent graduates to seek out the IMA. For instance, they organized dozens of study groups for students and instructors at the medical schools at Cairo University and Ayn Shams University (both in Cairo). The IMA also established, with the help of a donation from the Kuwaiti Ministry of Religious Endowments, a library that also included a copier for students to use to reproduce educational materials.[25] This focus is why, in addition to Futuh, a number of other young doctors and medical students who benefited from the IMA's outreach would go on to become prominent figures in the Brotherhood. This list of luminaries included Hilmi al-Gazar, 'Isam al-'Ariyan, and Sana' Abu Zayd (Futuh 2012, 49, 93).

As they sought to grow the organization, the IMA's founders were forced to wrestle with a key question: How should they relate to the Egyptian regime?

Should they acquiesce to the extensive legal and bureaucratic mechanisms, such as Law 32 of 1964, that were designed to circumscribe their ability to oppose the regime? Or should they attempt to remain informal, trading greater freedom to maneuver for larger risks of crackdown?

Supporting or Subverting the State

The Islamic Medical Association emerged in the context of Anwar al-Sadat's decision to use nonstate providers to assume some of the burdens of public welfare. Before delving further into the development of the IMA, I pause to assess another important implication of the theory: that while the regime encourages these organizations to build up their social service capacity, it simultaneously uses an array of bureaucratic and administrative devices to limit their ability to mount a political challenge.

This exercise also offers the chance to assess alternative explanations for the Brotherhood's apparently unique ability to transform social service activism into political mobilization under conditions of authoritarianism. Recall that there is a common argument in the literature that the group seeks to operate in interstices outside the state's control. Sheri Berman, for example, tells us that "the dispersed and local nature of [Islamists'] associational life has made it difficult for the Egyptian state to monitor their activities" (2003, 262). Malt and his colleagues indeed first coalesced in an informal medical committee. If they desired to do so, there seems little reason why they could not just have remained informal (and unregistered) in order to remain under the radar. This was a common tactic for many associations: Janine Clark (2004, 53–54) estimated that as many as seven unregistered associations existed for each registered one. According to Tamir Moustafa, "nearly every . . . human rights group . . . registered as civil companies [instead of under Law 32 of 1964]" (2007, 152). The reason these groups made the decision to avoid registering under Law 32 was their "belief in the illegitimacy of the regime" and their "hostility or suspicion to existing political parties and to state institutions" (Pratt 2005, 124, 131, 133). Put simply, it was a viable alternative to remain informal and thus attempt to keep the organization off the radar of the regime.

A welter of official regime documents, however, shows how the IMA took proactive steps to do the opposite. Malt and his colleagues grounded the medical committee on what he described as a "legal foundation" (*al-qā'ida al-qanūniyya*) by registering it with the Ministry of Social Affairs under Law 32 of 1964 (Malt 1993, 175). This required submitting to the regime extensive documentation on the IMA leadership, aims, goals, sources of funding, and membership. In fact, the first mention of the IMA in the Muslim Brotherhood's monthly magazine *al-Daʿwa* (in an issue four months after the 1977 bread riots) was a summary of this paperwork, listing nine goals of the organization as well as describing the funding it hoped to receive.[26] By laying the internal operations of the organization open to authorities, Malt and his colleagues were effectively admitting that they would not politicize the work of the Islamic Medical Association.

Malt and others in the Brotherhood were fully aware that they were trading off legal registration and above-ground operation in exchange for toleration. In his memoirs, the former member of the Muslim Brotherhood Sayyid ʿAbd al-Sattar Maligi reproduces a series of internal memos that he sent to the Brotherhood's leaders. In one, he uses the example of the IMA to make a point about how the Brotherhood operated its social enterprises. "In fairness, we must recognize that all of the [social] activities of the Muslim Brotherhood are organized according to the law, and the state encourages and approves of them [*shajjaʿathā al-dawla wa-wāfaqat ʿalayhā*]. The clearest example of this is the Islamic Medical Association, which Dr. Ahmad al-Malt founded and which today operates dozens of clinics and hospitals that operate completely normally and are not targeted by the state, unless they are used as sites for something other than medical activity" (2009, 360). In his memoirs, the former IMA president ʿAbd al-Muʿnim Abu al-Futuh echoes this sentiment, using the specific example of Malt and the IMA's legalism to point to the importance of a gradualist approach to social change, what he calls "the trend of building and not of coups" (2012, 98–99).[27]

In October 1977 the process of legal registration came to fruition as the Ministry of Social Affairs accepted the IMA's registration, and the IMA was written into the official Egyptian government gazette, *al-Waqaʾiʿ al-Misriyya*.[28] For its part, the Brotherhood proudly reprinted these government registration documents in the December 1977 issue of *al-Daʿwa*.[29] In his memoirs, Malt justified the decision to register by emphasizing that the IMA had nothing to hide; it was a nonprofit, apolitical organization designed to serve Egyptians of all stripes (1993, 175). There were no hidden agendas and accusations that the Brotherhood was using its services to "undermine the state" (*taqwīḍ al-dawla*) were, according to Malt, baseless (1998, 134–35).

The Brotherhood chose a fundamentally accommodationist, legalist path for its activism, gambling that "legal status, while offering no guarantees, at least offer[ed] some protection" (Hamid 2014, 50). This strategy provoked an intense reaction from other segments of the Islamist opposition, particularly those committed to underground and revolutionary activism, who claimed that the Brotherhood's strategy would end up doing little more than reinforcing the state. For instance, in his famous pamphlet *The Neglected Duty* (*al-Farida al-Ghaʾiba*, c. late 1970s/early 1980s) that justified the assassination of

Anwar al-Sadat, 'Abd al-Salam Farag (1986) walked readers through a series of arguments designed to justify his decision to use violence. Along the way he sharply criticized the Brotherhood's legalist strategy of social and civic activism, arguing that the regime's ability to monitor these associations rendered this approach pointless:

> There are those who say that we should establish societies that are subject to the state and that urge people to perform their prayers and to pay their *zakāt* [charity] tax and to do [other] good works. Prayer, zakāt and good works are [all equally] commands of God–Exalted and Majestic He is–which we should not at all neglect. However when we ask ourselves: "Do these works, and acts of devotion, bring about the establishment of an Islamic State?" then the immediate answer without any further consideration must be "No." Moreover, these societies would in principle be subject to the State, be registered in its files, and they would have to follow [the State's] instructions (184).

The IMA's emphasis on providing medical care dovetailed perfectly with the regime's desire to encourage nonstate providers to shoulder the burden of social welfare. And while the requirement to remain legal providers—rather than turn their energies underground—dissuaded some groups, there was also potential assistance to be had from taking the regime's hand. The Brotherhood opted to do so and, as the next section shows, benefited considerably.

Building the Islamic Charity Hospital

As part of a strategy to reduce the state's distributive burdens, Anwar al-Sadat began to encourage nonstate providers to step up their operations. His regime did so in a variety of ways: by providing seed funding (as with St. Mark's Hospital), by trumpeting its work and offering rhetorical support (as with the Rightly Guided Caliphs Association), and by easing these organizations' efforts to register with government authorities (as with the Islamic Medical Association). All these mechanisms braid together in the history of the IMA's flagship hospital, the Islamic Charity Hospital (*al-Mustashfa al-Khayri al-Islami*).

Concurrent with its registration with the Ministry of Social Affairs in 1977, the IMA began to plan a nationwide network of facilities. But in the pages of *al-Da'wa* it emphasized the flagship Islamic Charity Hospital project.[30] As Malt described it, this 350-bed, four-story facility would be "an Islamic landmark at an important entrance to Islamic Cairo, the city of a thousand muezzins [those who perform the call to prayer]."[31]

The project brought together a diverse cast of characters that highlighted the interrelated interests of the Islamic movement, the regime, and the private sector, challenging arguments about these groups' purported desire to work in the shadows. On one side were Islamic associations. One key partner was the aforementioned Rightly Guided Caliphs association, which—as we saw—the regime was trumpeting as an exemplar of the newly empowered Islamic social sector (Malt himself had earlier been involved in the medical efforts of the Rightly Guided Caliphs' Association [Maligi 2009, 149]).[32] The Badr Foundation, which had been founded in the mid-1970s, was another Islamic social service provider involved in the effort.[33] From the private sector came 'Uthman Ahmad 'Uthman, whose prominent Arab Contractors Company would build the facility ('Uthman was also a close friend of Sadat, whose youngest daughter was married to 'Uthman's oldest son).[34] Sadat's government also ensured that the IMA's hospital project would get off to a running start. Following the IMA's registration, the Egyptian Ministry of Defense donated to the group a plot of land 20 km[2] in area on the outskirts of Cairo—what had been the Armed Forces Club—on which to build the hospital.[35] And mirroring his involvement in the St. Mark's hospital, Anwar al-Sadat himself laid the cornerstone of the Brotherhood's flagship hospital.[36] Accompanying him during the ceremony were other regime luminaries, including the then-vice president Hosni Mubarak as well as the country's defense minister.[37]

The following chapter shows that the majority of the IMA's operations were based on providing care for a paying clientele rather than on donations. One exception to this was the capital campaign that followed the IMA's announcement of the Islamic Charity Hospital. Beyond the Egyptian military's gift of land, Malt began to appeal for donations in the pages of al-Da'wa, telling readers that "the treasury of the Islamic Medical Association . . . is the pockets of charitable Muslims."[38] To handle donations in multiple currencies, the IMA set up accounts in the state-owned Banque Misr and Bank Ahli, as well as in the Faisal Islamic Bank.[39] Key to this appeal was securing religious approval for the IMA to receive zakāt donations. To this end, Malt obtained a fatwa from the prominent Islamist scholar Yusuf al-Qaradawi that paying zakāt to the hospital project was a legitimate religious expenditure. In the fatwa, reprinted in al-Da'wa, Qaradawi explained that the Islamic Charity Hospital

> represents a citadel among citadels defending Islam, preserving the doctrines of its sons against the onslaught of missionary and evangelical hospitals and foundations. Every aid to it, physical or moral, is considered an act among the acts of jihad in the cause of God. For jihad is not only by the sword, and not only limited to military service, as

many think. But it is an act toward the triumph of Islam, enabling it and defending it in every arena, and by every means. For this reason I think that counting the zakāt toward the erecting of this charitable hospital is "in the cause of God and for the triumph of Islam."[40]

Even as they appealed for donations to build the hospital, Malt and his colleagues had envisioned that the IMA would ultimately operate more or less as a business, catering to paying Egyptians. From a religio-legal perspective this raised a question: Was it justified to use charitable contributions to support an essentially commercial enterprise? To elide this issue, as part of the fatwa Qaradawi engaged in a little bit of legal gymnastics. Because a minority of the bed space in the facility (20 percent) would be reserved for the poor, he reasoned, this qualified the facility as a worthy recipient of zakāt funding.

With backing from the unlikely bedfellows of Egypt's military and the Islamist luminary Yusuf al-Qaradawi, the Islamic Charity Hospital campaign quickly achieved tangible success. A January 1981 article in al-Da'wa charted the progress of the construction. Not only had walls around the property been constructed, but a foundation of forty thousand square meters had been dug at a cost of approximately 80,000 EGP.[41] By June of that year work on the foundation had been completed.[42]

Work ceased that fall. Amid mounting criticism over his economic policies and rapprochement with Israel, Sadat launched a widespread crackdown on his opponents, including many of the Islamists he had so recently courted. In fact, on Sadat's list of groups whose funds he ordered frozen, the Islamic Medical Association was second (the Rightly Guided Caliphs Association was first).[43] The IMA's assets, a second decree stated, were transferred to the Red Crescent society (equivalent to the Red Cross).[44]

Generous financial, bureaucratic, and symbolic support from the Egyptian government had given the Brotherhood an important head start in its mission to reenter Egyptian society. Although the relationship between the Islamic Medical Association and Sadat ended on a sour note, the IMA—like many of those arrested during the Autumn of Fury—was rehabilitated by Hosni Mubarak in the early months of his term. As the following section discusses, this was a key juncture. Mubarak's decision to restore the assets of the IMA and tolerate its operation, driven partially by his own economic pressures, effectively ensured that any future attempt to extract the Brotherhood from Egypt's increasingly variegated social welfare landscape would be a difficult task. This dilemma emerged most starkly after the 2005 elections, when Mubarak would begin targeting the Brotherhood's social services in a last-ditch, and ultimately unsuccessful, effort to secure his hold on power.

What to Do When Your Hands Are Tied

Empowering nonstate providers had allowed Sadat to escape the immediate consequences of economic reforms. It was difficult to foresee how this strategy might, decades later, end up empowering a group that, in the late 1970s, was quite weak.[45] His successor, Hosni Mubarak, in contrast, was the one forced to navigate between an increasingly politically assertive Brotherhood and a state treasury that remained unable to meet the needs of its citizens.

Sketching out the general trajectory of Brotherhood-regime relations under Mubarak, and in particular how and why this relationship degraded from the relative comity enjoyed under Sadat, illustrates a key theoretical point. Were we to simply drop in on regime-Brotherhood relations in the early 2000s we would be hard-pressed to explain Mubarak's continued willingness to tolerate such an obviously disadvantageous situation, in which the Brotherhood was presiding over a vast network of social services that were obviously playing a key role in its increasingly assertive political mobilization against the regime.

This question of why Mubarak would tolerate such a situation resolves when set in a longer timeline. Under Mubarak, the Brotherhood's social service networks began to furnish the group a powerful social base from which it was able to launch an effective electoral challenge. But Mubarak's hands were largely tied—Egypt's economic situation remained problematic, and suppressing the Brotherhood's extensive network of nonstate providers would risk the very turmoil that Sadat had hoped to avoid. Further adding to the pressure, powerful international financial institutions were pressuring Mubarak in the opposite direction, suggesting he devolve even more power to the NGO community to compensate for needed structural reforms. This equilibrium held for a surprisingly long period of time, but it began to collapse after the 2005 elections, as the Brotherhood's pointed electoral challenge coincided with a looming regime transition as Hosni Mubarak schemed to pass power to his son Gamal.

Throughout the 1980s Egypt's financial position weakened amid falling oil prices, increasing foreign debt, and growing unemployment (Richards 1991). Mubarak began negotiations for a loan package with the International Monetary Fund, one condition of which was to begin adjusting the country's balance sheet to reduce social spending (Momani 2005). This program of structural adjustment had significant implications for Egypt's health care market and thus consequences for the relationship between the Islamic Medical Association and the Mubarak regime. One of the World Bank's new priorities for health care in developing countries involved shifting more financial responsibility for care to individuals so that the government health sector could tackle larger and public problems. "Individuals are generally willing to pay for direct, largely curative care with obvious benefits to themselves and their families," the authors of a key 1987 report noted. "Those who have sufficient income to do so should pay for these services. The financing and provision of these private types of health services (which benefit mainly the direct consumer) should be shifted to a combination of the nongovernment sector and a public sector reorganized to be financially more self-sufficient" (Akin, Birdsall, and deFerranti 1987, 2). An important part of this new strategy was the idea of "cost recovery," which encouraged medical facilities to begin charging citizens for aspects of basic care that had earlier been borne by the government (World Bank 1993).

The international donor community was not blind to the increasing demands on the citizenry these reforms would imply. A key part of structural adjustment was, as the aforementioned quote suggests, engaging the nongovernmental sector in social service provision (a recommendation that was doubly copacetic in light of the post–Cold War emphasis on growing civil society as a means of democratization). So simultaneous with the pressures to reduce the role of the state in social service provision, international donors were encouraging the Egyptian government to make it easier for NGOs to operate. A 1991 World Bank report on Egypt noted that "the most urgent need is to expand [NGOs'] scope by relaxing some of the red tape which surrounds their fund raising operations" (145). The authors later returned to this point, concluding that Egypt's "NGOs could greatly increase the scale of their operations if their capacity to raise funds were not so restricted" (147).

Forcing more of the social welfare burden onto NGOs would mirror a strategy that was already at work in the private sector. During the 1990s Mubarak began to remind Egypt's fat cats that their wealth required them to assume certain responsibilities toward their less affluent countrymen and women (Kandil 2012, 211). Presumably to blunt the impact of Islamic groups' relief efforts (see below), Suzanne Mubarak herself spearheaded an effort following the 1992 earthquake to enroll prominent businessmen in relief efforts (Soliman 2011, 127). Later in the decade Mubarak would chide businessmen that their "personal wealth entailed social obligations," effectively coercing them to provide public services, such as refurbishing public schools (Kienle 2004, 288). This "coerced charity," as Stephen King put it, allowed the regime to potentially redirect some small part of the extensive gains of privatization toward those suffering under its deprivations (2009, 14).

Yet while this "coerced charity" essentially amounted to squeezing funds from cronies, enrolling NGOs in social welfare efforts would play right into the hands of Mubarak's most potent political challenger. Not only was the Brotherhood notching notable gains in parliamentary elections, but its increasing presence in syndicate politics made it appear as if the Islamists were on the verge of a breakthrough (Wickham 2002; Shehata and Stacher 2006; Brownlee 2010a). By the early 1990s the Brotherhood, as Asef Bayat put it, "seemed to be looming at the state's backdoor, ready to pounce" (2007a, 143).

The Brotherhood's reaction to the devastating October 1992 earthquake that struck central Cairo highlighted Mubarak's dilemma. With the regime nowhere to be seen, the Muslim Brotherhood's web of organizations and services sprang into action. Within hours the group had made its presence felt among the victims, handing out food and water, providing shelter, and making medical services available (Awadi 2004, 149–53). The group's effectiveness was a striking counterpoint to the government's embarrassingly sclerotic response. The Brotherhood also could not resist the urge to attempt to make political hay out of the episode, deploying its readily recognizable campaign slogan, "Islam Is the Solution," as part of its relief efforts, plastering it across Brotherhood banners and tents (it had earlier been deployed during election campaigns). One member of the Brotherhood later reported a private conversation with a security official, who praised the Brotherhood's humanitarian efforts but condemned the group for pairing the social service provision with political propaganda and warned that the state would not accept this interaction (Awadi 2005, 73–74). Indeed, a number of analyses of the deterioration in relations between the Brotherhood and the Mubarak regime in the 1990s reference the Brotherhood's politicization of its earthquake response as an important factor in the tension (Abed-Kotob 1995; Campagna 1996; Awadi 2005).

Starting under Sadat and through to Mubarak, the primary strategy the regime used for maintaining control over the Brotherhood's social service networks relied upon the various bureaucratic and administrative organs of the state. In addition to the overall oversight role of the Ministry of Social Affairs, for instance, the Central Accounting Agency (al-Jihaz al-Markazi li-l-Muhasabat) had authority to inspect the accounts of the organization and monitor financial irregularities. The Ministry of Health constantly inspected all facilities for cleanliness and sanitation. Finally, particularly for those medical facilities that rented property from religious endowments (for instance, renting space in a mosque complex), both the Ministry of Religious Endowments and the Administrative Control Authority (Hay'at al-Riqba al-Idariyya) also have oversight jurisdiction (Sullivan 1994, 17).[46] This web of bureaucratic organizations gave the regime a variety of subtle avenues through which to ensure that the Brotherhood's social service networks remained domesticated, and the tools with which to warn them back if they refused.

A concatenation of events in the mid-1990s—including the Cairo earthquake, growing Brotherhood visibility in civil society and associational life, and increasing a sense that the Brotherhood's social service network was fueling its political challenge—began to show the limits of this more restrained strategy of control. Although the regime's need to preserve social stability limited its ability to fully crack down, lower-level confrontations between the IMA and the regime grew more common as Egypt's economy continued to stress many of its citizens. As an official from state security told the administrator of a Brotherhood hospital during an inspection in the mid-1990s, "If you weren't helping us carry the load, we'd haul all of you into prison."[47]

Eventually, the regime began using blunter coercive measures in its interactions with the social sector (Kienle 1998; Awadi 2005). In the civic sector, the security agencies increasingly took charge of dealing with social organizations and NGOs while sidelining the relevant ministries, for instance, the Ministry of Social Affairs (Tadros 2011). As the Brotherhood's political challenge sharpened during the 2000s, the regime's approach shifted to targeted repression specifically designed to blunt the presumed electoral impact of the Brotherhood's social services. Surprise visits from the authorities and nitpicking inspections had been a fact of life for the IMA for years, but beginning around 2005 the regime stepped up its interventions, ranging from petty harassment and temporary closure on one end to forced reorganizations, abrupt denial of permission to operate new facilities, and the seizure and destruction of existing facilities at the other (Gabas 2005, 229–30). Some of the first salvos of this new offensive were fired shortly after the 2005 elections, when the Brotherhood lodged an unprecedented victory against the regime by sending eighty-eight deputies to parliament. IMA facilities, both on the drawing board and in operation, would be casualties of this clash.

One tactic was to simply deny the IMA permission to open new facilities. In late 2005–early 2006 the IMA began to prepare a modest new medical facility in the delta town of Itay al-Barud, situated around 125 km northwest of Cairo. After years of planning and working with the regime and the town's citizens to get the plans approved, the IMA began converting a two-story building in the city center into a clinic that would eventually hold fifteen beds and two examination rooms, in addition to an on-premises pharmacy. At that point State Security stepped in and stopped the process. "You already have the Dar al-Salam hospital in [nearby] Damanhur," the agents told the IMA. "You'll have to erect this one over our dead bodies." After freezing the process, State Security eventually allowed the project to proceed after the IMA agreed to hand the entire enterprise off to the less politically active al-Jam'iyya al-Shar'iyya. Now the facility serves as one of that organization's medical centers treating premature infants.[48]

Another tactic of the regime was to expropriate facilities for its own use. The IMA's first clinic was in the lower-middle-class Cairo district of Sayyida Zaynab. The clinic began when a group of Muslim Brotherhood doctors cleaned out a room used to store trash behind the famous Sayyida Zaynab mosque and started seeing patients a few nights a week.[49] In the 1990 elections a talented lawyer and National Democratic Party functionary, Fathi Surour, was elected from the district. He would later become the chairman of the People's Assembly, a position he would hold until 2011.[50] After the 2005 elections, Surour maneuvered to expropriate the Muslim Brotherhood's Sayyida Zaynab clinic for himself, in order "to prevent the spread of the Muslim Brotherhood, and to prevent their communication with the people" according to an IMA official (who had himself started with the organization by working in the Sayyida Zaynab facility).[51]

What they were unable to stop or seize, the regime simply destroyed. Despite Sadat's high-profile inauguration of the Islamic Charity Hospital, the facility did not last a decade. In 1986 Hosni Mubarak confiscated the facility, reportedly because he was incensed by the hospital's high-profile location on a main artery into Cairo's downtown (the facility is now a military hospital).[52] In compensation for the seizure, in 1991 the regime gave the IMA a smaller plot of land a short distance away, near the current City Stars commercial complex.[53] After building up a small outpatient clinic there, in 1993 the group began to work on an ambitious new expansion of the facility. At that time Ahmad al-Malt laid the foundation stone for the new facility, accompanied by Shaykh Muhammad al-Ghazali, whose sermon two decades prior had ignited in Malt the idea of the Islamic Medical Association.

Construction slowed during the 2000 parliamentary elections while inspections and general harassment increased (Shammakh 2011, 86).[54] The IMA navigated these difficulties, and in 2006 it launched a new expansion expected to cost over $7.3 million and scheduled to be completed in time for the 2010 parliamentary elections.[55] Even as the group began to construct new floors and purchase new equipment, the regime stepped in to destroy the building, allegedly for violating zoning restrictions. In December of 2009 workers armed with picks, sledgehammers, and heavy equipment descended on the facility to destroy it from the inside out.[56] Although a sit-in of doctors and patients opposed the regime, the workers began around-the-clock demolition efforts that eventually stretched over a week.

The Brotherhood and the IMA scrambled to stop the demolition. In addition to filing emergency appeals with the Cairo courts, the IMA also tried to appeal to Hosni Mubarak through his wife, Suzanne, and attempted to place advertisements in the media (it claims newspapers rejected the ads under regime pressure). As one senior figure in the IMA claimed, "We told Mubarak 'please, if you don't want us to have it, take it for yourself! There's no need to destroy it!'"[57] This was "a political case" claimed the Brotherhood parliamentarian, Mohammed Beltagy.[58] The Brotherhood's parliamentary deputy from the district, 'Isam

Mukhtar, led a delegation to plead the case with the Cairo governorate. After failing to stop the demolition, he exasperatedly told the press, "It seems this is a new strategy by the regime . . . to pull the rug out from under the Brotherhood's feet in advance of the upcoming parliamentary and presidential elections, despite the damage it will do to the ordinary Egyptian."[59] Eventually the IMA's lawyers were able to stop the destruction but not before two floors had been wrecked and a number of delicate machines had been rendered unusable.[60] As late as 2013 the top floors remained closed amid exposed rebar concrete and blown-out walls, scars from the attempted destruction.

The type of targeted repression visited on the Central Charity Hospital was, as Mukhtar intuited, part of a much larger strategy to prevent the Brotherhood from building on their gains from the 2005 parliamentary election as the 2010 contests approached. As those elections drew nearer, inspectors forced IMA facilities to close for the smallest infractions. For instance, the security services showed up at Sharabiyya Hospital in October 2010 and shut the entire facility down over a leaky faucet.[61] Shortly thereafter, regime agents visited Tawba Hospital in northern Cairo and forced it to close because the fire suppression system was judged to be deficient. The facility remained closed for the duration of the parliamentary elections and in fact reopened only after Mubarak stepped down in February 2011.[62] Similarly, Hadi Hospital, south of Cairo, was forced to close because an employee left a dirty uniform on the floor.[63] Muwasat Hospital in the delta was also closed during the 2010 elections.[64] Not only that, but the hospital's parent association (Muwasat Association) came under tremendous pressure for allegedly campaigning on behalf of Brotherhood candidates, to the point that the district governor even demanded the association be dissolved.[65]

The harassment against the Brotherhood's medical network got so bad that the group felt the need to address it as part of a larger formal statement explaining its participation in the 2010 elections (most opposition groups refused to participate in the elections and, although the Brotherhood initially refused to join that boycott, it would ultimately withdraw its candidates after unprecedented fraud in the first round). The Brotherhood urged the regime to

> desist in mobilizing the state's institutions against its opponents, especially the unjustified use of security services which have carried out dozens of arrest campaigns against the Muslim Brotherhood around the country, in addition to raiding dozens of offices, as well as branches and hospitals of the Islamic Medical Association around the country, which is all an illegal attempt to cripple the candidates of the Muslim Brotherhood. [66]

The crackdown on the Muslim Brotherhood was part and parcel of Mubarak's larger effort to regain control over a society that had grown increasingly restive

(Mahdi 2008; Beinin 2009). This culminated in the wave of blatant abuse during the 2010 parliamentary elections, which observers dubbed as "the most fraudulent in the country's history" (Stacher 2012b, 203). Of course, rather than a deft restabilization, this spasm of repression that further deprived an already put-upon citizenry was the prelude to the upheaval of the January 25 revolt.

Legacies of Economic Crisis

This chapter has analyzed the economic and political conditions surrounding the founding of the Islamic Medical Association in 1977. A variety of new qualitative material supports one key implication of the theory: that autocrats, in response to acute economic crisis, can gain breathing room by devolving social service provision to nonstate providers. Yet to retain a degree of social control they will use legal and bureaucratic means to render this activism visible. Anwar al-Sadat reacted to the nationwide rioting of 1977 by increasingly enrolling nonstate providers, prominent among them religious organizations, into efforts to deliver social services. Among these was the Islamic Medical Association, which Muslim Brotherhood leader Ahmad al-Malt founded as a way to reconnect with Egyptian society after a long period of absence.

Malt and his colleagues immediately grounded the Islamic Medical Association on a legal basis, putting the organization in compliance with Egyptian Law 32 of 1964. By signaling their acquiescence to the existing political order, they were able to access many of the incentives that Sadat was offering nonstate providers to get them to step up their social welfare responsibilities. This included financial assistance as well as rhetorical and symbolic support, as when Sadat laid the foundation stone at the IMA's flagship hospital. This evidence is "doubly decisive" in the sense that as it supports one hypothesis, it casts doubt on another (Van Evera 1997, 32). Specifically, it suggests that little about the Islamist social service enterprise took place away from the eyes of the state. Instead, the regime was deeply involved in the origination of these activities and remained actively aware of their scope through 2011.

The final sections of the chapter traced the relationship between the Islamic Medical Association and the regime through the January 25 uprising to highlight one additional implication of the theory. Regimes that decide, in a moment of crisis, to encourage nonstate providers to accelerate their activism will experience a steady erosion of their ability to curtail this activism in the future. In this way, the 2010 scuttling of the bargain that allowed the Brotherhood a relatively free hand to proliferate social services was a harbinger of the end of the regime itself. In the 1970s the Brotherhood was willing to bet that, in the long term, the benefits of its above-ground and legal provision of social services would out-weigh the costs of submitting to regime supervision. In contrast, the regime's future discount rate was very low: Sadat was willing to risk the possibility that he was nurturing a long-term challenge to his regime in exchange for staving off what was in the late 1970s a more imminent threat of popular mobilization. In the end, Hosni Mubarak found himself facing the worst of both worlds: while the Brotherhood attempted to leverage its electoral power to secure a permanent place in the regime as it stood, protesters in Tahrir Square were attempting to tear it all down.

INSIDE THE ISLAMIST ADVANTAGE

Two trajectories instantiated in the 1970s combined decades later to produce the conditions under which the Muslim Brotherhood's social service provision would generate political support. Sadat's decision to back the government out of its social obligations triggered a cascade of fairly predictable consequences for the public sector. Not only was the quality of government facilities slowly degrading, but the corruption that was leaching into myriad state-society interactions was particularly pronounced in the health sector. Against this backdrop, the Islamic Medical Association's particular style of provision made it an increasingly popular option for Egyptians who could neither bear the indignities of a visit to public facilities nor afford the exorbitant fees at a private one.

This chapter combines a variety of new historical material with contemporary fieldwork and interviews to provide the first detailed examination of the way that the Muslim Brotherhood's vaunted social service network operated. One key finding is that a consistent stream of revenue, itself a bequest of the IMA's founders' initial decision to target more affluent customers, allowed the IMA to hire talented staff and helped managers ensure that all employees were invested in the mission to provide quality and relationally enjoyable care. This allowed the IMA's provision to make a pronounced impression on the citizens who patronized the group's facilities, an effect that would increasingly bear political fruits.

The first half of this chapter illustrates the decline of quality and spread of corruption in Egypt's public health sector that stemmed from Sadat's decision to reduce the state's role. It then identifies the mechanisms behind the IMA's style of provision, specifically the ways in which its focus on a paid customer base gave the organization the tools with which to generate and maintain a decent standard of care that appealed to a middle-class audience. The chapter's final sections use three case studies of non-Brotherhood providers to show how initial decisions influence whether or not social service provision can be used for political effect.

Egypt's Public Health Infrastructure Frays

In a moment of fiscal crisis, the Egyptian president Anwar al-Sadat gambled that encouraging the proliferation of nonstate actors would help mitigate the potentially disastrous political consequences of economic reform. But while this strategy did help prevent a repeat of the 1977 bread riots, the detrimental effects on the health sector were notable. Under the combined stresses of population growth, urbanization, and budget pressures, Egypt's public health sector increasingly struggled to maintain basic services and competencies. The effect was to trap Egypt's middle class between two bad options: attempt to access an increasingly out-of-reach private sector or endure humiliation and pain at one of the country's overburdened public facilities.[1]

The state's reduced emphasis on social services (and medical provision in particular) was not simply a question of declining *access*; the quality of the available services also fell precipitously as "irksome chaos and corruption [spread] at all levels of admin."[2] This generated further inequalities among Egypt's increasingly divided population.[3] On the one hand, these deficiencies were partly the consequence of unavoidable structural factors, such as rapid population growth that put immense strain on facilities. On the other, the way that these problems metastasized across the sector were part of a broader and deliberate government strategy to push a portion of the citizenry off the public budget (Waterbury 1983, 218–23; Tadros 2006, 247). "Unable to reform or upgrade the public medical service," Ray Hinnebusch argues, "the strategy of the Sadat regime was to neglect [the public health sector] and encourage the development of a quality private sector" (1988, 272). But the private sector that emerged was instead heavily tilted toward the wealthy, leaving middle-class Egyptians without a clear option for care (Chiffoleau 1990). A joint Egyptian government/Harvard analysis charted how the market began to separate. "Approximately 89% of private beds are in first or second class accommodation," the authors argued. "This indicates that the private sector provides for the upper end of the market, either those who can afford to pay or are willing to pay in order to be treated in the private sector. On the other hand, [Ministry of Health and Population] and university facilities assign the majority of their beds to free care and the least to first class accommodation" ("Egypt Provider Survey Report (Draft)" 1994–95, 3).

So instead of selecting upwards into private options as Sadat hoped, the infitāḥ squeezed the middle class downward into crumbling public facilities already swollen with the ranks of the poor (Bayat 2006, 139). This was a painful reckoning. As the Egyptian economist Galal Amin notes, in the wake of the infitāḥ "the Egyptian middle class suffered a series of blows that slowed its growth rate sharply, lowered its standard of living, and made it even less distinguishable from the lower class" (2011, 96–97). The psychological effects of this downward mobility were considerable, especially for those for whom education and employment (not to mention exposure to Egypt's burgeoning consumerism) had bred expectations of a particular middle-class lifestyle. For the longtime Brotherhood leader 'Abd al-Mu'nim Abu al-Futuh, himself a young doctor at the time, the choice was particularly galling. "The poor people would have to go to the governmental service, and it was humiliating," he conceded. "But what about a judge . . . or a new doctor like me? If someone like us would have to go to the government [public] service, we would be humiliated. But we can't afford the private hospitals."[4]

A 2002 study of Egypt's health service providers, cosponsored by the Egyptian Ministry of Health and Population, showed the dire state of public-sector facilities, even in basic metrics of quality, such as functioning latrines and general cleanliness. As the report summarized, "Among all facilities, only 49 percent had all client amenities and a regular supply of water and electricity. . . . Only 55 percent of general service hospitals and 53 percent of fever hospitals had all of these items" ("Egypt: Service Provision Assessment Survey 2002" 2003, 26). A World Bank–directed survey of facilities in Alexandria and Manufiyya governorates captured in a more systematic way the failings of the country's health care system. Over three surprise visits, the enumerators found almost half of the full-time staff (42 percent) were absent at least once (World Bank 2010, 61). The facilities themselves often lacked basic materials: only around 30 percent of facilities possessed a working electrocardiogram, just over 40 percent had the materials to measure blood pressure, fewer than half (48.4 percent) could find a hammer to test reflexes, and the surveyors also noted a general lack of basic materials with which to educate patients. The enumerators—all trained physicians—sat in on exams and pronounced doctors' inability to follow basic hygiene practices (hand washing, using gloves, disposing of items between patients) as "alarming" (63). When asked why they were unable to improve services, the largest percentage of facility managers (43 percent) cited "low staff motivation," while other common laments were lack of supplies (39 percent) and lack of qualified staff (37.5 percent) (63).

Provider surveys repeatedly find Egyptian governmental facilities at the bottom of both perceived and actual quality. Winnie Yip and Aniceto Orbeta used data from the Household Health Care Utilization and Expenditure Survey to generate an index measure of perceived quality based on respondents' ratings across dimensions of access, structure, and process.[5] The Ministry of Health and other public facilities scored on the low end of the spectrum, while private facilities scored the highest (1999, 10). Their findings echoed an earlier report (an earlier series of the same underlying surveys) that found the same hierarchy across the three rough dimensions (quality, interpersonal relations, and time spent with patients), although the ratings were based on trained enumerator observations rather than patients' self-reported perceptions ("Egypt Provider Survey Report (Draft)" 1994–95, 27).

As urbanization, population growth, and mismanagement ground Egypt's health infrastructure into the dirt, a visit to one of the country's public facilities became a grim joke. "People believe that the quality of services in Bulaq Public Hospital and the old Kasr el Aini Hospital have deteriorated so much," reported Mariz Tadros, "that those requiring in-patient care would rather die at home than be admitted for in-patient care" (2006, 252). A 2012 report from *al-Ahram* sketched a dire scene at Hilwan's general hospital, just south of Cairo:

> The building looked like it had been abandoned for decades. It was an island in a huge pile of rubbish. Grey paint was peeling off its walls and a sewage drain had erupted near the entrance filling the air with an abominable stench. The only indication of what the structure was used for was a tattered sign reading "Kidney Dialysis Centre." . . . The horror continued inside: the stone stairs are broken, dirt blackens green walls, the bathroom is filled with broken chairs and more rubbish, and puddles fill the corridors leading to the wards.[6]

As if the worsening quality in Egypt's facilities wasn't bad enough, the increasing financial strains bred corrupt practices, as public servants offered those who paid bribes and offered favors a chance "to get a little ahead, a little extra, a little quicker" (Jain, Nundy, and Abbasi 2014, 4184). This "tyranny of corruption" (Naggar 2009, 44) spread to nearly all aspects of the Egyptian health care system, and anecdotes abound of patients and their families being accosted for bribes and pressured to call in favors at nearly every level of care, from the lowliest attendant to the loftiest administrator (Badrawi and Yusuf 2007). One report on government corruption in Egypt, prepared by the country's Central Auditing Authority and leaked to the media in 2016, contains a litany of examples of managerial and bureaucratic corruption in the health sector.[7] Concluding that corruption contributes to "severe weakness" in administration of the health sector, the report highlights insufficient oversight of building and operations of hospitals, contractor misconduct, and how foreign aid and local charitable contributions were rerouted to pay bonuses to bosses instead of to fulfill their directed purpose (Central Accounting Authority 2015, 204–6). Kefaya, the anti-Mubarak reform coalition that was formed in late 2004, described in its own report how the health sector's pervasive corruption rendered receipt of medical care in public facilities "a journey of torture riddled with red tape and complicated procedures" (Kefaya Movement 2006, 103).

Systematic data on corruption in Egypt's health facilities is difficult to come by, but certain indicators are available. While it did not query respondents specifically about corruption, a 2003 provider survey found that government facilities were the least likely type of providers to have fixed, all-inclusive, and publicly posted fees for delivery services ("Egypt: Service Provision Assessment Survey 2002," 2003, 265). One effect of this, presumably, would be to increase opportunities for bribery by allowing medical personnel to manufacture ad hoc costs for materials and procedures that would end up in their pockets (Lewis 2007). In the 2013 round of the Afrobarometer survey, respondents *were* asked about the extent of corruption, specifically, "In the past year, how often, if ever, have you had to pay a bribe, give a gift, or do a favor to government officials in order to get treatment at a local health clinic or hospital?" Of the 809 Egyptian respondents who needed the services of a local health clinic or hospital, over half (52.16 percent) had to pay a bribe at least once.[8] And in the 2013 Global Corruption Barometer survey, 73 percent of the Egyptians sampled judged the country's medical sector either "corrupt" or "extremely corrupt."[9]

Middle-Class Targeting

Against a public sector where filth, disinterest, and corruption made dying at home a conceivable option, the Brotherhood's Islamic Medical Association stood out for its reliable, affordable, and compassionate care. But this care was not universally available; the IMA's leaders made a conscious decision to orient the organization toward middle-class Egyptians who found themselves trapped in the aforementioned public-private gap in the market. The Brotherhood's interest in this social stratum was driven by various calculations, including historic ties to the country's middle class (Brooke and Ketchley 2018), a desire to fill a need among the population, and a recognition that, at the time the group was conceptualizing its social service provision outreach it simply lacked the movement resources to support an effort aimed at providing free or low-cost care. The effect of this decision would be to ground the group's social service provision in an especially durable and self-sufficient foundation. This, in turn, would allow the Brotherhood to stand out in especially vivid tones amid both failing state institutions and proliferating private providers.

An emphasis on providing for Egypt's struggling middle class runs through the IMA's documentary record. As the IMA's founder, Ahmad al-Malt, explained, the proliferation of private hospitals during the early years of the infitāḥ had encouraged Egyptian doctors to see their knowledge as a financial commodity to be sold rather than a gift with which to alleviate human suffering. This, he argued, had forced ordinary Egyptians to choose between sacrificing their dignity at overburdened and underfunded public facilities or "selling the clothes off their own back" to enter a private facility (Malt 1993, 177). He envisioned the IMA would split the difference by offering "reliable care without exploiting the patient."[10] In his memoirs Malt elaborated: "We are able to preserve the dignity of those who cannot bear standing in line at a public hospital only to receive substandard care, or who cannot go to a private hospital because they lack the ability to pay. . . . At the IMA we have Muslim doctors who work for Allah's pleasure, with solid qualifications, who respect the rights of the patient and are sensitive to that patient's ability to pay" (1993, 178).

'Abd al-Mu'nim Abu al-Futuh, one of the early members of the Islamic Medical Association, recalled a similar justification for the organization's creation: "At that time [the late 1970s] we saw two paths for medical care in Egypt—the governmental, weak, fraying system, and the investment [private] system, which was for the rich. . . . So the reason behind founding [the IMA] was to offer medical service, moderately priced and decent. . . . So when a middle-class person comes for an operation, they can afford it and they'll have a clean place to stay. [The IMA] is not as good as a private hospital, but it is also not humiliating like a public one."[11]

As Malt and Futuh intimate, the IMA was established to run on a quasi-commercial basis, although the organization was quick to specify in its founding documents that profits were not the goal of the enterprise. A 1977 al-Da'wa article introducing the IMA specified that the association would not be "a business or profit-making venture. All the revenue will be spent to improve the services of the association and maintain and improve the facilities. Nothing [no profits] will go back to the members or sponsors but the pride in their good deeds and the reward of Allah."[12] This orientation continued through the life of the organization, and the IMA never took a profit from its facilities; instead it used any end-of-the-year surplus to reinvest and grow the network.

This practice enabled the IMA to build itself independently and mostly from scratch, beholden neither to the whims of donors nor the commitment of volunteers. At IMA facilities common services are not prohibitively expensive: to see either a general practitioner or a specialist individuals purchase a ticket upon entering the facility. The prices of these tickets fluctuate somewhat depending on the socioeconomic area of the hospital but usually average around three or four dollars for a generalist. More extensive care, however, entails additional expense. In these situations, the patient will usually split the outlay between the doctor and the facility. For instance, for surgeries half of the patient's fee goes to the hospital while half goes to the doctors themselves.[13] Nearly all facilities also include an associated pharmacy where commonly prescribed drugs are for sale at competitive prices.[14] According to one IMA executive interviewed in early 2013, patient fees accounted for approximately 98 percent of the organization's total budget.[15]

The IMA's prudent financial management style that matched competent care to populations willing and able to pay generated fairly consistent organizational growth. During my fieldwork I obtained from the IMA a series of audit sheets for the network's hospitals, which show that the vast majority of visitors paid, in cash, for the services they received. The audit sheets I was given (years 2005–11 inclusive) confirm the historical record that catering to a middle-class, paying clientele was a characteristic of the organization. For each facility these documents provide the raw number of "poor" patients who received care (e.g., free or subsidized care). As figure 4.1 shows, during this period, never more than 5 percent of patients at the IMA's network of medical facilities fell into this category.

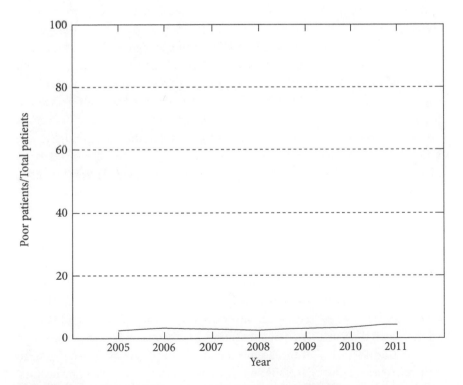

FIGURE 4.1. Annual percentage of poor patients, 2005–11

Authors and analysts often attribute the social activism of groups like the Muslim Brotherhood to an "egalitarian impulse" that drives them to focus on the poor (Davis and Robinson 2006). A declassified CIA report from 1986 even claimed that the Brotherhood, led by Malt, had been establishing "free medical clinics in Cairo slums."[16] A variety of qualitative and quantitative evidence complicates these arguments, showing instead that the overwhelming number of those benefiting from the Brotherhood's largest social service enterprise paid for the services they received. This is, obviously, quite different from what we would expect were the organization engaged in either clientelism or charity. The IMA did provide a limited amount of free care to indigent patients, but they were required to navigate a relatively extensive bureaucracy in order to access it. Most of the poor patients served by the IMA were referred through an existing mosque, charity organization, or wealthy persons in the area known for their sponsorship of the poor (*ahl al-khayr*, lit. "charitable people").[17] If poor patients did walk in, they were still eligible for charity care, but they were first extensively investigated by the specific hospital's "public relations" committee to determine whether or not they are truly needy.[18] The point of this extensive bureaucracy made sense for an organization concerned with balancing income and expenses, and worried about the fiscal consequences of providing free care to whoever simply asked for it.

The IMA's emphasis on providing care to paying audiences shaped the atmosphere at its facilities in a number of ways. One key mechanism had to do with hiring and firing. Without a predictable and independent flow of resources from paying customers, the organization could not entice the best staff. Instead, it would have been forced to use only those willing to work for reduced or even no salaries (i.e. volunteers) and to provide care only when those individuals could make time to work. Managers, for their part, would also have been hindered in their ability to enforce standards because they would have little leverage to discipline or fire employees who flouted them.

The IMA could be choosy about whom it hired because it was known to offer competitive salaries and, in general, because the association had a reputation for being well run and offering good opportunities for professional advancement.[19] Reflecting Janine Clark's observation that "interpersonal bonds come first and then ideology, not the reverse" (2004, 25), hiring often occurred through personal networks rather than ties to the Brotherhood's organizational or ideological milieu. The IMA often recruited at medical schools (particularly outside Cairo) and also placed ads in its internal publication, *al-Hikma*.[20] In fact, the presence of a preexisting network of medical professionals in an area sometimes exercised an influence over where the IMA sited a brick-and-mortar facility.[21] As one hospital director explained, people would usually travel long distances for their main job (e.g., in a government or university hospital). But in his experience it was incredibly difficult to convince them to do so for a second job as well.[22] Many of the employees I spoke with—particularly the nurses and technicians—were from the neighborhoods in which the facilities were located. For instance, at one facility I noticed a sign for a 5 percent discount for residents of the area stashed in the corner of an office. I asked an employee how she knew if someone was a resident or just trying to get the discount, and she explained that the hospital employees knew all the families who lived there because they were their neighbors.[23]

Employees noted that the IMA had a reputation among their peers for being a desirable workplace both because of the good pay and because of the ways that employees were encouraged to build their skills in the organization. One common way the IMA did this was to encourage talented and dedicated staff to apply internally for management positions, even if they had started at lower or midlevel positions in the facilities. For instance, the assistant manager in one facility had joined as a nurse and had worked her way up.[24] A doctor had started out of medical school in the emergency department, was promoted to assistant manager, and then to manager.[25] Another explicitly compared the IMA's willingness to cultivate talent against government hospitals' sclerotic bureaucracy. In the public sector, he argued, age (he was in his early thirties) would essentially determine his position in the organization's hierarchy. In contrast, the IMA managers "do not discriminate against us because of our age, only if we are skillful, good with patients, good managers."[26] A doctor in an IMA facility in the delta concurred, noting that his salary and the scope of his responsibilities were "based on skill."[27]

The IMA's careful hiring practices—facilitated by its ability to offer competitive salaries and thus choose among a pool of interested applicants—ensured a high-quality, technically proficient, and motivated workforce. Equally important was the active role of management and continual monitoring to ensure that the IMA's standards lived up to what Malt envisioned when he founded the organization. Managers strove to create a "flat" style to personally invest the employees in the success of the facility. As one described, encouraging employees to bring problems and suggest improvements to their superiors ensured a "family-like" atmosphere.[28] According to one young doctor, there was a "familiarity between employees, everyone is in good spirits, and the facility is well organized."[29] A lab manager explained the type of ethos he brought to his job: "We should not just work here for the money, we should belong to it, feel like we have to make it better—to take ownership of it."[30]

The Islamic Medical Association relied on a series of internal mechanisms to monitor the atmosphere in its facilities, keep up employee spirits, and troubleshoot problems. There was a practice of frequently shuttling doctors and managers around to different hospitals in the IMA network. One employee in the

Cairo area worked three simultaneous jobs for the IMA, managing diagnostic labs in Hilwan, Giza, and Maʿadi. Another managed both an IMA hospital and a dialysis center in addition to working a day job in a government hospital (his day, he claimed, began at 4:30 a.m.). On a number of occasions I encountered a manager hard at work at one facility whom I had met earlier in my fieldwork at a different facility. Not only did this acquaint the employees with all facilities and their respective clienteles and prevent burnout, but it also identified and diffused best practices across the network. One employee related how he had developed a procedure for tracking lab chemicals in one facility and, after monitoring its success, was encouraged to implement it in other facilities.[31] In another instance, the IMA had piloted a digitized system to track patient health records at two facilities in Cairo before extending the project to the rest of the network.[32]

As part of the effort to make employees feel invested in the facilities, the managers also encouraged friendly competition among the facilities. Officials from the IMA's headquarters in Cairo constantly assessed the individual facilities and independently ranked them according to twenty-five criteria, across areas such as cleanliness, service, staffing, fiscal health, and patient satisfaction. Facilities were sorted into three categories, "exceptional," "satisfactory," and "below average," and the facilities at the top were recognized and the staff rewarded for their efforts. Those facilities at the lower end of the spectrum were not punished but instead were singled out for extra attention by the organization. In cases where the facility was plagued by consistently low rankings, a specialist team of experienced managers would be brought in to check for deeper problems and make the necessary changes to bring the facility's rating back up.[33] Finally, the management at the facilities recognized the contributions of exceptional employees and held events (such as company retreats and celebrations) to bring together the families of employees.[34] These practices all helped to cultivate a shared sense of mission and accountability that pervaded the organization's facilities.

Operating more or less as a business meant that the IMA did not need to explicitly politicize its provision, either by tying receipt to political support as clientelism or by using access to social services as "selective incentives" to recruit new members (Rubin 1990, 26; Ibrahim 1997, 52; Munson 2001). Just the opposite was true: a variety of evidence shows that the IMA explicitly rejected the idea of discrimination. In the historical record, Malt repeatedly noted that the IMA would never condition care on political allegiances.[35] In one column, he drew parallels between the IMA's mission and the Brotherhood's supposed treatment of Jews wounded in fighting at Ramla and Ramallah during the 1948 Palestine War to highlight that the organization would never discriminate in the realm of medical care, even against its political enemies (Malt 1993, 178).[36] The Islamic

Charity Hospital, he told readers of *al-Da'wa,* "is open to every sick person regardless of color, nationality, or denomination."[37]

The IMA's credo was also prominently posted in each facility I visited: "To draw closer to God the Almighty through medical work . . . with compassion for the patient without respect to his ability to pay, social status, type of disease, without discriminating on the basis of color, nationality, or religion" (Shammakh 2011, 86).[38] In interviews, doctors and managers not only rejected the idea of discrimination but bristled when asked about it. As one of the IMA's executives claimed, "We give care to all the people; the services of the Islamic Medical Association are for all. It is not about whether you are a Christian or Muslim, a Muslim Brother or not a Muslim Brother."[39] Muhyi al-Din al-Zayit, director of the Central Charity Hospital, explained that "yes, we are Muslim Brothers, but here I am a physician. I remove any political affiliation. . . . The patient here is a human being, and I am a physician. There is no [consideration of] political orientation or social class" (Brooke 2013, 19). And Futuh warned,

> It is a disaster to mix charity work with politics. I consider this *harām* [forbidden]. . . . This is like committing a crime. . . . It is very regrettable and disgusting to use [a human being's] needs to achieve a political target. And this is unfortunately what Christian missionary organizations are doing. And we hope that Islamic missionaries, they won't do the same thing. The [Christian] missionaries, when they go to Africa, they use the poverty of the people to force them to be Christian, and this is wrong; you cannot use charity to spread religion, either Christianity or Islam.[40]

There was only mild evidence of politicization in the vicinity of IMA facilities. Posters around the exterior of the facility sported the Brotherhood's logo and slogans urged religious adherence, e.g. "*Aqim Ṣalātak, tan'im bi-ḥayātak* (Say your prayers and your life will be blessed)," and "*Ṣayyim 'asharat ayyām Dhū al-Ḥijja* (Fast for ten days during the month of Dhū al-Ḥijja, an especially auspicious stretch during Ramadan for performing good deeds and charity).[41] Explicit political propaganda was largely absent, and in fact I found that the IMA's management expended significant efforts to get their employees to keep the facilities depoliticized (including officially reprimanding those who were actively campaigning inside the facilities). As the internal disciplinary letter referenced in the introduction showed, IMA officials were alert to the potential for politicization of their facilities and acted quickly when it was brought to their attention.

It is possible that managers, doctors, and staff were able to conceal their discrimination either in favor of the Muslim Brotherhood or against the group's political opponents. In chapter 6 I use a nationwide survey of Egyptians to systematically show that even the Brotherhood's self-confessed political opponents both used the Brotherhood's facilities and gave the atmosphere in those facilities high marks. But these impressions are grounded in the historical and contemporary materials, which show how the group's founders abjured the idea of discriminating, either in favor of the group's members or against opponents, and in the contemporary interviews, which revealed how managers strictly policed their employees to prevent the use of IMA facilities for partisan ends. Of course, above and beyond IMA members' own intrinsic commitments to offer social services purely out of a desire to do good, Egypt's strict civil society laws provided a hard external constraint on politicization (Hamid 2014, 50–52). But a key factor that kept the IMA depoliticized was that the enterprise was financially self-sufficient. It did not exist to recruit new members or to sway voters through the provision of free or reduced-cost benefits, so it could operate without a constant reference point to an ideology, political party, or election campaign. In fact, one reason citizens appreciated the facilities is that they knew that they could use them without being badgered to support the Muslim Brotherhood at the polls. Indeed, we can imagine how allowing staff free rein to stump for the Brotherhood to a captive audience would probably have resulted in a *decline* of customers willing to tolerate this imposition.

Alternative Models of Social Service Provision

The IMA's model of businesslike operation generated a series of benefits, including preserving their independence, attracting a reliable workforce, providing tools with which to maintain a consistent standard of care, and allowing them to remain above the political fray. But other organizations adopted different styles of social service provision. This section probes three of these alternatives. The first comparison shows why common arguments about the benefits of close affiliation with a social movement do not hold in a nondemocratic context such as existed in Sadat's and Mubarak's Egypt. The second uses the case of an Islamic party that provides social service provision as a type of clientelism to identify explicit differences in form and function with what the IMA offers. The final comparison identifies a unique case through which a provider can offer relatively high-quality care to poorer customers but must do so by sacrificing its political ambitions. The point of each is to isolate how initial choices about how to operate and whom to serve shape the subsequent *quality* of social service delivery, and thus the ability to realize—or not—political benefits from that provision.

In certain contexts, affiliation with an organizationally dense movement affiliate can provide a series of key political advantages. For instance, the movement can provide a pool of individual or financial assets that could help the party surmount certain structural disadvantages (Van Cott 2005; Thachil 2014a). As Paul Staniland argues, this is a natural progression for an organization: "Social services tend to follow organizational cohesion, given that an organization must exist in the first place to provide services" (2012, 174). The Egyptian Muslim Brotherhood certainly had such an organizationally dense and cohesive structure, so it is worth examining the initial circumstances surrounding why the group chose the pay-for-service model rather than just exploiting its reach as a social movement to extend provision.

Two factors made this option impractical for the Brotherhood. First, the Brotherhood of the mid-1970s was a shell of the organization it had been prior to Nasir, or would become under Mubarak. Beyond a few charismatic but elderly leaders (including Ahmad al-Malt), the organization was bereft of ties to society and was consumed with contentious internal debates (Zollner 2007; Rock-Singer 2016). "There was no organization," as one of the leaders described that period of the group's history.[42] Stripped of a cadre of ideologically committed members to rely on, the group's founders were effectively forced to choose a relatively businesslike, self-sustaining focus, as it was one of the few ways that they could build social service networks absent a strong and dedicated social movement.

Such a commercial orientation made sense for other Brotherhood activities that emerged during Sadat's rule. For example, prior to the Nasirist repression, member contributions had almost entirely supported the Brotherhood's newspapers and magazines.[43] But because it lacked the movement resources to duplicate that approach in the 1970s, the Brotherhood pivoted to a business model, aggressively selling advertising space to a variety of businesses in order to support the publication of its flagship magazine, al-Da'wa (Rock-Singer and Brooke 2018).

Adopting a business model was also a nod to the political conditions. In the authoritarian context of Egypt, an explicit affiliation with the Brotherhood tended to hamper—rather than facilitate—the provision of social services. Even though the IMA tried at all points to keep the Brotherhood at arm's length, the simple fact of an affiliation led to problems. The IMA "was an institution accountable to the Muslim Brotherhood," claimed the former IMA president Futuh. "And that's why [the regime] harassed us."[44] "My presence [in any social service institution] is a burden," another prominent Muslim Brother told Tarek Masoud in 2007 (2014a, 75). In early 2013 I (somewhat naively) asked one executive if he had ever experienced any harassment by the authorities on account of the relationship between the IMA and the Brotherhood. He leaned back in his chair and laughed out loud. "Everyone who has sat in this chair before me has been arrested" (after the 2013 military coup he too was arrested).[45]

This affiliation with the Brotherhood created numerous difficulties for the IMA when it came to accessing alternative resources. Futuh explained that "any source of outside funding was scrutinized, and attempts to raise money through other channels were denied. If [the IMA] wanted to get a permission from the Ministry of Social Affairs to raise funds they would say no. Or to register a new hospital they would give us a hard time (lit. "they pulled our eyes out"). We would try to get a construction permit, and they would not approve it."[46] While it was difficult to go after the IMA's finances, given that a majority of the group's income came from payment from individuals for services rendered, the regime was always on the lookout for ways to tamper with sources of financial support to curtail the Brotherhood's reach. Amr Darrag, a longtime Brotherhood activist, described this approach as *siyāsat tajfīf al-manābi'*, which he translated as "the policy of drying out the [Brotherhood's] resources and avenues of activity" (2017, 222).

So instead of waves of men, money, and material freely crossing between the Muslim Brotherhood and the IMA, the reality was substantial segregation. For example, the IMA erected an extensive tracking system for donations with numbered and itemized receipts so that potential contributors could donate with confidence that the act would not later be used by the regime as evidence of their support for a technically illegal organization (the Muslim Brotherhood).[47] In fact, individuals were encouraged to make in-kind donations of equipment rather than cash for precisely this reason.[48] Effectively, the IMA's essentially businesslike basis of operation allowed it to distance itself from the Brotherhood and thus maintain in Egypt's authoritarian environment a freedom to operate that close affiliation to the movement would have precluded.

Examining the differing fates of Islamist and "secular" parties in the Arab World, Marina Ottaway and Amr Hamzawy suggest that Islamist parties are advantaged over their counterparts "because they can hire professional, full-time organizers" (2007, 17). Their rationale tracks with Michels's argument for why German socialists were so organized and effective: they paid party operatives for their contributions rather than relying on unpredictable volunteer labor ([1915] 1966, 137). The following short case study shows what happens when parties rely on volunteer labor and volatile donations—rather than paid professionals and a steady stream of receipts—to finance their social service provision.

During the fieldwork for this project I visited one of the medical clinics of the Asala party in a run-down Cairo neighborhood. Asala is a largely Cairo-based Salafist party that emerged following the fall of Mubarak. It achieved modest success in the 2011–12 parliamentary elections by winning three seats as part of the Islamist bloc, headlined by the larger Salafist Nur party (Lacroix 2012, 2). Like the Brotherhood, Asala emphasizes its Islamic identity, which furnishes important leverage over alternative arguments laying the success of the Brotherhood's social service provision at the feet of its Islamic identity.

Asala's clinic occupied the second floor of an old apartment building and consisted of a cluttered waiting room (the old living room/kitchen), a bathroom that doubled as a supply closet, and the doctor's office/examination room in what was once the bedroom. A sign with the party logo sat in a corner, waiting to be hung outside. When I arrived for my appointment, the waiting room was already filled with exasperated mothers and sick children, and the doctor was nowhere in sight. After waiting in vain for thirty minutes or so, I decamped to the cafe next door and sipped tea underneath a giant banner showing the National Democratic Party's (NDP) candidates for the district in the 2010 elections (the cafe owner thought so highly of the men that he had kept the banner up, long after the NDP's collapse and despite the Muslim Brotherhood's rise).

An hour or so later I saw a harried, middle-aged doctor dash in, and eventually we were able to talk. The clinic in which we sat was, as he explained, his own way of serving the political party. Although he was now a successful doctor, he was originally from the area and had established the clinic in consultation with party leaders to try and "bridge the gap" between ordinary people's lives and the rhetoric they heard from politicians. Using donations, he had opened the facility, and only a few patients paid. He was the only doctor who worked there, and, as I had witnessed, he came by once or twice a week when he could spare the time from his main job at a university hospital and his secondary job running his own successful private clinic in a wealthier part of the city.[49]

After spending months visiting the Muslim Brotherhood's facilities, I found the scene here particularly jarring. The divergent levels and quality of care were notable, but what particularly drew my interest were the underlying differences in the way that the facility was organized and managed. There was no real organization or structure to the operation. The doctor (who was also the manager) kept irregular hours, was usually late, and sometimes simply did not show up at all. The clinic was tidy but not particularly clean, and there were very few medical supplies or dedicated pieces of medical equipment. The doctor examined children by laying them on his desk. If the problem was particularly acute or difficult, he would have to simply send the family elsewhere for care.

The doctor was obviously doing his best in a tough situation, and the party would likely be able to wring some political support from the enterprise (indeed, it was also quite open about its hope to do so). But these divergent experiences highlight how the poor clientele shaped the broader atmosphere at the facility. Asala had made a conscious decision to locate its clinic in a poorer area and rely on volunteer labor from party activists to support the endeavor. This was a classic clientelist strategy. Indeed, Asala's clinic was embedded in precisely those poorer neighborhoods where, as the next chapter will show, the NDP's clientelistic networks had historically been most effective under Mubarak—witness the cafe owner beside the clinic who had kept up his NDP banner into the spring of 2013. But without a sustainable income stream the clinic was prevented from providing anything more than basic care. So while the doctor at Asala's clinic was committed to helping citizens of the area, the services would likely never be better than rudimentary, the equipment was and would remain lacking, and the hours would probably never be routinized. The whole effect was to confirm Janine Clark's description of the plight of those medical facilities that provide largely for the less affluent: "Those services targeted explicitly for the poor are often of inferior quality and are inconsistent on a year to year basis. . . . [Poor] areas are dominated by clinics that have one doctor, have few or no supplies or equipment, are often inconsistent in their operational hours, and teeter on the verge of closure" (2004, 38).

The point of this brief comparison with Asala is not to make a general claim about what types of social service provision will or will not produce political support. Instead, it is to help us understand how initial decisions about *how* to provide social services influence both the character of that provision and the mechanisms through which this provision translates into political support. The Brotherhood made an early decision to ground its provision on a base of paying customers, which allowed it to offer a competitive salary to attract trained staff, provide extensive and relatively modern services, and hold reliable hours. This, in turn, helped the group maintain the higher quality of care that, as chapter 6 will show, spoke directly to the concerns of middle-class voters. Asala, in contrast, had chosen to appeal to the poor via clientelism, which bound its provision to the whims of donors and the vagaries of party volunteers' hectic schedules. This influenced the *character* of the party's provision in a quite predictable way: it was limited in scope, not particularly high-quality, and unreliable. This is not to say that Asala's venture would produce zero benefit on election day, only to suggest that whatever political impact this provision produced would probably more resemble the contingent, episodic exchange of clientelism than the reputational effect that proved so powerful for the Brotherhood.

Asala was openly hoping to use its social service networks to spur political mobilization through a mechanism approximating clientelism. A social service provider that is far more circumspect about its politicization is the vast Islamic association al-Jam'iyya al-Shar'iyya, which has around three thousand branches nationwide (Jam'iyya al-Shar'iyya n.d., 10). In 1912, Shaykh Mahmud Khattab al-Subki, a graduate of al-Azhar, established al-Jam'iyya al-Shar'iyya to train preachers, build mosques, and combat the intrusion of what he saw as *bida'* (innovation, heresy) and *khurāfāt* (superstitions) into religious practice.

Al-Jam'iyya al-Shar'iyya provided social services from its outset, including hospitals and clinics offering reduced prices, as part of its mission to bring "practical Islam" to the people (Da'ud 1992, 132–35; 148–52; Yunus 2006, 40). Late in his term as president, Gamal 'Abd al-Nasir used Law 32 of 1964 to effectively freeze the operations of al-Jam'iyya al-Shar'iyya, a decision that Sadat reversed soon after assuming power (Da'ud 1992; Ben Néfissa 2002; Tahir 2006; Yunus 2006).

Unlike the Muslim Brotherhood or Asala, al-Jam'iyya al-Shar'iyya is not a political organization (in the sense that it does not field candidates in elections), so it is difficult to extrapolate what the electoral effects of its social service provision would be. It is also difficult to make sweeping statements about al-Jam'iyya al-Shar'iyya because of the variegated and decentralized nature of the organization. But as "the most important Islamic charity organization in terms of social and political power, and in geographic spread" it is worth considering what insights al-Jam'iyya al-Shar'iyya's style of social service provision can provide into the mechanisms discussed in this book (Ben Néfissa 2002, 134). In particular, what happens when an organization makes the decision to provide for the poor rather than offer a commercial service for more affluent citizens?

At first glance a comparison with al-Jam'iyya al-Shar'iyya would seem to trouble the mechanisms through which the IMA was able to produce high-quality and consistent care. On the one hand, al-Jam'iyya al-Shar'iyya tends to provide charity care for a high proportion of poor patients. Morroe Berger found, for instance, that beneficiaries of al-Jam'iyya al-Shar'iyya social services were "generally very poor" (1970, 119). On the basis of his more recent fieldwork in a popular quarter of Cairo, Mohamed Fahmy Menza found the same, noting that al-Jam'iyya al-Shar'iyya's provision of welfare programs "has firmly established its standing within the Cairene popular quarters as an advocate of the poor and the disenfranchised classes" (2012, 332). Salwa Ismail's research in the lower-class Cairo neighborhood of Boulaq also supports this conclusion (2006, 78). At al-Jam'iyya al-Shar'iyya clinics I visited I found a pretty similar scene: there was a higher proportion of poor patients than at IMA facilities, something that was particularly evident in poorer areas. On the other hand, the *quality* of the provision was decent, equipment was older but in working order, the facility was clean, and staff kept a fairly predictable schedule. How is al-Jam'iyya al-Shar'iyya able to provide generally decent care while focusing on generally very poor patients who would struggle to afford what the organization provided?

The proximate cause was the same: like the IMA, those working at al-Jam'iyya al-Shar'iyya clinics were paid for their labor. I was surprised by one manager at a clinic in a poor area who expressed exasperation at the high salaries he had to pay his doctors. This manager complained that many of those who worked for al-Jam'iyya al-Shar'iyya saw the job opportunistically, as a way to build a clientele that they could later take with them when they established their own private clinics. He believed that he had to counteract this dynamic by offering higher and higher salaries to keep doctors the patients knew working at his clinic; otherwise the constant turnover would cause the residents of the area to desert the facility.[50] He admitted that this had somewhat put him in a bind because the young doctors he had hired at a relatively cheap salary years before were now established professionals who commanded a considerable salary. He felt compelled to pay them, he continued, lest he be forced to start over and, in the process, risk his longtime patients' trust when they were suddenly handed over to new doctors.[51]

But unlike the IMA, which relied on cash payments from customers to sustain its operations, al-Jam'iyya al-Shar'iyya's steady revenue stream came from donations, namely, zakāt funds from the mosque and local notables.[52] This gave the organization access to a tremendous amount of discretionary funding that could support provision directed toward the indigent (Ibrahim 1998, 38). To give one idea of the scope of these resources, a government study from the late Mubarak era reportedly noted that Egyptians contributed approximately $800 million to charity in 2009, a large portion of which consisted of zakāt funding.[53]

In interviews, al-Jam'iyya al-Shar'iyya officials discussed how they tended to be a preferred organization for donations from Muslim Egyptians seeking to discharge their zakāt obligations. They went on to explain that another sizable chunk came from wealthy individuals who wanted to donate money to some good cause but were unsure of how to maximize their contributions. Because they had either heard of al-Jam'iyya al-Shar'iyya or encountered its work in passing, they trusted the organization to handle the donation professionally and see it disbursed correctly.[54] Hani Nasira charted the activities of a number of al-Jam'iyya al-Shar'iyya branches, including financial support for the indigent, marriage arrangement, prisoner services, care for the sick, dialysis clinics, care for premature babies, literacy classes, burn centers, and specialized X-ray facilities. These were extensive programs—some served thousands of patients monthly—and according to Nasira all were financed by donations (2003, 14–19). Mona Atia relates that al-Jam'iyya al-Shar'iyya's "fund-raisers are so efficient at collecting donations that they told me that they raised 35 million EGP [about $6 million] for their cancer hospital" (2013, 62).

Any organization able to access the resources of the zakāt box would be in prime position to generate considerable sociopolitical mobilization (Wiktorowicz 2001, 64). The regime clearly understood this and took steps to prevent the Brotherhood from accessing these funding streams, in particular by blocking it from accessing the country's ubiquitous mosques. As one Brotherhood spokesman put it, "We were never allowed to have papers or media channels or even mosque sermons because we had a political agenda involved."[55] A former

Brotherhood member lamented that Mubarak's repression had been so comprehensive that, during those years, "some of our youth would have killed to be able to say a brief word after *aṣr* [late afternoon] prayers in a small *zāwiya* [prayer room] in a remote village" (Darra 2011, 30–31).[56]

The regime displayed no such worry about al-Jamʿiyya al-Sharʿiyya's access to this valuable resource because of the organization's quiescent posture vis-à-vis Egypt's political leadership. In fact, the regime actually facilitated al-Jamʿiyya al-Sharʿiyya's control over Egypt's religious administration to such an extent that the group became, in Sarah Ben Néfissa's words, a "parapublic" institution (2002, 155). Under Sadat, al-Jamʿiyya al-Sharʿiyya gained responsibility for training imams and supervising mosques, and this strategy became further ensconced under Mubarak (Da'ud 1992, 149). As Dr. Muhammad ʿAli Mahgub, Director of the Ministry of Religious Endowments, described the regime's relationship with al-Jamʿiyya al-Sharʿiyya in a 1994 interview, "I included [al-Jamʿiyya al-Sharʿiyya] with us in running and maintaining the mosques. Some of [the members of al-Jamʿiyya al-Sharʿiyya] are even members of the Higher Committee for Religious Enlightenment in each governorate, and they comply with the sermons we supply them. . . . [Al-Jamʿiyya al-Sharʿiyya is] committed to the state's plan in terms of the content of the Friday sermon, technical supervision, and field inspection of preachers at these mosques by the ministry's inspectors."[57] This tight and officially sanctioned connection gives al-Jamʿiyya al-Sharʿiyya unique access to a consistent and substantial charity-based revenue stream that allows the organization to produce higher-quality social services than those relying purely on volunteer labor or the sporadic interest of party volunteers.

As the dependence on outside financial support would suggest, the organization was constantly on the lookout for new sources of revenue. As the value of a parliamentary seat increased, al-Jamʿiyya al-Sharʿiyya seized on the opportunity to trade its influence over networks of (mostly poor) beneficiaries for resources from opportunistic politicians. Mirroring its emphasis on using mosque-based resources to support its social service activism, al-Jamʿiyya al-Sharʿiyya began to accumulate favors from those wealthy businessmen and potential parliamentarians that sought to benefit from their expansive networks (Ben Néfissa 2002). As one Egyptian voter summarized, "I consider them [al-Jamʿiyya al-Sharʿiyya) incredibly crafty because they play the game of politics correctly. They don't care who wins or loses because they know quite well that the candidate, once he wins, forgets all his promises and ignores al-Jamʿiyya al-Sharʿiyya or the people of the district. Thus they take their cut from the candidate before the elections, regardless of whether he wins or loses" (Ben Néfissa and Arafat 2005, 214).

This brief sketch of al-Jamʿiyya al-Sharʿiyya supports two points of the argument that middle-class provision is important to political mobilization in nondemocratic environments. First, although the *quality* of the provision offered by al- Jam'iyya al-Shar'iyya is generally decent, the *beneficiaries* tend to be poorer Egyptians. This suggests that were al-Jam'iyya al-Shar'iyya to attempt to leverage its social service networks in a challenge against the regime—consider a scenario in which the group nominated opposition candidates—it would still be competing for the votes of those least able to defect from the regime: poorer Egyptians. Indeed, al-Jam'iyya al-Shar'iyya's embeddedness among this sector was one thing that made it so attractive to candidates seeking to buy large blocs of votes as part of a classic clientelistic strategy.

Second, al-Jam'iyya al-Shar'iyya would assumedly refrain from openly challenging the status quo, for instance by supporting opposition candidates in elections. Not only would such an orientation risk its ability to train imams and supervise mosques—a responsibility that puts it in a privileged position vis-à-vis its competitors in the Islamic field—but it would also strip the group of its ability to access the material resources furnished by Egypt's extensive religious charity system.[58]

Sources of the Islamist Advantage

This chapter uses historical and qualitative material to trace the longer-term trajectories of two decisions introduced in the prior chapters. First was the regime's decision to begin withdrawing the state from the field of health care, which contributed to sharp declines in quality and basic sanitation even as it supercharged corruption and malpractice. But while the public sector was cratering, the Islamic Medical Association was thriving. From day one the IMA aimed to provide decent service to a paying clientele, an impetus that continued to define the organization as it expanded to serve millions of Egyptians per year.

The empirical material in this chapter illuminates, for the first time, the inner workings of the Brotherhood's social service facilities. These findings support an important implication of the theory: that grounding provision in a middle-class customer base offers a series of benefits for the particular character of their operations. Chapter 6 will examine how this management influences an individual's experience in an IMA facility and the ways this influences perceptions of the Brotherhood's candidates for elected office. But this chapter showed how paying customers provided a reliable and consistent stream of resources that allowed managers to hire qualified staff and effectively monitor the performance of employees. All of this is a precursor to being able to produce the *character* of care that can generate political effects.

The next chapter transitions from the Islamic Medical Association to the society in which it is rooted. It specifically picks up on a spatial implication of the emphasis on paid provision that runs through the above pages: that these facilities will cluster in wealthier areas because that is where the customers are. This spatial implication connects social and political activism because of the ways that Egypt's electoral map split the country into uncompetitive poorer districts and the middle-class ones where the Muslim Brotherhood's candidates made consistent political gains.

THE POLITICAL GEOGRAPHY OF ISLAMIST SOCIAL SERVICE PROVISION

The Brotherhood's decision to target social services at the country's middle-class citizens bore electoral fruit because of how Egypt's authoritarian electoral system bifurcated the country's socioeconomic geography. The passage of a new electoral law in 1990 triggered a flood of money into the electoral process as a motley of longtime National Democratic Party (NDP) patrons and nouveau riche businessmen bid for political power. But these clientelist networks did not lie evenly across the landscape: while electoral monopolies emerged in poorer districts, opportunities for competition emerged in middle-class ones.

In these wealthier neighborhoods and towns three largely independent streams effectively converged to politically benefit the Muslim Brotherhood: one sprang from the way Egypt's electoral geography created competitive enclaves in middle-class districts. Into this flowed a second stream, welling from the Islamic Medical Association's (IMA's) years of prioritizing these areas because they were the sole places that could support the style of care the group provided. Third, the Brotherhood tended to run its parliamentary candidates in middle-class districts, precisely because this gave the organization a fighting chance at representation. The result, as this chapter shows, is that in those districts the Brotherhood was able to build on its preexisting and social service–based presence to win the support of middle-class Egyptians and thus set the conditions to politically challenge the regime.

Beyond shifting from the causes of social service provision to its effects, this chapter also introduces new spatial data to supplement earlier insights gained from historical and qualitative research. "Political behavior," John Agnew tells us, "is intrinsically geographical. The social contexts provided by local territorial-cultural settings (neighborhoods, towns, cities, small rural areas) are crucial in defining distinctive political identities and subsequent political activities—from votes to strikes to street violence" (2014, 6). Building on Agnew's intuition, I assemble new evidence—on subnational electoral competition, activities of the Brotherhood's candidates for elected office, and the spatial distribution of the IMA's facilities—to track the confluence of these three processes.

I open the chapter with a brief description of the proliferation of clientelist activity following a change in electoral laws in 1990. I then show how this trans-formation systematically shaped patterns of subnational competition, restrict-ing competition in less affluent districts while facilitating it in wealthier ones. An original data set tracking where the Brotherhood ran candidates for Egypt's lower house of Parliament from 1995 to 2010 shows that the organization fol-lowed this logic by disproportionately fielding candidates in these middle-class districts. The third piece of the puzzle is a data set of the locations of all IMA "brick and mortar" (Cammett and Issar 2010) facilities, which allows a more complete analysis of how these facilities nested in Egypt's underlying socioeco-nomic and electoral geographies. As the earlier discussion of the IMA's empha-sis on providing for a middle-class audience would suggest, these facilities were disproportionately located in middle-class areas, in many cases in the same dis-tricts where the Brotherhood most frequently fielded candidates for parliamen-tary office. The chapter's final sections use highly disaggregated Cairene election data from Egypt's 2012 presidential election, waged between the Muslim Brother Mohammed Morsi and the former regime official Ahmed Shafiq, in order to identify the local effects of social service provision on political support for the Muslim Brotherhood.

The Political Economy of Egyptian Clientelism

Clientelism is practiced by regimes and oppositions throughout the Middle East, and it perseveres under political systems that are both competitive and hegemonic (Lust 2009; Blaydes 2011; Corstange 2016). Samer Shehata summarizes the per-vasiveness of the practice, arguing that throughout the Middle East, "people do not vote primarily on the basis of party affiliation, electoral program, or ideology, but rather on the provision of services, including individual services provided to district residents" (2008, 95). Egyptian clientelism stretches back to landown-ers who presided over large agricultural estates (Binder 1978; Springborg 1979). But the phenomenon became pervasive when a change in electoral rules in 1990 abolished a mixed-party list/single-candidate system of 48 districts and replaced it with 222 two-member districts open to independent candidates.[1] Egypt's new capitalist class pounced, pouring ever greater sums of money into parliamentary elections in an attempt to join the political elite and reap its accompanying perks (Kassem 1999; Ouda, El-Borai, and Abu Se'ada 2001; Blaydes 2011; Soliman 2011; El Tarouty 2015).

Beyond cash and traditional items such as foodstuffs and cooking gas, many candidates also provided a variety of social services to poorer voters in their districts. These candidates found that they could amass significant political support by building or refurbishing mosques, setting up charity clinics, and assuming sponsorship of widows and orphans (Arafat 2009, 71; Menza 2013). For example, Shahinaz El-Naggar, scion of a wealthy family in the capital and husband of the NDP bigwig Ahmed 'Izz, operated a charity clinic in her Cairo district of Maniyal as part of her profligate campaign (El Tarouty 2015, 81). Lisa Blaydes and Safinaz El-Tarouty summarize the role played by social services in another Cairo district:

> In poor areas of in the Kasr El Nil district in Cairo Governorate, such as Boulaq, many constituents did not have tap water, and [NDP candidate Hisham Moustafa Khalil] paid for water to be connected to their houses. In addition, he paid for the repair of streets and painting of houses in the area. In the al-Aini area of the Kasr El Nil constituency, he also paid for 1,500 meters of sewage pipe to connect the residents of this area. His opponent, [NDP candidate Hossam] Badrawi, also provided social services. His two NGOs in the district provided for four hundred orphans, and he also provided free medical care at a local clinic. (2010–11, 80–83)

As the above examples imply, certain types of voters were more prone to be targeted by this type of social service provision than others. This style of contingent spending, including free medical care at candidate-sponsored clinics, is a particularly effective way of attracting the support of poorer voters (Auyero 2001; Thachil 2014a; Szwarcberg 2015). But those voters with "economic autonomy" also have options (McMann 2006). Because their day-to-day survival is less tied to maintaining access to free health care or a weekly bag of food from a local vote broker, they are better able to allocate their political support on the basis of their ideological or programmatic preferences (Magaloni 2006).

These divergent political logics scale up beyond the particular party-voter linkages to patterns of competition across the electoral map. Particularly where one party has a resource advantage, the end result is often a depression of competition (McMann 2006; Mahdavi 2015). As Mariela Szwarcberg summarizes, "Low levels of electoral volatility result from the consolidation of machine politics" (2015, 3). Rebecca Weitz-Shapiro's research suggests the other half of this dynamic: "The presence of a large middle class should create incentives [for politicians] to abandon clientelism" (2014, 63). These logics did not simply exist in theory; they were embedded in the ways that Egyptian candidates and their campaigns thought about voter outreach. As one longtime NDP figure explained his campaign strategy, "We look at the districts (*shiyākhāt*) within the constituency . . . then, in accordance with the dominant social and economic statuses of these districts, we start designing our plan. For starters, the relatively well-off areas are less important than the ones with harsher socio-economic conditions, as they don't have those potential voters who are willing to go through the hassle of voting in order to reap the benefits of voter clientelism. Conversely, those who reside within the low-income communities are more willing to do so" (quoted in Menza 2013, 134).

Given the importance of clientelistic relationships in Egyptian elections, we should expect to find a systematic relationship between district wealth and competitiveness, with poorer districts playing host to electoral monopolies, while their wealthier counterparts have more lively levels of electoral contestation.

Electoral Markets and Electoral Monopolies

The great Egyptian author Tawfiq el-Hakim's 1937 novella *Yawmiyyat Na'ib fi al-Aryaf (Diary of a Country Prosecutor)* follows a judicial prosecutor as he investigates a murder among peasants in Egypt's Nile delta. The tale is a biting satire of colonialism and cultural conflict, as the new Egyptian-British state bureaucracy attempts to expand its control over a bewildered rural population. In one section, the prosecutor falls into a conversation with a local official who goes on to explain how he conducts elections in his village. "I let people vote as they like" the official says, "right up to the end of the election. Then I simply take the ballot box and throw it into the river and calmly replace it with the box which we prepare ourselves" ([1937] 1989, 112). The torrent of reports and news stories chronicling the fraud, violence, and manipulation of successive Egyptian elections since then would suggest that not much has changed.[2] Given this reality, how can one generate a defensible, *ex ante* measure of competitiveness across Egypt's electoral districts?

Kenneth Greene (2010) uses the winner's vote margin over the first loser to track electoral competition in single-party regimes. While a natural measure of competitiveness, this is not possible in the Egyptian case as the regime did not release vote totals for losing candidates. And though it would be possible to create a vote share measure—winner's vote share over district population or turnout—this might not compensate for the possibility—if not likelihood—of *ex post* alteration of voting statistics (Simpser [2013] provides a general discussion of why nondemocratic regimes may tinker with voting statistics, and Wickham [2002] and Soliman [2006] provide critical investigations of turnout statistics in the Egyptian case). Furthermore, this type of manipulation is something that was likely especially pronounced in those districts where the Muslim Brotherhood's candidates were running (see below).

Instead, I approach the question of how to measure competition deductively. I begin with the assumption that citizens weigh a candidate's orientation vis-à-vis the regime when considering for whom to vote. Specifically, they will tend to view opposition candidates more skeptically than proregime ones because they doubt those opposition candidates' ability to provide continued access to clientelist resources. There is a variety of qualitative evidence to this effect. In his study of Egypt, Raymond Hinnebusch noted "the tendency of many voters, out of hope for advantage or deference to authority, to support candidates known to have government approval and avoid those in disfavor" (1988, 171). Similarly, Ellen Lust noted that "voters do not elect candidates whom they perceive as unable to work with the government" (2009, 239).[3] Summarizing the dominance of one powerful proregime political family in its "private fiefdom" of an electoral district in Alexandria, one group of researchers observed that "any independent candidate who would try to challenge the family would not only have to meet them in a political struggle, but would also have to be able to convince the voters that he had the means to secure the continuous flow of hand outs to the inhabitants" (Danish-Egyptian Dialogue Institute 2012, 12).

I also assume that there exists common knowledge among citizens, including potential candidates, about when a race includes candidates who can use their resources—either from their own pocket or via a connection to the regime—to simply outspend most opponents. In these cases, many potential challengers will simply sit out the election rather than expend resources to register their candidacy, campaign, and mobilize supporters. The implication of the foregoing is that districts with large swaths of poor voters, where the path to victory effectively runs through clientelism, will manifest as political monopolies with depressed competition. In contrast, where fewer poorer voters portends political competition based more on programs or ideology, levels of competition will be notably higher.

At this point I exploit a convenient feature of Egyptian law to generate an *ex ante* proxy measure of district-level competitiveness. According to Egyptian law, all candidates in parliamentary elections must publish their names in a national newspaper prior to the election. I coded pre-election issues of the state Arabic-language dailies to assemble information on the number of candidates who entered races in each electoral district for five consecutive lower-house parliamentary elections: 1990,[4] 1995,[5] 2000,[6] 2005, and 2010.[7] From these five elections I produced a district-level outcome variable charting competitiveness, consisting of the median number of candidates entering the race in that *dā'ira* (district).

To assess how patterns of electoral competition relate to levels of socioeconomic development I draw on Egyptian census data.[8] I manually assigned each *qism* (urban) and *markaz* (rural) (Egypt's second subnational unit, roughly akin to American counties) to specific electoral districts, based on Egyptian Law 206 of 1990 (Majlis al-Sha'b 1990).[9] Then, to create the key independent variable, I generated an electoral district-level asset index based on eleven common household items to measure wealth ($\alpha = .8983$).[10] Figure 5.1 plots the effects of district wealth on competitiveness from a simple regression analysis, holding control variables at their means.[11]

Keeping in mind the caveats about the reliability of the measure, figure 5.1 suggests that the qualitative evidence about differential effects of wealth on district competition was on the mark. Simply, Egypt's poorer districts had systematically lower levels of political competition, as measured by number of candidates in the race, than wealthier ones ($p < .001$). Put in substantive terms, moving from one standard deviation below the median value of district wealth to one standard

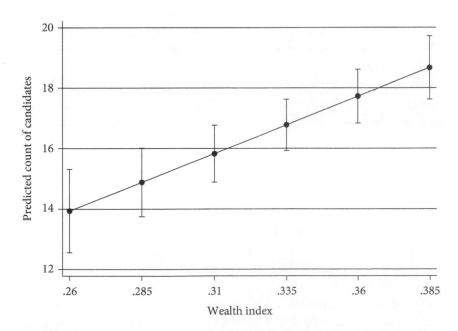

FIGURE 5.1. Competition vs. electoral district socioeconomic profile, 1990–2010

deviation above increases the predicted number of candidates who would enter the race by almost 40 percent. While the lack of detailed vote share statistics should be kept in mind, figure 5.1 suggests that any ambitious opposition politician would be wise to seek his or her political fortunes in Egypt's comparatively more affluent cities and provincial towns, and steer clear of ones with a predominance of poorer voters.

While electoral competition petered out in Egypt's poorer districts, it hummed along in wealthier ones. In *Counting Islam* Tarek Masoud (2014a) finds that one reason the Muslim Brotherhood experienced such electoral success under Mubarak was that its largely middle-class identity was attractive to middle-class voters upset with the regime but who could not bring themselves to cast a ballot for leftist parties clamoring for redistribution. I now build on and systematically assess his argument, using new data on the entry of each Brotherhood candidate for four lower-house (*Majlis al-Sha'b*) elections since 1995. This allows a test of a key spatial implication of the Brotherhood's middle-class identity: a disproportionate tendency to field candidates in middle-class districts, in precisely the types of places where opposition candidates would have the best chances of electoral success.

Shifting from aggregate rates of political competition as in figure 5.1 to the specific question of the Brotherhood's electoral history still courts data availability problems. For example, lists of Muslim Brotherhood *winners* (i.e., parliamentarians) do exist, for instance in the directories produced by the al-Ahram Center. But coding on candidate success would risk inflating the problem of suspect data: the regime frequently visited at times comical forms of manipulation, fraud, intimidation, and violence on the opposition, including the Brotherhood's candidates and supporters (Stacher 2006; Brownlee 2007, 136; Hishmat 2011; Blaydes 2011, 53). Thus coding on success, specifically where the Brotherhood candidates won elections, could systematically skew attempts to identify those locales where the group was most powerful.[12]

To generate a measure of *Muslim Brotherhood* competitiveness I borrow from the same logic as above and focus on Muslim Brotherhood candidate *entry*. Using a variety of Arabic and English-language sources, I compiled an original data set of all the Brotherhood's candidates, including the districts in which they ran, for the lower house elections of 1995, 2000, 2005, and 2010 (n = 548).[13] This allows a comprehensive examination of where the group felt itself able, and the underlying structural conditions propitious, to mount an electoral challenge against the regime.[14]

Figure 5.2 reproduces the key elements of figure 5.1, charting the effect of shifts in socioeconomic profile (the wealth index) on Brotherhood candidate entry, again holding all other variables at their means. Note that here (figure 5.2),

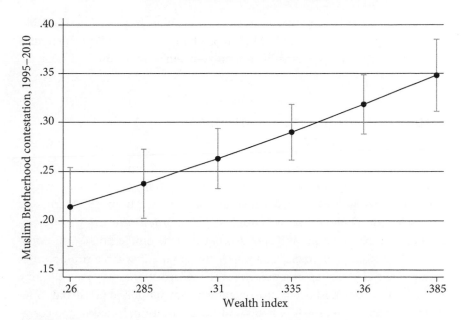

FIGURE 5.2. Brotherhood political participation vs. electoral district socioeconomic profile, 1995–2010

the outcome variable (the y-axis) charts the percentage of times a member of the Muslim Brotherhood appeared as a candidate in the electoral district. For example, if there was a Brotherhood candidate in 1995, 2000, and 2005—but not 2010—that district receives a score of .75.[15]

Egypt's overarching authoritarian electoral institutions combined with the country's underlying economic structure to powerfully shape patterns of electoral competition. Figure 5.1 shows how poorer districts tended to host political monopolies while more affluent ones emerged as hotbeds of electoral competition. Figure 5.2 shows how the Muslim Brotherhood was also shaped by this logic: its candidates systematically appeared in competitive middle-class districts while avoiding less affluent ones ($p < .001$). And again the shift across standard deviations in the wealth index is substantial, nearly doubling the Brotherhood's predicted involvement in these races.

Figures 5.1 and 5.2 use new data to effectively confirm Masoud's (2014a) argument that the Brotherhood was successful because it overwhelmingly ran in middle-class districts. In the next section, however, I begin to outline an alternative explanation for *why* the Brotherhood was so successful in those places. I show that instead of essentially serving as a receptacle for the protest votes of middle-class Egyptians opposed to the regime and unnerved by leftist parties, the distribution of the Islamic Medical Association's brick-and-mortar facilities maps in a predictable way onto this spatial segregation of electoral competition. By providing affordable, competent, and enjoyable care, the Muslim Brotherhood gave the Egyptian middle class something to vote *for* rather than simply something to oppose.

Local Determinants of Islamist Medical Services

Under what conditions did the Muslim Brotherhood provide social services? Many media reports on the eve of Egypt's winter 2011–12 parliamentary elections contained at least a cursory mention of how the Muslim Brotherhood's extensive network of social services would drive the group to victory. One Associated Press dispatch, for instance, pointed out that the Brotherhood's "machine" would "appeal to poor voters" and power the group's inevitable triumph. But toward the end of the report a resident of the village of 'Ilwan, a "poor farming community, where most people live on government-subsidized bread and suffer from poor sanitation, roads, schools and hospitals," complained to the correspondent that "the Muslim Brotherhood never helped here."[16]

Prior chapters should give us a clue why the group had never helped in 'Ilwan: despite the fact that its efforts there were sorely needed, it was unlikely that this poor farming community could support the style of social service provision that the Brotherhood prioritized. But in another dispatch on those same elections, *PBS Newshour's* Margaret Warner opened her report from the Islamic Medical Association's bustling Faruq Hospital in the southern Cairo suburb of Ma'adi. Medical facilities like this, Warner surmised, were part of the reason the Brotherhood was expected to succeed in the upcoming elections.[17] Ma'adi, the report did not mention, is one of Cairo's more upscale suburbs, home to diplomats, expats, and many of Cairo's Westernized elite. Together, these two anecdotes tend to confirm earlier chapters' insights into how the IMA decided to deploy their social services. But how representative of the entire network are these two reports?

Qualitative evidence helps identify the process by which the IMA decided whether to open a facility. Largely because of its reputation for providing high-quality care, the IMA was deluged with requests and opportunities to open facilities. In nearly all extant cases, individuals or associations came to the IMA with available property and petitioned the group to open a facility there. In some cases, groups or individuals were operating a facility under another name but were either losing money or unable to competently manage the enterprise. Rather than close it down, they looked to the IMA to take over the management and operation. In fact, nearly every one of the Islamic Medical Association's hospitals or medical centers was housed in a building owned by a local community association. Faruq Hospital operated in a building the Association for Developing West Ma'adi owns, and the IMA paid rent to that association.[18] Jam'iyyat al-Sharif (the Sharif Association) owns the building housing 'Adil Hospital in Shubra, and the IMA paid rent to the Sharif Association. At both Sharabiyya and Tan'im Hospitals in Shubra and Basatin, respectively, the IMA rented the premises from the Islamic association al-Jam'iyya al-Shar'iyya.[19] The IMA's Ibn Sina Hospital in Banha had been a preexisting and independent medical facility until the IMA took it over in 2006. When I visited the hospital in 2013, the original owner still lived on the top floor and received rent from the IMA.[20]

The IMA turned down most of these opportunities to operate a facility. As the emphasis on fiscal responsibility suggests, these initial offers triggered a lengthy IMA investigation and assessment process designed to discern whether opening a facility in that specific area would be a fiscally sound decision. During this review, IMA staff would visit the property to examine its condition and quality, canvass the residents of the area to see if they needed (and could financially support) a facility, identify the competition (government facilities, private ones, and other associations), and investigate whether there were enough potential employees in the area to staff the venture.[21] In many cases they simply found no room in the market for the IMA. For example, one individual offered the group the opportunity to open a hospital on a piece of property he owned in al-Tajammu' al-Khamis, a wealthy exurb east of downtown Cairo. When the IMA investigated, it found an extensive array of private providers in the area, which caused it to doubt its ability to compete. The group ended up turning down the offer.[22] One reason the Tan'im facility in Basatin was attractive was that potentially competing services in the area were so weak (Brooke 2013). This particular assessment helped alleviate other concerns of the IMA management, who had worried that the lower socioeconomic status of the area and lack of access to convenient transport options might imperil any initiative's fiscal solvency.[23]

The emphasis on fiscal sustainability continued even after a facility began seeing patients. The IMA almost always started small and cautiously, first opening a small clinic or basic hospital facility to ensure that the area can support the facility. If the venture was profitable, the surplus was used to expand the facility: to rent new floors, buy new equipment, or hire new staff. Faruq Hospital in Ma'adi had started as a one room clinic and, over twenty years, had expanded to take over an entire building. At Ibn Sina Hospital, the IMA had been slowly renting new floors as the patient base grew.[24]

If a facility was consistently unprofitable, then the IMA considered scaling back or shutting it. For instance, the IMA operated for a short time a specialized facility geared toward psychological rehabilitation. But the facility struggled to remain solvent, largely because it was located in downtown Cairo, on a piece of land sandwiched between Ramses Train Station (the country's main rail hub) and the chaotic Sixth of October Bridge (one of the capital's main thorough-fares). This turned out to be a particularly infelicitous location for a psychologi-cal care facility, and, unsurprisingly, fewer and fewer patients used it. The IMA ended up closing the facility and was exploring more bucolic settings in which to reopen the facility at the time of the 2013 military coup.[25]

Dialysis centers posed an acute sense of the dilemma between expanding the organization's reach into the population and maintaining solvency. Kidney dis-ease is rampant in Egypt, and dialysis services are both poorly managed and con-stantly in demand (Sayed et al. 2000). Yet while this offered the IMA a potentially valuable avenue through which to reach large swaths of the population, it also forced the group to balance this opportunity against the reality that its dialysis centers would likely be unsustainable. In southern Giza, a local man offered the IMA an empty basement in which he hoped the group would open a dialysis cen-ter. The IMA assessed the area and judged it unfit because it was a relatively poor area. However, it made an exception and opened the center because its investiga-tion showed that there was such a high need for the services that its clinic might reach profitability (when I visited the facility, every bed was occupied).

But the IMA miscalculated and was losing as much as $8 per patient per month because it was subsidizing the care of many who were too poor to pay their own way. This is because of how the dialysis sessions were supported: three sessions per month cost provider organizations an average of roughly 220 EGP (approx. $20 in 2013). Although in theory the Egyptian government would reimburse the costs of these three sessions, budget constraints meant that it would reimburse providers (including the IMA) only two-thirds of that. Many providers—both public and private—thus cut corners to avoid a shortfall in their own budgets. For instance, some restricted patients to two monthly sessions, asked the patients to pay for the third session out of pocket, or even reused disposable equipment such as filters and tubing, with predictably catastrophic public health conse-quences (Sayed et al. 2000; Kefaya Movement 2006, 106). But the IMA ended up subsidizing this third session for those who could not pay, putting the orga-nization further into the red the more patients it served. This particular clinic had consistently flirted with insolvency, and it was probably, an IMA member noted in early 2013, a mistake to open it.[26] Each of the IMA's four dialysis centers struggled to break even.[27]

This evidence further challenges arguments that a drive to provide services to the poor was paramount in the IMA's motivations. Instead, the organization was forced to constantly temper its desire to offer care to its fellow citizens with the reality that it could not do so while maintaining a healthy balance sheet. Muhyi al-Din al-Zayit, director of the IMA's Central Charity Hospital in Nasr City, put it starkly. "We simply cannot accommodate the requests from associations across the country to open new facilities, so we endeavor to open one a year, and as for the rest [of the requests] we can only apologize."[28] Another official agreed: "I cannot make a hospital in all the places that need services."[29] Futuh highlighted the same factor: "You may have twenty places that require our services, but our finances limit us. We cannot offer our services everywhere."[30] To the extent that this calculation is systematic—and there is no reason to suspect it is not—one spatial implication is that these facilities should exist in wealthier areas because those are the places where they will be financially viable. And this should securely tie the Brotherhood's social service provision into the patterns of electoral competition isolated above.

Prior to 2011 the IMA operated thirty-one facilities across Egypt. These consisted of hospitals, dialysis and eye centers, an institution for Egyptians with special needs, and a fertility clinic. A circa 2012 listing of facilities was available both on the group's website and in the IMA's in-house (uncirculated) journal *al-Hikma*.[31] Through fieldwork I also identified additional facilities that had been opened but had been closed or seized prior to 2011 (such as the Sayyida Zaynab clinic referenced in chapter 3). From these lists I used a combination of open-source research methods to identify the precise latitude and longitude of each facility. As a first stage, I cross-referenced the facility name with the results of an internet search. This usually turned up a directory listing, Facebook page, or website for the facility in question that provided the address or, more likely, a nearby landmark. Occasionally these facilities or nearby landmarks were also tagged in Wikimapia, a crowd-sourced geo-referencing website.[32] In other cases satellite maps identified prominent landmarks and intersections referenced in these facilities' promotional or online materials. In many cases, the above methods located accurately the latitude and longitude of these facilities. However, in some particularly difficult cases the open-source information was not sufficient to pinpoint the location of the facility with any confidence. In these cases, I physically traveled to the facilities and, while there, used my smartphone to hand-log the GPS coordinates. Later I correlated these measures with a satellite overview of the area to confirm the location.

Figures 5.3 and 5.4 present the locations of these facilities, first on a nationwide scale, and then zooming in to focus on the Cairo metropolis.

For Egypt's opposition more broadly, and the Muslim Brotherhood specifically, all the electoral action was occurring in middle-class districts. And the qualitative evidence suggests that the Islamic Medical Association's drive for fiscal sustainability led it to establish brick-and-mortar facilities into those same areas. How much do these trends overlap?

Using a spatial join I assigned each IMA medical facility that was open prior to 2011 to the census district (markaz or qism) in which the facility was located.

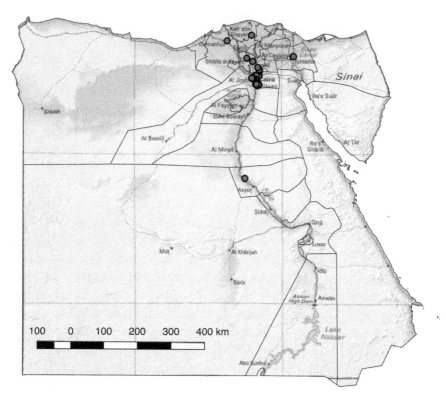

FIGURE 5.3.   IMA facilities (nationwide)

I then generated a dummy variable (0/1) denoting whether or not an IMA facility fell within the borders of that census district.[33] Because the census districts are nested within larger electoral districts (analyzed in figures 5.1 and 5.2), I am also able to assess the likelihood that a medical facility will appear in a given markaz or qism within a given electoral district. This exercise will help show how the Muslim Brotherhood's electoral ambitions, as noted in figure 5.2, and the quali-tative evidence suggesting the importance of fiscal sustainability as part of the IMA's calculus on where to place facilities overlap.

Figures 5.5 and 5.6 plot the predicted probability of an IMA facility's appear-ing in a census district as a function of the wealth index (this time computed at the level of the census district) as well as the larger electoral district-level vari-able charting how often a Brotherhood candidate appeared in that district (the outcome variable from figure 5.2 above).[34]

Figure 5.5 supports a key quantitative implication of the qualitative and histor-ical evidence: that the Islamic Medical Association's middle-class focus anchored it in middle-class neighborhoods and towns. Specifically, the wealth of a markaz

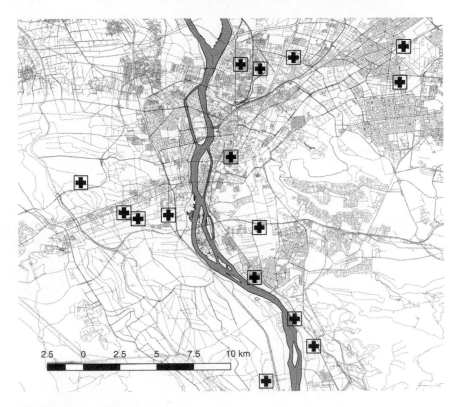

FIGURE 5.4. IMA facilities (Cairo metropolis)

or qism was positively and significantly correlated with the likelihood of one of the Islamic Medical Association's facilities existing in the district ($p < .001$). And as the relationship depicted in figure 5.6 suggests, the relationship also extended to those districts where the Brotherhood was putting forward candidates for elected office. Frequency with which a candidate from the Brotherhood appeared in an electoral district was also positively correlated with a likelihood that an IMA facility would exist there ($p < .10$). This state of affairs meant that not only were those Egyptians most able to vote their political preferences in sustained daily contact with the Brotherhood's social service networks, but that, on election day, Brotherhood candidates were there to receive those voters' support.

The qualitative data can help us better understand the correlation in figure 5.6. One implication of the relationship between IMA facility existence and the frequency of a Brotherhood candidate's appearance in that district is that there should be direct linkages between specific Brotherhood candidates who ran in those districts and IMA facilities located there. Candidate biographies indeed show these relationships. In the 1980s a number of Muslim Brotherhood

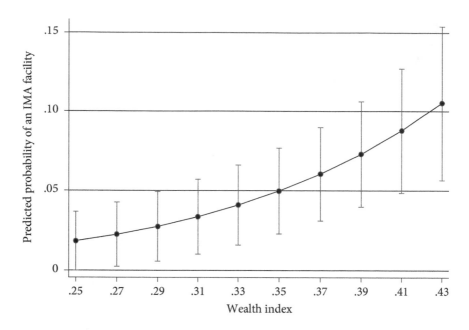

FIGURE 5.5. IMA facility existence vs. wealth index (markaz/qism)

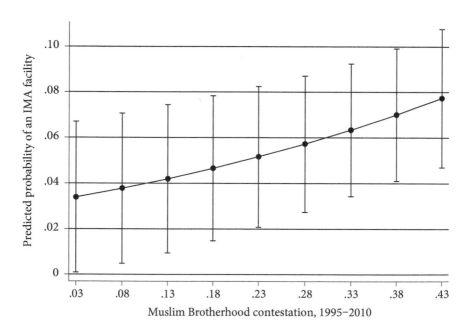

FIGURE 5.6. IMA facility existence vs. Brotherhood electoral contestation (electoral district)

candidates played critical roles in the establishment and operations of the IMA and its satellite facilities. For instance, the imam of the Sayyida Zaynab mosque in Cairo, Muhammad Mitrawi, helped establish the IMA's clinic at that mosque and would later emerge as a powerful member of the Brotherhood's parliamentary bloc (Hilal 1987, 172).[35] The former IMA president Lutfi Shahwan ran in the Nile delta governorate of Sharqiyya's first district in the 1987 elections at the top of the Islamic Alliance's list.[36] 'Isam al-'Ariyan and Hilmi al-Gazar, prominent early members of the IMA, ran for seats in Giza in the 1987 elections.[37] A picture on the Brotherhood's online encyclopedia *Ikhwanwiki* shows the 1983 founding of Salah al-Din Hospital in Khanka, in Qalyubiyya governorate, and includes the IMA's founder, Ahmad al-Malt, 'Izz al-'Arab Fu'ad, who in 1987 would be elected to parliament from the district in which Salah al-Din Hospital was being built; Gamal Hishmat, who would be elected multiple times from Buhayra; and 'Abd al-Mu'nim Abu al-Futuh.[38]

Turning to the period 1995–2010, many of the Muslim Brotherhood's candidates for office were prominently linked to IMA facilities. In the Delta they included the aforementioned Gamal Hishmat, who served not only on the IMA's national board of directors, but also as founder and president of the board of directors of the IMA's Dar al-Salam Hospital in his district.[39] The four-time Muslim Brotherhood candidate Ashraf Badr al-Din, from Manufiyya, was founder, member of the board of directors, and past president of the Muwasat Association, in addition to being the "founder of Muwasat Hospital."[40] Muhammad 'Ali Bishr, who ran for parliament in 2005, had also been president of the Muwasat Association.[41] In 1995 (and again after the fall of Mubarak) Hisham al-Suli contested elections for the Brotherhood in Ismailiyya, where he worked as director of the IMA's Amal Charity Hospital.[42] In the upper Egyptian governorate of Assiyut, the Brotherhood candidate Muhammad 'Abd al-Raziq touted his role as "one of the founders the Abu al-Nasr Charity Hospital."[43]

The relationships were also dense in the Cairo-Giza metropolis. 'Abd al-Mun'im Dahrug helped establish the IMA's Tawba Hospital in the same Cairo district where he ran in 2005.[44] The longtime Brotherhood candidate Hazim Faruq, from the central Cairo district of al-Sahil, is a member of the board of directors of the Jam'iyyat Sharif (Sharif Association). The Sharif Association owns the building housing the 'Adil Hospital in his district.[45] As one IMA employee there put it, "'Adil Hospital is affiliated to both the IMA and the Jam'iyyat Sharif."[46] In the south Cairo district of Hilwan, al-Muhammadi 'Abd al-Maqsud was also president of the association "that established the Hadi Charitable Hospital."[47] Across the Nile in Giza, Abu 'Ila Qarni stood for parliament in al-Hawamdiyya in 1995 and 2000, during which time he was the director of the IMA's hospital in that district (he was also that hospital's founder).[48] Another member of the Qarni family,

Gamal, won the 2005 elections as the Brotherhood's candidate in that district, helped along by Abu 'Ila's campaigning on his behalf (Gamal would contest, but lose, the 2010 elections).[49]

This brief compilation of candidate-facility linkages should raise confidence that the statistical analysis reported in figure 5.6 reflects a relationship that manifests on the ground. This convergence of candidates and facilities, however, raises a question of endogenity: Did the group run candidates where it had hospitals, or build hospitals where it ran candidates? I argue that in many cases the relationship was the result of a mostly fortuitous convergence rather than strategic decisions by the Brotherhood and its leadership to maximize political support by strategically establishing centers of social service provision (Masoud 2014a, 181). It is also the case that the qualities that the Brotherhood knew would make a given candidate politically competitive were linked to its operation of a social service enterprise in that district. Thus the political logic seems to follow the social service one; an individual would become known and respected through social service provision and then use that social capital to compete for elected office.

For example, in the spring of 2013 I traveled to Banha, in the Qalyubiyya governorate north of Cairo. I went there to interview Muhsin Radi, one of the Brotherhood's veteran parliamentary deputies (he had run in the 1995, 2005, 2010, and 2011–12 people's assembly elections, winning in 2005 and 2011–12) and the author of an important book on the Brotherhood in parliament (1990). Radi had only been elected, he said, after he had spent extensive time working in the district, building up his profile and reputation through social services, and helping solve people's problems. In fact, one of the ways Radi was known in the community was through his position as founder and chairman of the Brotherhood's al-Fath School, which enrolled over two thousand children. Close by Radi's office was one of the IMA's hospitals, and the Brotherhood also operated an orphanage elsewhere in Banha. "It is critical to be able to offer services to people who have been deprived of those services by the regime," Radi answered when I asked why he was so active in the Brotherhood's social service endeavors.[50] Radi's "homestyle" (Fenno 1978) illustrated the way that political ambitions tended to flow from social activism, and not the other way around.

Further support for this argument comes from the fact that the effort the Brotherhood put forth to understand how best to exploit the electoral landscape is well documented. Long before election day the group reviewed the results of prior contests, studied the characteristics of the district, identified the positions and strengths of potential opponents, and gauged the interest of local Brotherhood members who might run (Anani 2007, 252–54). Media efforts were carefully calibrated to reach particular constituencies and tailored to highlight relevant strengths of candidates (Tammam 2009). We might expect that as part of its pre-election research, the Brotherhood would have realized that those members already known in the community and respected for their work in social service provision would make formidable candidates for elected office.

The Brotherhood's strict disavowal of politicization in the facilities themselves also indicates that they did not conceive of social services as an instrumental way to maximize electoral support, but rather as a tool with which to realize broader sociopolitical change. Interviewees universally rejected the notion that the IMA's social service provision was specifically designed with an eye towards elections. For example, when I asked 'Abd al-Mu'nim Abu al-Futuh, the former IMA president, how the IMA decided where (and where not) to open facilities, he discussed the emphasis on fiscal sustainability (cited above). He then paused and added, "It wasn't a political thing, if that is what you meant by your question. It wasn't like we needed the votes of the people in this electoral district so we constructed a medical service there; that wasn't the aim at all."[51] His denial mirrored what IMA officials and Brotherhood members told me at other points.

Egypt's protean electoral map also suggests that political concerns were not the driving force, in the sense that it was impossible to anticipate what the electoral landscape would look like by the time a brick-and-mortar facility was fully operational. To wit: the IMA was established in 1977. At that time Egypt's electoral map was based on Law 38 of 1972, which set 175 two-person districts under the new Egyptian constitution.[52] Then, in advance of the 1984 elections, Law 114 of 1983 transformed Egypt into a party-list system in which voters from 48 newly established constituencies elected 448 parliamentarians.[53] After a legal challenge, the 1987 elections added to each district a single first-past-the-post (FPTP) seat.[54] This mixed system was ruled unconstitutional, and then, in preparation for the 1990 elections, a new law set a nationwide system of 222 electoral districts composed of two FPTP seats that continued until the 2010 elections. Prior to those contests (2010), the regime carved out three new governorates—Luxor, Hilwan, and 6 October—and again rearranged a portion of the electoral map on the basis of these changes.[55] And of course, after Mubarak was pushed out in 2011, the Supreme Council of the Armed Forces completely redrew the electoral map once again (Hassan 2013).[56] All this is to say that anyone who banked on the stability of the Egyptian electoral map for any real length of time—for instance, by erecting a brick-and-mortar medical facility in a promising district—was investing in an extremely volatile market.

Of course, the lack of political causes does not rule out political effects (indeed, the remainder of the chapter, and the book, explicitly focuses on the counterintuitive ways that depoliticized provision produced political mobilization). But the available evidence suggests that the Brotherhood's apparently unique ability to realize political benefits from social service provision can be traced to the fortuitous convergence of largely distinct processes: a decision made in the mid-1970s to target social services at a wealthier and paying audience, the coalescing of post-1990 electoral competition inside wealthier districts, and the Brotherhood's tendency to put forward candidates in those same competitive, more affluent districts.

Turning Out the Neighborhood

Does social service provision produce measurable effects on electoral outcomes? Authoritarian settings quite obviously make answering this question difficult. And even if one were able to somehow mitigate concerns about manipulation, the effect of social service provision is likely quite localized. It would be difficult, for example, to tease out the independent effect of a hospital in a large electoral district. Absent highly disaggregated electoral statistics, it is quite difficult to systematically satisfy this implication.

Few studies have attempted to isolate and test out the exact relationship between Islamic social activism and pro-Islamist voting, but two attempts stand out. In *Counting Islam* Tarek Masoud finds mixed support for the hypothesis connecting the organizational density of Islamic institutions—including social service facilities—to the political success of Islamist parties and, notably, no evidence that this network helped Mohammed Morsi (2014a, 168–76). And using data on pre-1990 elections, 'Imad Siyam (2006) finds that the three governorates with the highest concentrations of Islamic associations (Cairo, Alexandria, and Giza) sent the majority of Brotherhood members to parliament in the 1984 elections. For the 1987 elections he turns to voting statistics and finds that the top eight governorates in terms of the largest share of "Islamic associations" (Cairo, Alexandria, Giza, Manufiyya, Sharqiyya, Minya, Aswan, and Qalyubiyya) yielded the most seats for the Muslim Brotherhood's "Islamic Alliance." From this, he concludes that Islamic associations constituted the Brotherhood's "base of support" and that there was a "clear link" between Islamic associations and the political success of the Islamic trend (95). But in addition to sidestepping the issue of electoral fraud, Siyam is examining the relationship at such a high level of aggregation (governorates are akin to American states and contain millions of residents) that it is difficult to take his results as anything more than suggestive.

Usage statistics, culled from both the IMA's internal documents and a representative survey of Egyptians, provide the first indication that the Brotherhood's medical services reached widely enough to plausibly have some effect on elections, especially disaggregated to the local level. In addition to providing information on poor and nonpoor beneficiaries, the IMA's audit sheets (referenced in chapter 4), give aggregate numbers of total patients seen at the IMA's hospitals. In line with public statements from IMA leadership figures themselves, these audit sheets show that around 1.5 million Egyptians per year visited the IMA's facilities.[57] Third-party data generally confirm these numbers; in an original survey of Egyptians, discussed at more length in chapter 6, respondents were asked if they or a member of their family had used the Muslim Brotherhood's brick-and-mortar facilities. Over 7.5 percent (7.65 percent) of the sample responded yes.[58] Were we to translate these results to the broader population, this would approximate over six million Egyptians who had benefited from this provision. On the one hand, Egypt's large population should certainly be kept in mind in attempting to extrapolate to how this distinct minority of citizens could have swayed the electoral balance of power. But on the other hand, the apathy and institutional engineering that marked elections in Mubarak's Egypt made it "possible to do well . . . with relatively small vote shares" (Masoud 2014a, 95). To the extent that this is true, even a relatively small group of committed supporters, applied acutely, could have disproportionate political effects.

A unique data set of geo-located precinct-level electoral returns from Egypt's first competitive presidential election, in the summer of 2012, can also help indicate how social service provision influences local patterns of electoral mobilization. While the nature of these data—limited as they are to the Cairo governorate and with natural control variables unavailable—is worth keeping in mind, it helps to understand the electoral effects these facilities could plausibly produce in their local communities.

Campaigning for Egypt's first democratic presidential election began in the spring of 2012 with a crowded field of competitors. After two days of voting, the Brotherhood's candidate, Mohammed Morsi, led with 24.78 percent of the vote. Ahmed Shafiq, a former Air Force general and Hosni Mubarak's last prime minister, was close on his heels with 23.66 percent support. Because no candidate had obtained 50 percent of the vote, Morsi and Shafiq headed to a two-man nationwide runoff. On June 16 and 17 Egyptians again headed to the polls, electing Mohammed Morsi by a slight 51.7 to 48.3 percent margin.

Official voting data for the second-round (runoff) election between Morsi and Shafiq were publicly released down to the markaz/qism level. From the French Centre d'Études et de Documentation Économiques, Juridiques et Sociales (CEDEJ) I obtained geo-located ballot box data for all 1,328 ballot boxes in Cairo.[59] Included for each ballot box are the total number of registered voters, the total number of votes cast, the number of spoiled (invalid) ballots, and the totals for Morsi and Shafiq, respectively. For the below tests I collapse all co-located ballot boxes into the precinct to produce a basic turnout measure for Mohammed

Morsi: total Morsi votes per precinct divided by total registered voters per precinct. Unfortunately, there exist no socioeconomic data fine-grained enough to produce potentially relevant control variables at this level of analysis, and this must be kept in mind when interpreting the results. However, I also generate a measure of the number of boxes aggregated into the precinct, on the assumption that the size of precinct may be related to the outcome (min = 1, max = 7).

While the availability of data rather than a disciplined process of case selection drove the choice of both the geographic unit (Cairo governorate) and the specific election (the second-round presidential elections), the potential pitfalls of the following analysis should be judged against the potential insights to be gained. Primarily, given the difficulty of obtaining data on Egyptian elections, particularly at the local level, this effort proves a notable step forward. And the Cairo governorate is a particularly prominent case. Not only is it Egypt's largest city and center of political, economic, and cultural influence, a number of the IMA's medical facilities were located there. Further, it encompasses neighborhoods of both ostentatious wealth and striking poverty, as well as areas of Islamist political power and historic strongholds of antipathy toward Islamists. Overall, Mohammed Morsi lost Cairo to Ahmed Shafiq by more than eleven percentage points (44.3 to 55.7 percent).

To produce the key variables, I overlaid the map of all 497 precincts (composed of all ballot boxes located at those latitudes and longitudes) in the Cairo governorate with the coordinates of all Cairo-based IMA facilities that were open during the runoff between Mohammed Morsi and Ahmed Shafiq. I then generated circular catchment areas around each medical facility at 500 meters (approximately a five-minute walk), 750 m, and 1,000 m, respectively.[60] Figure 5.7 illustrates the process in a section of the Cairo governorate (Hilwan), although for demonstration purposes it includes only the 500 m buffer).[61]

While a rough measure, the buffers help to identify how proximity to the Brotherhood's social service institutions might influence electoral support for the group. For each of the buffer zones I created a dummy variable. Precincts that fell within one of the catchment areas of an IMA facility received a one, while those not falling in any received a zero. To briefly restate the empirical implication this analysis is meant to test: precincts in the vicinity of IMA facilities will yield measurably higher margins of support for Mohammed Morsi than precincts outside the vicinity of the IMA facilities.

Figure 5.8 plots the coefficients on pro-Morsi turnout, drawn from a regression analysis, as a function of whether or not that voting precinct is located inside the buffers of the listed distance (Jann 2014).

Although Morsi lost the Cairo governorate overall, his performance seems to have improved the closer one moved to a Brotherhood social service institution.

FIGURE 5.7. 500 m buffer, Cairo governorate (Hilwan)

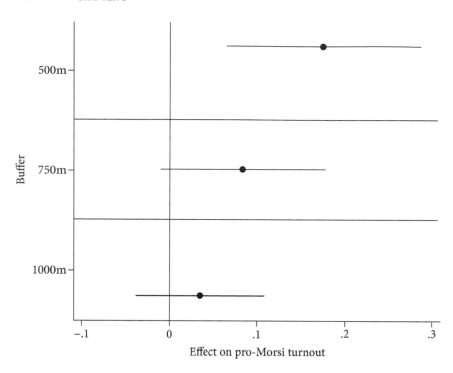

FIGURE 5.8. Effect of proximity to IMA facilities on pro-Morsi turnout

Within 500m the coefficient on pro-Morsi turnout is positive and statistically significant ($p = .003$). And the strength of the relationship degrades as one moves farther and farther away from the IMA facility ($p = .085$ at 750m and $p = .353$ at 1000m).

A recognition of the weaknesses of these data must temper interpretation of the results. Not only is the buffer measure crude, but the lack of socioeconomic control variables leaves open the possibility of confounding. We cannot rule out the possibility that the observed relationship is driven by other variables that, because of the granularity of the data, simply cannot be accounted for in the analysis. However, in conjunction with the information presented over the prior chapters, these results are at least suggestive of the possibility that the Brotherhood's social service provision generated an on-the-ground effect on election day.

It is also possible that this analysis *underestimates* the on-the-ground electoral effect of the Muslim Brotherhood's social service network. The Morsi-Shafiq contest from which these data were drawn was highly ideological and particularly polarized, framed as a choice between the secular remnants of the old regime and the Brotherhood's new Islamic order. Yet as we have seen, local and parliamentary elections usually turn on relatively more mundane concerns such as service delivery or prior relationships with the parties or the politicians. It is likely that the ideologically charged nature of the 2012 presidential election vitiated some portion of the social service–driven pro-Brotherhood effect that might manifest more strongly in a different electoral context.

Spatial Dimensions of the Islamist Advantage

This chapter investigated the spatial implications of two components of the theory. From the sender side, it extended the prior chapters' investigation of the IMA's emphasis on middle-class care into the realm of geography. As an array of historical and qualitative material would lead us to expect, the IMA's brick-and-mortar facilities disproportionately clustered in more affluent areas. Viewed in isolation, this is not surprising—targeting areas where the market is sufficient to support operations is a quite logical choice for an organization that places a priority on generating and sustaining revenue.

The IMA was, however, more than a business. Its focus on more affluent customers proved a political boon as Egypt's post-1990 political system mapped onto the contours of the country's dominant socioeconomic cleavage. Proregime patrons established durable monopolies in poor districts, where robust clientelist networks consolidated sturdy bases of support and dissuaded opponents from lodging an electoral challenge. Electoral competition in middle-class districts was more freewheeling, as opposition politicians—the Muslim Brotherhood among them—sought to make their mark among citizens who were willing and able to vote for them.

Disaggregated spatial data from Egypt's brief democratic interlude escaped the question of fraud to explore a natural extension of this argument: that the location of these facilities influenced electoral outcomes. While tentative and lacking obvious controls, the investigation suggested evidence of a local effect of these facilities on the Brotherhood's ability to win elected office. Combined with the prior qualitative evidence, the chapter's final section should increase confidence that social service provision is at least theoretically able to generate a measurable effect on electoral outcomes.

The next chapter develops the microlevel investigation of provider-citizen linkages. After using qualitative material to show how the IMA builds and sustains high-quality and compassionate care, it introduces an original survey experiment to examine the precise ways in which this atmosphere informs Egyptians' perceptions of the character of Brotherhood candidates and, in turn, their willingness to vote for those candidates on election day.

ELECTING TO SERVE

Mohammed Galal, from the delta town of al-Qanatir al-Khayriyya, was very sick. Lacking the capacity to handle his case locally, his doctor recommended that he go to the Islamic Medical Association's Talibiyya Hospital in Giza. The surgery there was successful, and after a few days in recovery Mohammed could go home. Before he left, however, he effusively praised the hospital and its staff. "Words cannot describe them," he claimed. "They are very good, they are excellent, and they care about me." The whole experience made him feel as if he was in a "five star hospital . . . in terms of their continuous care, their promptness, the cleanliness, and their organization. . . . Every section performs their jobs in an excellent way without begrudging me."[1] This chapter shows how Mohammed Galal's experience was broadly representative of the IMA's standard of care. It goes beyond this vignette to show why his experience at the Talibiyya Hospital would likely have redounded to the Brotherhood's benefit on election day.

Prior chapters have traced out the IMA's development under the umbrella of the Egyptian state, the ways that IMA managers ensured consistent and quality care, how these facilities nested within the country's particular economic and political geography, and their potential to produce an electoral effect. This chapter uses a variety of qualitative material to vividly illustrate the patient experience, showing particularly how the IMA emphasized the very traits that Mohammed Galal noticed—professionalism, humility, organization, and nondiscriminatory care—as keys to patient satisfaction. The second half of the chapter uses a nationwide survey experiment of over 2,400 Egyptians to gain insight into how these characteristics might have influenced citizens to vote for Brotherhood candidates. Additional data drawn from the survey, including Egyptians' own descriptions of their experiences at the Brotherhood's facilities and a causal mediation analysis, show how a key part of the vaunted "Islamic Advantage" runs through a social service-generated reputational mechanism (Cammett and Jones Luong 2014; Masoud 2014a; Pepinsky, Liddle, and Mujani 2012).

Illustrating the Patient Experience

The IMA tailored its advantages to that stratum of Egyptians caught between a collapsing public health system and an unaffordable private one. The IMA's marketing materials echo this sentiment: the brochure for the flagship Central Charity Hospital promises, on the front cover, "high-quality medical care at an affordable price," while a similar brochure for the Faruq Hospital in Ma'adi trumpets the facility's commitment to "safety, mercy, competency."[2] One result was to help convince Egyptians that the IMA's facilities were set up to do the simple things that make a visit to the doctor less harrowing than it already is.

Throughout IMA facilities were brochures—equally available to both employees and patients—in which the IMA discusses certain traits and characteristics that it prioritized in the atmosphere of its facilities and behavior of its staff (Zayd 2006). These pamphlets usually include a brief discussion of one particular trait relevant to medical care, framing it in terms of that particular trait's relationship to Islamic values. The brochures also contain short cartoons illustrating what these traits mean in practice and why specifically they are valuable in a medical setting.

Figure 6.1 presents a sample of some of these cartoons dealing with organization-level attributes.[3]

The IMA's facilities were not spotless, and occasionally they struggled to meet patients' expectations. But think of how the basic characteristics in figures 6.1A and 6.1B might be attractive to Egyptians facing the pathologies apparent elsewhere in the Egyptian health care system: the IMA's emphasis on cleanliness against the prevalence of dirty dialysis machines in government facilities, which led to the catastrophic spread of crippling diseases; publicly posted hours during which doctors and specialists would be available, versus the situation at the Asala party clinic, where one could wait for hours for a doctor who never showed up.

The general atmospherics at the IMA's facilities were one side of the coin; the other was the specific interpersonal qualities that managers looked for in potential employees and encouraged in current ones. Ahmad al-Malt claimed that IMA employees needed to possess technical skill, good character, and dedication to social and civic improvement. In introducing the Islamic Medical Association

FIGURE 6.1A. Brochure title: "Cleanliness [al-Niẓāfa]." Q: "What's their secret? Why is the hospital always so crowded?" A: "Because of how clean it is."

FIGURE 6.1B. Brochure title: "Organization [al-Niẓām]." Q: "Is a female gynecologist working now?" A: "The doctors' schedules are posted on that board."

to readers of *al-Da'wa*, an inside front cover advertisement touted that the association's flagship hospital would offer "all specialties, provided by Muslim doctors with the highest levels of knowledge, integrity, and trustworthiness."[4] A few months later, Malt explained to readers that the relationship between practitioner and patient would differentiate the IMA in an era in which "exploitation and negligence in treatment proliferate."[5]

As an indicator of how seriously the IMA valued the relational aspect of care, the formal hiring process began by assessing the extent to which the applicant was in tune with the organization's general mission, and only later in the process did the hospital manager assess the employee's technical skill.[6] One IMA executive stated that he aimed to hire employees who "present a good image to the people, are well trained, understand how to deal with the patients and the people, and they must be honest. . . . Our employees have to smile, have to be able to sympathize with the patient's pain, and things like that."[7] "The most important person in our hospitals is not the director, or the employees, but the patient," another executive summarized when asked to elaborate on his hiring philosophy. "We all exist to serve the patient."[8] The manager of one dialysis center even claimed that if he found someone of good character but lacking experience, he was willing to hire the person and train him or her himself—he found that many job seekers had the technical skill to work in his facility, but the proper attitude was much harder to come by. He went on to explain that one way he judged the success of this policy was that a number of wealthy Egyptians preferred to travel to his clinic rather than visit private clinics much closer to their homes, where the technical standards of care were high but the relational aspects were lacking.[9]

On the one hand, the IMA's emphasis on strong interpersonal skills tended to incentivize the use of personal networks (rather than open calls) for hiring. A number of managers noted that they tended to use their (and their employees') networks when they needed to fill a position because it allowed a better degree of prescreening for the particular attitudes and demeanors that the IMA sought out.[10] On the other hand, the IMA's reputation for upholding a particular standard of patient care and being a good place to work generally also acted as a type of filtering mechanism by attracting those frustrated by real or perceived shortfalls at other types of facilities. For instance, one employee explained her decision to join the IMA by contrasting the experience with her prior job, at a public hospital. "I left because there we treated patients like cattle, not like people." The IMA, she continued, had a good reputation for treating both patients and employees with dignity, which is why she sought them out.[11]

The IMA recognized that a key part of its advantage over alternative providers, in both the public and private systems, was its employees. The brochures extensively note this, and a selection of these individual characteristics is presented in figure 6.2.

FIGURE 6.2A. Brochure title: "Sincerity [al-Ikhlās]." Caption: Businessman: "Praise to God! You've treated the doorman the exact same way you treated me!" Doctor: "This is what our religion guides us to do."

FIGURE 6.2B. Brochure title: "Trustworthiness [al-Amāna]." Caption: Q: "Why don't you apply that new procedure you wrote about in your dissertation?" A: "I don't apply any new procedure until after it has been tested and verified."

FIGURE 6.2C. Brochure title: "Trustworthiness [al-Amāna]." Caption: Father: "He lost his voice after the surgery!" Doctor: "This was my fault and I will pay for his treatment at the best hospital."

FIGURE 6.2D. Brochure title: "Modesty [al-Tawāḍuʿ]." Caption: Doctor: "Peace be upon you all." Man: "Do you see his humility?!"

The IMA emphasized the interpersonal, relational side of the endeavor just as much as technical side. Staff were expected to execute common procedures with expertise, admit when they were out of their depth, and be friendly, humble, and nonjudgmental when interacting with patients. Many of these traits are especially notable for how they can be counterposed against the problems that were rife among doctors and medical personnel in other types of facilities: haughtiness, a tendency to freelance, and an unwillingness to take responsibility (or be held accountable) for errors (Kefaya Movement 2006, 111–24).

Of course, these cartoons were not produced by an objective observer. They do, however, help to illustrate that the IMA understood that its advantage over competitors stemmed from the patient experience it offered, a quality that encompassed both technical expertise and interpersonal relationships. The combined effect was to produce a memorable experience for the millions of ordinary Egyptians—men and women like Mohammed Galal—who benefited from the IMA's facilities annually.

The Power of Depoliticized Provision

The IMA was able to offer high-quality and relationally enjoyable care that stood out especially starkly against failures elsewhere in Egypt's health care ecosystem. These types of normal, depoliticized, and highly personal interactions—based on obtaining medicine for an aging parent, mending a child's broken arm, or finding relief for one's own debilitating illness—generated powerful feelings of affection for the provider organization. Other organizations could have realized political support from their social service provision, for instance through the contingent, episodic exchange of clientelism, but the depoliticized, reputation-based mechanism generated by the quality of the care at the IMA's facilities was different.

An important aspect of this mechanism was structural, based on the particular types of patients served by the IMA. Had the IMA relied on a more clientelist, politicized style of provision, it would no doubt have alienated middle-class Egyptians. In her study of politician-voter linkages in Argentina, Rebecca Weitz-Shapiro identifies an important trade-off: "While clientelism garners support among the poor, this comes at the cost of lost electoral support from non-poor voters" (2014, 50). As she goes on to note, clientelism alienates middle-class voters—in this case, the type of people who disproportionately visited the IMA's facilities—not only because they have moral qualms with its transactional nature, but also because they see it as an indicator that the politician would prefer to trade resources for votes rather than concentrating on winning political support through enacting popular policies and governing effectively.

In fact, the IMA rejected many of the trappings that the classic clientelist model would lead us to expect. As we have seen, it overwhelmingly provided for paying patients and strictly forbade employees from politicking on the job. Instead, the Brotherhood benefited from the perception that it was going about its social activism detached from immediate political or electoral considerations, what Marie Vannetzel calls "the symbolic economy of disinterestedness" (2016, 49). Political support thus became a "residual effect" of social service provision rather than a calculated outcome (Wiktorowicz 2001, 85).

The Brotherhood relied on more subtle interactions, both purposive and coincidental, to connect its social service provision to political support. We have already seen, for example, how many of the Brotherhood's candidates for elected office also played prominent roles in IMA facilities in their districts. One former member of the Brotherhood explained that there was no quid pro quo, threats, or discrimination against recipients of social service provision who did not support the Brotherhood. Instead, on election day those individuals who were known in the community for their work providing social services would simply be involved in voter mobilization efforts.[12] Chapter 5 relayed a conversation in which the former IMA president Futuh rejected claims that the organization adhered to a political logic about where to place the facilities. I followed up and asked whether he thought the IMA's provision generated a political *effect*:

> Of course, it has a big [political] effect, because in the end, the man who is offering the service for the Brotherhood, if it is done the correct way, he is the same man who comes through during the election campaign to ask the people for votes. So the affection [between the people and the candidate] comes from here, whether this is intended or not. In many cases [the connection] is unintended because this guy is offering a service simply out of a desire to do good [*li-wajh Allāh*, lit. "for the face of God"]. . . . So it's not as if on election day he will show up to the neighborhood and say to the people, "Listen up, you bastards![13] I gave you this and that, and so come vote for us." No, this is not how it works, it is more spontaneous. Because the people themselves, if this is a good man offering services for them, which is the same man who is a politician, [it is natural that] he will gain all of their votes.[14]

Maintaining this thin but plausible separation from politics was neither easy nor natural, and sometimes it failed, particularly around election time, when the pressures to let the two realms merge was strongest (Fayed 2017, 247–48). Managers and administrators had to constantly monitor the situations at each facility in order to make sure zealous employees (or managers) did not cross the line into blatant politicization. But so long as their interactions remained generally depoliticized, as part of a larger atmosphere of reliable and professional care, visitors to these facilities tended to passively associate their positive experience at the Brotherhood's social service institutions with the Brotherhood's candidates for elected office. Particularly for middle-class voters, these traits would exercise a powerful influence on election day.

From Medicine to Mobilization

To go beyond intuitive but vague statements about how the Muslim Brotherhood's particular style of social service provision generated political support, this chapter now reports an original and nationally representative (n=2,483) telephone survey of adult (18+) Egyptians. In an attempt understand precisely how social service provision influences political attitudes, I embedded in the survey an experimental component. Specifically, a brief prime modulated basic factual information about medical service provision in Egypt for a random selection of respondents, then subsequently tested their attitudes on a variety of relevant political outcomes against a control group.[15]

This survey experiment necessarily simplifies the complex and inherently social process of receiving medical care but does so with a series of trade-offs in mind. First, the nationally representative survey format facilitates the systematic collection of ordinary Egyptians' experiences with the Brotherhood's social service networks, furnishing ostensibly independent data with which to test implications of the theory. Second, the experimental component, in this case a priming design, assists in causal inference. Because respondents are randomly divided into treatment and control, concerns about potential confounders are lessened, and confidence in the precise causal effects of the treatment is heightened (Shadish, Cook, and Campbell 2002; McDermott 2011; Mutz 2011; Druckman et al. 2011). Finally, the extent to which the experimental manipulation builds on both this book's broader theoretical logic as well as the variety of historical, qualitative, and spatial evidence presented over the preceding chapters should somewhat ameliorate concerns about the admittedly artificial nature of the manipulation.

To help identify the causal effect of the Brotherhood's provision of medical services on political outcomes, I borrow experimental designs developed in American politics. In their landmark study of race and affirmative action, Sniderman and Piazza sought a simple way to stimulate and measure citizens' attitudes that might otherwise remain latent. In their case, they designed an experimental manipulation that could "simulate the kinds of conversations that ordinary people undoubtedly have about affirmative action and the characteristics of blacks.

The basic idea is to determine whether references to affirmative action can, in and of themselves, excite negative reactions to blacks" (1995, 110).

This book adapts this design to the Egyptian case, using a brief informational prime about the Muslim Brotherhood's medical services in order to stimulate and capture respondent attitudes about the group's candidates for elected office. This "mere mention" design has the benefit of being a fairly unobtrusive way to examine—on a large scale—the attitudinal effects of exposure to the Brotherhood's social services (but see also Lenz 2009). One fairly obvious implication of the information presented up to this point is that being stimulated to think generally about the Brotherhood's medical provision would induce a positive shift in respondents' assessment of Brotherhood candidates' and deputies' character traits in line with the types of characteristics that predominated in the IMA's facilities. This, in turn, would increase electoral support for the group.

In the specific construction here, all 2,483 survey respondents received an informational prime in the form of four questions about medical provision in Egypt. However, the content of the four questions differed based on the survey form to which the individual had been randomly assigned. While those respondents in the control version were asked about the Ministry of Health's medical services, respondents in the treatment condition received questions about the Muslim Brotherhood instead. The treatment and control batteries, where modulated text appears in italics, are as follows:

Control

Now I would like to ask you some questions about the *Ministry of Health* and their activities in the field of medical provision in Egypt. The *Ministry of Health* operates many hospitals and clinics in all parts of the country, and these facilities provide a wide range of medical services to millions of Egyptians every year, among them the poor and destitute. Have you heard about these facilities before?

Have you or a member of your family visited a hospital or clinic operated by the *Ministry of Health* before?

Treatment

Now I would like to ask you some questions about the *Muslim Brotherh*ood and their activities in the field of medical provision in Egypt. The *Muslim Brotherhood* operates many hospitals and clinics in all parts of the country, and these facilities provide a wide range of medical services to millions of Egyptians every year, among them the poor and destitute. Have you heard about these facilities before?

Have you or a member of your family visited a hospital or clinic operated by the *Muslim Brotherhood* before?

The *Ministry of Health* organizes medical caravans that provide medical services to areas lacking hospitals or clinics, where they focus on specialized problems such as glaucoma. Have you heard about these before?	The *Muslim Brotherhood* organizes medical caravans that provide medical services to areas lacking hospitals or clinics, where they focus on specialized problems such as glaucoma. Have you heard about these before?
Have you had a checkup, received medicine, or undergone a simple medical procedure at one of the *Ministry of Health's* medical caravans before?	Have you had a checkup, received medicine, or undergone a simple medical procedure at one of the *Muslim Brotherhood's* medical caravans?

The lack of a natural control made it particularly challenging to produce a prime that was both anodyne and relevant (the chapter's final sections as well as the appendix discuss—and ultimately rule out—potential alternative mechanisms at work). Other competing politically active service providers, such as the aforementioned Wafd and Asala parties, were comparable in neither scope nor scale to what the Brotherhood was offering.[16] This could end up exacerbating one of the flaws of the experimental approach: that the artificial nature of the manipulation might produce an effect quite detached from what actually obtained on the ground. And it would be difficult to specify a private-sector provider or network that all respondents in the nationwide sample could immediately identify, risking confusion in that subgroup. So for simplicity's sake the remainder of this chapter refers to the Ministry of Health battery as the control, although it is better conceptualized as a second prime (Gaines, Kuklinski, and Quirk 2007).

Following the treatment battery, all respondents answered a question about their self-reported propensity to vote for the Muslim Brotherhood and then a three-question battery designed to capture their perception of the traits of the Muslim Brotherhood's candidates. The first question, regarding vote choice, was designed to probe the basic theory articulated in this book: that the Brotherhood's social service provision benefited the group at election time. The subsequent three-question trait battery was specifically designed to test the hypothesized reputation-based causal mechanism: that the Brotherhood's social service provision caused recipients to view the character of the Brotherhood's candidates more positively.[17]

Respondents were first asked, "If the Brotherhood did participate in the upcoming elections, how likely would you be to vote for their candidates?" (Very unlikely, unlikely, likely, very likely.)[18] Respondents were then asked the extent to which they agreed with three traits that purported to describe the Muslim Brotherhood's "candidates and [parliamentary] deputies": "honesty [al-ṣādiqūn]," "capability [akfā']," and "modesty [al-mutawāḍiʿūn]" (strongly disagree, disagree, agree, strongly agree). Each of the three trait questions was asked independently, although they tapped into a common underlying sentiment (Cronbach's α = .8296). Thus in the figures below (6.4–6.5) the results of this question are compiled into a single index measure, "reputation."[19]

Historical, qualitative, and spatial evidence suggested that there was a notable bias against the poor in these facilities. Founders of the IMA proclaimed their intention to target middle-class Egyptians, internal balance sheets recorded only limited visits by poor patients, and these facilities were predominantly located in wealthier areas. So, in order to specifically explore how well this bias toward the more affluent manifested at the level of the individual, each respondent answered whether or not she belonged to a household that owned an automatic washing machine and whether the household owned a car. "Poor" households owned neither. "Non-poor" households owned either an automatic washer and a car, or just a car.[20]

The remainder of this chapter presents the results of the experimental manipulation, as well as additional qualitative and quantitative information drawn from the survey instrument. To briefly restate the expectations: First, Egyptians exposed to information about the Muslim Brotherhood's medical initiatives would rate Muslim Brotherhood candidates higher on perceptions of honesty, capability, and modesty. Second, Egyptians exposed to information about the Muslim Brotherhood's medical initiatives would report themselves more likely to vote for the Muslim Brotherhood's candidates. Third, the causal effect of social service provision on political support would operate by influencing perceptions of Muslim Brotherhood candidates' honesty, capability, and modesty (in other words, these traits mediate the relationship between priming related to the Muslim Brotherhood's medical initiatives and political support for the Muslim Brotherhood's candidates). And fourth, this effect should generally manifest more strongly among more affluent respondents than among their poorer counterparts.

Figures 6.3 and 6.4 summarize the results of the experimental manipulation on the entire sample as well as the posited differential effects according to socioeconomic class. For each question and subgroup, the figures report the difference of means (treatment minus control) and the 95 percent confidence intervals, where asterisks represent a statistically significant difference between treatment and control group means.[21]

Figure 6.3 shows that priming respondents with information about the Brotherhood's medical provision increases electoral support for the group. Specifically, those in the treatment group report themselves significantly more likely to vote for the Brotherhood than those in the control group ($p < .01$). This satisfies one of the basic predictions motivating the use of the experimental design and shows

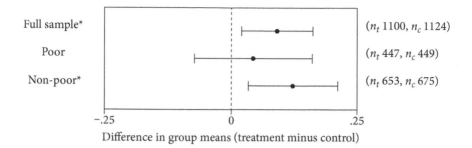

FIGURE 6.3. Propensity to vote for the Muslim Brotherhood

how receiving basic information about the Brotherhood's social service provision can shift the outcome of interest, here captured with a question about propensity to vote for the Brotherhood's candidates in a hypothetical upcoming election. The differential effects are also noteworthy: restricting the sample to the "poor" respondents—that is, comparing only poor respondents in the treatment group with poor respondents in the control group—causes the effect to drop beyond the standard threshold of statistical significance ($p < .05$), suggesting a weaker effect of the informational prime on political attitudes among this subgroup. In contrast, those "non-poor" respondents were more strongly influenced by the treatment ($p < .01$). In sum, while being primed with information about the Brotherhood's social services made non-poor Egyptians more likely to support the Brotherhood in elections, the effect was notably weaker on poor Egyptians.

Figure 6.3 helps support this book's argument about a general relationship between social services and voting. Figure 6.4 begins to identify the particular reputation-based causal relationship by reporting the results of the same prime on the three-question battery assessing respondents' perceptions of the traits associated with the Brotherhood's candidates and parliamentary deputies.

Figure 6.4 shows how the informational prime about Brotherhood social services *also* shifts respondents' perceptions about the personal qualities of the Brotherhood's candidates for elected office. In the full comparison, the mean score on the reputation index of the treatment group is significantly higher than the mean score of the control group ($p < .001$), showing that those receiving the prime systematically perceive the Brotherhood's candidates and deputies' reputation more positively than those in the control. The results when disaggregated by socioeconomic status are similar to what obtains in the voting measure charted in figure 6.3. When the sample is restricted to poor respondents, the strength of the prime's effect on aggregate perceptions of reputation diminishes, with the difference between treatment and control means falling just beyond the traditional threshold of statistical

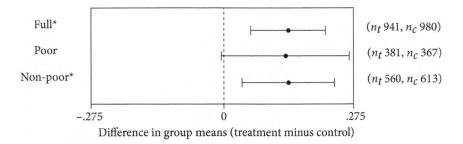

FIGURE 6.4.   Reputation of Muslim Brotherhood candidates and deputies

significance (p < .0581). But when the sample is subsetted to just non-poor respondents, those receiving the treatment do rate the reputation of Brotherhood candidates and deputies (a composite of three specific questions assessing their honesty, capability, and approachability) significantly higher than those non-poor respondents in the control group (*p* < .01). Given the prior chapters' information about the ways in which the Brotherhood's particular style of social service provision mostly bypassed the poor, the fact that the experimental manipulation produced weaker effects on poor respondents should not be particularly surprising.

Figures 6.3 and 6.4 support two key predictions of the theory: that respondents primed with information about the Brotherhood's social services would perceive the Brotherhood's candidates as more honest, capable, and approachable than those respondents in the control group and also report themselves more likely to support the Brotherhood's candidates at the polls. The theory suggests that these changes are interrelated, whereby Egyptians' assessment of Brotherhood candidates' honesty, capability, and modesty mediate those Egyptians' likelihood to vote for Brotherhood candidates for elected office. The "mediation" software package can help identify the extent to which this occurs by facilitating a causal mediation analysis (Hicks and Tingley 2011).

Briefly, the approach generates two models. The first generates predictions for the likability index as a function of (random) assignment to the treatment/control condition. A second model generates estimates for the propensity to vote for the Muslim Brotherhood's candidates as a function of both the treatment/control and the likability index. Model one's estimation of the values for likability under both the treatment and control feed into model two's estimates of the propensity to vote for the Brotherhood's candidates. Averaging the differences in the predicted values of this propensity as the predictions for likability shift under the treatment and control yields the average causal mediation effect (ACME) (Imai et al. 2011). Figure 6.5 maps the results of the causal mediation analysis onto a diagram of the hypothesized causal process.[22]

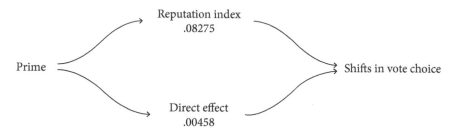

FIGURE 6.5.   Causal mediation analysis

Receiving the prime about the Brotherhood's social services produces a total effect of .08733 on a respondent's self-reported propensity to vote for the Brotherhood's candidates in a hypothetical election. As figure 6.5 shows, the reputation index mediates almost 95 percent of this total effect. Specifically, .08275 of the effect of the prime on vote choice operates through a shift in the perception of the candidates' reputation, while only .00458 occurs directly between the prime and the vote choice outcome. This supports the causal mechanism introduced above, whereby exposure to the specific type of atmosphere at the Brotherhood's facilities leads to an increase in perceptions of Brotherhood candidates' reputation, which in turn boosts willingness to support the group's candidates for office.[23]

The survey experiment and causal mediation analysis provide important microlevel support to the arguments presented over the prior pages, showing particularly how the IMA's style and target of provision could conceivably have influenced the beliefs (and potentially behaviors) of ordinary Egyptians. The artificiality of the experimental setup, using an informational prime to shift attitudes among a random subset of Egyptians, should be kept in mind when extrapolating to real-world interactions and more substantial outcomes such as voting. But it is plausible to think that the millions of Egyptians who had a much more intense interaction with the organization would react by supporting the Brotherhood in more tangible ways, up to and including a vote on election day.

The Islamist Advantage, Illustrated

A variety of material, both produced by the IMA and independently observed in the IMA's facilities, points to the high quality of care on offer. The survey instrument also offers a chance to assess how ordinary citizens perceived these facilities. Specifically, respondents who reported that they had used a Brotherhood medical facility were given the option to use up to five (separate) words or short phrases to describe their experiences there, which survey enumerators recorded in Egyptian colloquial Arabic. First, I dichotomously coded from the Arabic each of the 230 total words or phrases as either "generally positive" or "generally negative." A significant majority—86.1 percent—of the words or short phrases were generally positive, heightening confidence that the impressions generated by the IMA's historic and contemporary materials and my own site visits were a fair representation of the patient experience. To further illustrate how the survey respondents perceived their experience in the Brotherhood's facilities, figure 6.6 presents the rough English equivalent of these 230 terms arrayed in a word cloud (the size of the text indicates the frequency with which respondents used that word).[24]

Figure 6.6 vividly demonstrates the positive impressions that the Brotherhood's medical provision left on those who reported having visited. In addition to systematically bringing the perceptions of ordinary Egyptians into the investigation, these particular descriptive terms are also an important link in the proposed causal process (Brady and Collier 2010). First, there seems to be a conceptual association between the types of traits the IMA emphasized in its internal materials, including the cartoons in figures 6.1 and 6.2, and the open-ended respondent descriptions of the Brotherhood's facilities (e.g., "compassionate" and "professional"). Further, those characteristics tend to map onto the ways that Brotherhood candidates were described (e.g., honest, capable, and modest). While subjective, the word cloud evidence shows that respondents did absorb and focus on the technical and relational quality of care rather than its mere existence.

Collecting impressions of how a sample of ordinary Egyptians experienced the Brotherhood's medical facilities also heightens confidence that earlier qualitative findings about the atmosphere of these facilities was not the process of a selection bias (visiting hospitals only in wealthy areas, for instance) or of a cunning attempt by the Brotherhood to direct public scrutiny toward attractive but unrepresentative cases. Rather, the results here suggest that the Brotherhood's medical provision was generally high-quality, or at least systematically perceived as such by ordinary Egyptians who reported using it.

FIGURE 6.6. Respondents' descriptions of the Brotherhood's facilities

One objection that might be raised to this exercise is that a type of selection effect might have been at work, whereby only citizens who were already favorably disposed to the Muslim Brotherhood were disproportionately likely to visit its facilities. This is potentially also relevant in light of the alternative arguments, discussed in chapter 4, that the Brotherhood actively discriminated against its political opponents in its facilities. While the bulk of the qualitative evidence suggests that the Islamic Medical Association went to extensive lengths to avoid discrimination, if members were encouraged to attend (and opponents actively dissuaded from doing so), then the positive impressions in figure 6.6 would be misleading.

To assess this possibility in more depth, we can revisit the above descriptive exercise by constricting the sample to the Brotherhood's self-described political opponents, those who would have been most likely to be on the receiving end of any discrimination at the Brotherhood's social service enterprises. Before the respondents received the treatment (or the control), enumerators asked each of them an open-ended question: whether there was any organization, party, or individual for whom they would never vote. Out of the 2,483 respondents, 460 respondents answered with either the Muslim Brotherhood, the Freedom and Justice Party (the Muslim Brotherhood's political party), or Mohammed Morsi (the former president of Egypt, a Muslim Brother). Separating out these respondents allows the *ex ante* identification of a subgroup with the deepest antipathy toward the Brotherhood and therefore provides important insight into how the group's tough stand against discrimination actually reflected the ground truth. Figure 6.7 repeats the word cloud exercise, this time using only the descriptive terms *those self-described Brotherhood opponents* used when describing the Brotherhood's medical facilities.

The terms used by the Brotherhood's harshest political opponents to describe the Brotherhood's social service facilities were essentially similar to the ones used

FIGURE 6.7. Brotherhood *opponents'* descriptions of the Brotherhood's facilities

by those who expressed no prior hostility to the group. This evidence should put to rest arguments that the Brotherhood's brick-and-mortar facilities were biased against the group's opponents or were simply clientelism in a different guise. First and most simply, there were political opponents of the Brotherhood who reported visiting the Brotherhood's medical facilities. It is difficult to imagine a self-described opponent of the Mexican Partido Revolucionario Institucional (PRI) or the United Malays National Organization (UMNO) receiving material benefits from those parties. Providing high-quality services to one's political opponents is unthinkable in most electoral contexts, but it was a core of the Brotherhood's brick-and-mortar social service outreach. And second, the Brotherhood's opponents were, in the main, quite impressed with their experiences in the group's medical facilities. Like the facilities themselves, the opponents seemed able to separate their partisan inclinations from their impressions in the realm of social services.

The Reputational Advantage

By providing relationally enjoyable and technologically competent care, the Brotherhood's medical institutions were able to activate more subtle and reputation-based linkages connecting party and voter. Citizens did not walk out of these facilities dedicated to applying sharia law, convinced that the Brotherhood was their best bet for economic redistribution, or feeling compelled to repay the Brotherhood's charity at the ballot box. Instead, an original survey experiment of nearly 2,500 Egyptians showed that citizens believed the Brotherhood's honest, competent, and approachable style of social service provision offered a reliable indicator of what the party and its candidates stood for.

The survey also provided a variety of additional evidence about the particular character of the Brotherhood's social service provision. First, the poor are relatively absent from the story, in the sense that they are far less susceptible to the prime than their wealthier countrymen and women—a finding that should not be surprising in light of prior chapters. Second, the ways in which survey respondents described their own experiences in these facilities generally tracks the qualitative and historical narrative that these facilities did indeed provide enjoyable and consistent care. Finally, even self-described political opponents of the Brotherhood conceded the quality of care in these facilities, suggesting that the emphasis on nondiscriminatory care was more than just a story sold to credulous outsiders.

The next chapter follows the arc of the Brotherhood's social services through Egypt's abbreviated democratic transition. This period of within-case variation, in particular the rapid liberalization in political competition after Mubarak stepped down in early 2011, helps to identify how the institutional context shapes the style of social service provision. In particular, this political transition augured a systematic change in the country's electoral geography, which the Brotherhood responded to by reorienting its social services toward a style of voter outreach that essentially departed from the ways it had been run for decades under authoritarianism to more closely approximate classical understandings of clientelism.

MOHAMMED MORSI'S MACHINE

The collapse of authoritarian rule, Guillermo O'Donnell and Phillipe Schmitter famously observed, often triggers an "exultant feeling ... that the future is open, and that ideals and decisions count as much as interests and structures" (1986, 19). This certainly describes the atmosphere among the thousands of Egyptians who flooded Tahrir Square as Hosni Mubarak was forced from power in early 2011. Beneath the euphoria of the crowds, however, Egypt's long-standing authoritarian regime powerfully influenced the country's transition (Brownlee and Stacher 2011). In the summer of 2013 this influence broke into the open when the military deposed Mohammed Morsi from power and reinstituted authoritarian rule.

This chapter examines a massive Brotherhood social service campaign launched during Egypt's brief period of liberalized political competition, particularly as new parliamentary elections were being planned in the spring of 2013. As the prior chapters have shown, under decades of nondemocratic rule, the Muslim Brotherhood's social services passively produced political goodwill among middle-class Egyptians through an essentially fortuitous process: while proregime networks effectively monopolized poor voters, the Brotherhood's competent and depoliticized care attracted the support of middle-class citizens likeliest to support the opposition. But the collapse of proregime monopolies in 2011 supercharged electoral competition, and the Brotherhood responded to these shifting political opportunities by deploying highly politicized mobile medical caravans to establish essentially clientelist linkages with Egypt's poor.

The sections immediately following sketch out the Egyptian political scene in early 2013, focusing on preparations for new parliamentary elections and the emergence of the Salafist Nur party, which became the Brotherhood's closest political competitor. They then present qualitative evidence about the Brotherhood's social service–based strategy for the planned 2013 elections, the "Together We Build Egypt" campaign, and use the core theory to derive testable implications. A spatial data set of the Brotherhood's caravan activity during this period allows a systematic test of these arguments, and additional evidence from the previous chapter's survey provides important microlevel confirmation for the theory.

Monopoly Busting

Despite the Brotherhood's adept electoral performance during Egypt's transition, it never enjoyed a unified government. Roughly six months after the 2011–12 parliamentary elections had concluded, and on the eve of Mohammed Morsi's inauguration as Egypt's president, Egypt's Supreme Constitutional Court ruled the parliamentary electoral law (Law 121/2011) unconstitutional. The judiciary, backed by the ruling Supreme Council of the Armed Forces, then formally dissolved the Brotherhood-dominated parliament.[1] So when a new constitution passed a divisive nationwide referendum in late December 2012, serious preparations to reconstitute parliament through elections began.[2] Those new parliamentary contests were rumored at multiple points throughout the spring and summer of early 2013, and preparations continued until the July 3, 2013, military coup ended Egypt's democratic experiment.[3]

This period of intense politicization, from January to July 2013, offers an important opportunity to study how the Brotherhood's social service networks mobilized when the powerful proregime networks that had structured electoral competition for decades were reeling (Masoud 2014a, 166–68). Not only did a lustration law strip many of these patrons of their ability to participate in elections, but citizens' groups devoted to ferreting out their influence in politics emerged, and a fatwa from a respected Azhari shaykh, 'Emad 'Effat, argued that it was forbidden to vote for these figures.[4] With these traditional proregime patrons pushed into the background, poorer areas became a site of intense competition precisely because they offered parties with resources the tantalizing opportunity to move in just as the NDP had moved out.

Most of the newer Egyptian parties would struggle to mobilize these poorer voters because they lacked "the resources and organization of pre-existing institutional structures" that Adrienne LeBas found to be such an important determinant of party success in postauthoritarian environments (2011, 5). The

Freedom and Justice Party was one obvious exception to this rule, being able to draw on its affiliated social movement, the Muslim Brotherhood, as well as webs of Islamic institutions (Masoud 2014a). More surprising was the emergence of the group that would become the Brotherhood's closest competitor, the Nur party.

The social movement undergirding the Nur party, al-Daʿwa al-Salafiyya (the Salafi Call) had been around since the 1970s. In addition to drawing from a generally less affluent social class than the Muslim Brotherhood, its strict disavowal of electoral politics and willingness to operate social service networks protected it from regime predation. As Stéphane Lacroix points out, "The Salafi Daʿwa's stance against violence and refusal to engage in formal politics made it relatively acceptable to the Mubarak regime.... [The Salafi Daʿwa] also provided an array of social services in neighborhoods, thereby mirroring the activities of the Brotherhood. This allowed the group to establish strong ties with ordinary Egyptians, although most of its activities remained underground" (2012, 2). So when the NDP collapsed and most Egyptian parties had to scramble to assemble networks in the country's poorer areas, the Salafi groups simply had to reorient their already formidable social presence towards electoral mobilization (Rougier and Bayoumi 2016, 151). As the authors of one report put it, the Nur party was in some sense a "new" party although "the salafi movement behind the party was ... already known for its involvement in the Islamic call (daʿwa) movement, its charity and community work, and through its presence in the many mosques" (Danish-Egyptian Dialogue Institute 2012, 23).

The Brotherhood came out of the 2011–12 parliamentary elections a clear winner, taking 47.2 percent of the available seats in parliament. And not surprisingly, its nearest competitor was the Nur party, which leveraged its own considerable networks to gain 27.8 percent of the seats (Attallah 2017). So when this parliament was dissolved in the summer of 2012 and preparations for new parliamentary elections began in early 2013, Egypt's less affluent neighborhoods and villages emerged as a key battleground How would the Brotherhood seize this opportunity, especially given that its social service network had for so long been oriented toward more affluent citizens?

"Together We Build Egypt"

To commemorate the January 25 uprising (and conveniently coincident with the passage of the new constitution that triggered preparations for new parliamentary elections), the Brotherhood launched a massive social service initiative it dubbed "Maʿan Nabni Misr" ("Together We Build Egypt").[5] Often sited at local mosques and timed to access the large crowds after the communal Friday prayer, volunteers clad in Muslim Brotherhood and Freedom and Justice Party vests and T-shirts, underneath banners with logos from both organizations, provided medical care, cleaned streets, planted trees, refurbished schools, and established low-cost co-op markets and charity fairs. As an indication of the scope of Together We Build Egypt (TWBE), in May of 2013, after five months of the nationwide campaign the Brotherhood released a summary of its to-date efforts. These included over 2,000 medical caravans, over 250 veterinary caravans, 1,635 co-op markets, 1,534 school refurbishments, 827 beautification and cleaning efforts, and 257 craftsman convoys performing small household repairs.[6]

As these numbers indicate, the centerpiece of this campaign was the dispatch of thousands of medical caravans, essentially pop-up clinics that would spend a few hours or days providing free or highly discounted medical care to citizens of an area.[7] Figure 7.1 reproduces and translates the announcement for a caravan in the Upper Egyptian governorate of Minya.[8]

Although the Brotherhood had periodically operated medical caravans for decades, the group's efforts in the first half of 2013 were unprecedented.[9] For example, in May 2013 one caravan departed Alexandria for the Siwa Oasis (around 600 km southwest, roughly 50 km from the Libyan border) boasting specialists in "internal medicine, pediatrics, ear, nose, and throat, surgery, dermatology, and ophthalmology" provisioned with over $4,000 in medicines. Another caravan spent over $14,000 performing free glaucoma and cataract surgeries.[10] In the delta governorate of Kafr al-Shaykh, trucks equipped with loudspeakers roamed the streets drumming up interest in an upcoming medical caravan in the city.[11] In Buhayra, the Women's Section of the Freedom and Justice Party organized a series of seminars to raise awareness of breast cancer, provide information, and schedule early detection examinations.[12]

For decades the Brotherhood strove to keep social service provision and politics separate, but the high stakes of these crucial elections made it difficult to maintain the firewall.[13] While some Brotherhood officials reassured citizens that the TWBE effort was "unrelated to any election," other members claimed that the campaign was a direct response to the group's falling political popularity.[14] Some in the Brotherhood even claimed that the name of the campaign would be repurposed into the group's slogan in the upcoming parliamentary elections.[15] In many ways these mixed signals reflected the discomfort of many in the group with the new initiative and, in particular, with how it threatened the depoliticization that had been a hallmark of the Brotherhood's social service outreach for decades. But as the Brotherhood's political fortunes hung in the balance, these concerns were increasingly shunted to the side.

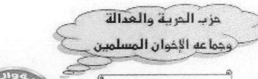

القافلة الطبية

بجمعية الوحدة الإسلامية بشاهين

جميع التخصصات

* أطفال – باطنه – جلدية – عظام – جراحة – أنف وأذن وحنجرة – مسالك بولية

* عمليات ختان الذكور (طهارة)

* خصومات على الأدوية والأشعة بجميع أنواعها

* نخبة من الاستشاريين والأخصائيين

قيمة الكشف ٣ جنية

تحت شعار معاً نبني مصر

للحجز والاستعلام مقر الوحدة الإسلامية وصيدلية الكوثر بعزبة شاهين

يوم الجمعة الموافق ١ / ٣ / ٢٠١٣

ت / ٠١٠٩١٨٩٣٠٨٢ – ٠١١٢١١٠٠٥٧٠

Freedom and Justice Party
Muslim Brotherhood

(FJP Logo)   Medical Caravan   (Brotherhood Logo)

At the Islamic Unity Association in Shahin

All Specialties

Pediatrics - Internal Medicine - Dermatology - Bones
- (Minor) Surgery - Ear, Nose, and Throat - Urology
Male Circumcision
Discounted Medicines and X-Rays of All Types

3 EGP for an Examination (approx. $0.50)

Under the Slogan "Together We Build Egypt"

For Registration and More Information Contact the Headquarters of
the Islamic Unity Association and Kawthar Pharmacy in 'Izbat Shahin
Friday, March 1, 2013
Phone: 01121100570/ 01091893082

FIGURE 7.1. Medical caravan flyer and translation, Minya Governorate

A Machine in the Making

Before systematically examining the Brotherhood's deployment of these medical caravans, it is worth pausing to consider how this mobile style of provision solved some of the dilemmas the group was facing in early 2013. One key problem for the Brotherhood was a lack of information about poorer Egyptians' preferences. Partly as a consequence of decades of nondemocratic rule, the Brotherhood tended to lack in poorer areas the local organizational branches that the former deputy guide Mohammed Habib described as "the eyes of the organization in the street" (2012, 121).[16] So when the collapse of the NDP opened these areas to political competition the Brotherhood was left with a dilemma: what did it need to do to mobilize voters it had so little information about? How could it ensure that those who received benefits upheld their end of the bargain in the voting booth?

The Brotherhood's dilemma in early 2013 was not that unique; all political machines thrive on information about voter preferences (Stokes et al. 2013, 19; Cox and McCubbins 1986, 377–78). Without an understanding of how "elastic" voter preferences are—whether citizens are latent supporters who need only a little prodding to turn out or staunch opponents who would demand extensive outlays to buy their support—parties could find themselves expending significant resources for potentially minimal political gains (Kitschelt and Wilkinson 2007a, 13). The Brotherhood in 2013 could have simply approached these areas the same way it had operated in wealthier areas for decades, using depoliticized brick-and-mortar facilities and relying on a reputational mechanism. But aside from constricted time horizons and likely problems with fiscal sustainability, another problem was that the Brotherhood might establish a brick-and-mortar clinic, only to find out that the recipients in the area were already in the tank for one of the Brotherhood's competitors.

Relying on mobile medical caravans to access less affluent voters helped the Brotherhood cope with this uncertainty in two ways. First, the caravans were a more conservative use of resources than the alternatives. At best, a brief caravan visit could provide information about voters while generating a potential bump in electoral support. At worst, it would reveal that the voters were opposed to the Brotherhood and thus best avoided. Second, the strategic deployment of mobile medical caravans—rather than fixed assets—allowed the Brotherhood to signal to those living in the area that, if they supported the group in the upcoming elections, they might expect bigger and better (or just continuing) medical caravan visits in the future (Chubb 1982). In contrast, if citizens of these areas failed to reciprocate the Brotherhood's politicized beneficence, then they would be much less likely to see caravans in the future. Put in formal terms, these revocable caravans better allowed the Brotherhood to play tit for tat with the residents of these districts—an iterated interaction that has proven crucial for the establishment of clientelist networks elsewhere (Stokes 2005).

Building Islamist Monopolies

The caravan strategy was seemingly designed with one eye toward gaining the support of less affluent voters through clientelism and another toward minimizing the waste should these citizens prove staunch Brotherhood opponents. This section systematically assesses the use of caravans in the Together We Build Egypt campaign to isolate this dynamic, first with qualitative evidence drawn from a review of the Arabic-language media coverage of the caravan activity, then with an original data set mapping the visits of these caravans across Egypt's underlying political and socioeconomic terrain.

A variety of anecdotal evidence suggests that the Brotherhood directed caravans at poorer areas and voters (in nearly all cases, the cost of the caravans was either free or offered for a tiny "symbolic price" (as shown in figure 7.1). One Freedom and Justice Party leader interviewed in the midst of a TWBE event in Buhayra, near Alexandria, explained to a Brotherhood newspaper that the party had "surveyed residents' needs in this village and found that the over 6,000 inhabitants here lacked both a school and a medical center."[17] Another report noted that a caravan, based at a mosque in Suez, had distributed hundreds of prescriptions for free.[18] As the Together We Build Egypt campaign reached the end of its first month, a disgruntled former member of the Freedom and Justice Party criticized the Brotherhood's supposed cynicism about the efforts: "The Brotherhood undertakes geographic studies of the poorest and most ignorant concentrations in the electoral districts" and directs provision toward those places, he claimed.[19]

When the Brotherhood inaugurated the IMA in the mid-1970s, it had little organization or social movement resources to speak of; this was one of the reasons that basing that organization on a commercial style of operation made sense. But by 2013 the Brotherhood boasted an organization with hundreds of thousands of members, among them some of Egypt's richest men.[20] So when social service provision directed at the poor emerged as a potentially useful political strategy, the Brotherhood did what political parties with sturdy social movement affiliates did in other contexts around the world: they drew upon their members' personal wealth, ideological commitments, and organizational loyalty to support the enterprise (Thachil 2014a; Van Cott 2005). As in those cases, the Brotherhood's medical caravan activity (as well as the other Together We Build

Egypt efforts) relied almost entirely on free activist labor of Muslim Brotherhood cadres and was financed from movement coffers. Brotherhood-affiliated doctors donated their time and/or waived fees, volunteers helped organize the caravans or offered space to hold them, Brotherhood member-owned pharmacies donated medicines, and the group simply used its own financial resources to buy supplies.[21] And along with this massive outflow of resources the Brotherhood also politicized the exchange to an extent far beyond what had been its trademark with the brick-and-mortar facilities. To make sure citizens understood their obligation on election day, the Brotherhood put its role in these endeavors front and center. Notice how in figure 7.1 the Brotherhood's logo (with crossed swords) is prominently displayed alongside the logo of their political party, the Freedom and Justice Party (opposite), while the banner (speech bubble) announces the medical caravan from both the FJP (top text) and the Muslim Brotherhood (bottom text). This blatant mixing of politics and social service would have been highly controversial in previous periods, but during the Together We Build Egypt campaign it became ubiquitous.

The Brotherhood extensively highlighted its TWBE efforts in the Arabic press, including in party and social media, presaging and reporting on its caravan visits with press releases and news articles and widely disseminating pictures and videos of the campaign. I rely on this rich trove of material—released almost exclusively in Arabic—to assemble an original spatial data set of the distribution of nearly five hundred of these medical caravan visits throughout the course of the Together We Build Egypt campaign.[22] Combining the distribution of caravan visits with the census data discussed in earlier chapters systematically shows how this provision differed, in theoretically predictable ways, from the IMA's brick-and-mortar efforts.

I started building the data set of caravan activity from event reports on the Muslim Brotherhood's official web page, www.ikhwanonline.com, then expanded it by including Arabic-language Twitter searches for the hashtag "Together We Build Egypt" as well as the terms "medical caravan" and "Freedom and Justice Party/ Muslim Brotherhood." Broader Google searches with the same terms returned results from Facebook pages, YouTube, and other media outlets.[23] At a minimum, each caravan required a specific physical location to be logged in the data set. I also compared each entry across available dimensions, including date, specializations, number of patients served, cost, and location to prevent double counting. I then checked photographs and videos of the events (where available) to help identify potentially duplicate reporting. After I compiled the information described in these dispatches, open source research yielded the approximate latitude and longitude for each of the caravan visits in the data set.[24] This process furnished 488 medical caravan visits, arrayed on the map of Egypt in figure 7.2.

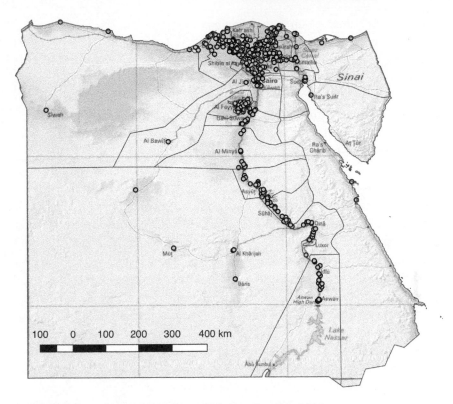

FIGURE 7.2.   Medical caravan activity, January–July 2013

These spatial data allow a more systematic investigation of how the Brotherhood targeted its medical caravans during the first six months of 2013. To understand this distribution I fit a negative binomial regression model where the outcome variable is a count of the number of caravans that visited the given census district (markaz/qism).[25] I also include at the markaz/qism level the same right-hand-side variables as used in chapter five (wealth index, electric hookup, percentage Muslim, and a logged crowding variable). And because it is likely that the medical caravan visits were in some ways correlated with the locations of brick-and-mortar medical facilities, I also include a dummy variable marking whether or not that markaz/qism also included a brick-and-mortar IMA facility.[26]

In addition to the markaz/qism-level variables we can add another set of relevant electoral district-level indicators by fitting a multilevel model. The Muslim Brotherhood's deployment of medical caravans in the Together We Build Egypt campaign was ultimately oriented toward winning upcoming parliamentary elections. Although they were never held, these elections were expected to effectively redo the 2011/2012 parliamentary contests—that is, occur across the same electoral district borders. Thus I can include in the model district-level statistics on outcomes in those elections.[27]

Following prior researchers, I focused on Egypt's party list districts rather than the dual member "first past the post (FPTP)" constituencies (Elsayyad and Hanafy 2014; Erle, Mathias, and Kjærum 2016). Not only did these districts send the bulk of representatives to parliament—two-thirds of the total representatives in the lower house (Majlis al-Sha'b) vs. one-third from the FPTP seats—but, as May El Sayyad and Shimaa Hanafy note, the dual-member constituencies are often highly idiosyncratic, based on the personality, resources, and personal history of the candidates (2014, 113–14). This was borne out in my review of the Together We Build Egypt material, in which specific candidates were almost never covered (this was largely because individual candidacies had not been announced, which would presumably happen after the actual election date was set). Instead, almost all coverage focused on the party.

These earlier electoral results should matter in the spatial distribution of the Brotherhood's medical caravans in light of the rich theoretical debate over how political actors should allocate limited resources. Some suggest that "core" constituencies should receive the lion's share of resources, while others propose that the smart strategy is to attempt to mobilize "swing" voters (Cox and McCubbins 1986; Lindbeck and Weibull 1987; Dixit and Londregan 1996; Calvo and Murillo 2004; Stokes 2005; Nichter 2008; Stokes et al. 2013; Gans-Morse, Mazzuca, and Nichter 2014). But this theoretical debate has more immediate implications when grounded in the specific dilemma the Brotherhood was facing in early 2013, as it geared up for a new round of parliamentary elections. Would the group seek to buck up its core supporters, funneling resources to those districts where it had triumphed in the 2011 contests? Or would it use the caravans to try to tip the balance in swing districts, places where the race had been much more closely run (usually against the Nur party)? The data set of caravan visits, coupled with the results of those earlier elections, allows a systematic empirical investigation of this question.

From the 2011 parliamentary contests I measure the Freedom and Justice Party's perception of electoral district competition by subtracting the vote share of the FJP from its nearest competitor (the FJP ran a slate in all forty-six districts, and in thirty-nine of these the closest competitor was the Nur party). I then take the absolute value of the statistic to ease interpretation, so that smaller numbers correspond to a tighter race (e.g., a "swing district"). Figures 7.3 and 7.4 draw from the regression model to display the effects of the wealth index and this measure of district competition in the district on the Brotherhood's allocation of caravans to that district.

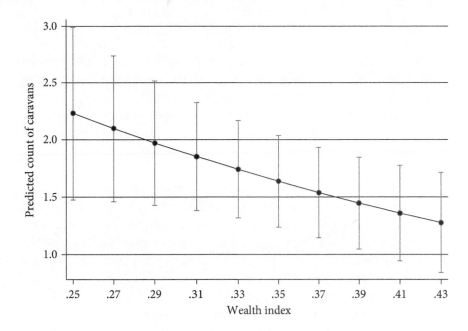

FIGURE 7.3. Caravan targeting as a function of socioeconomic status (markaz/qism)

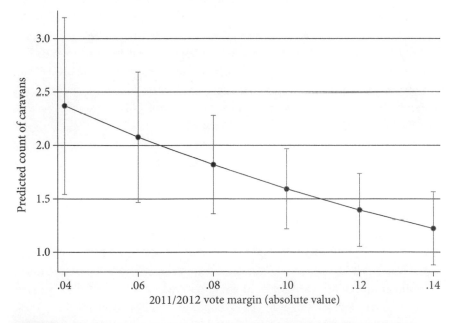

FIGURE 7.4. Caravan targeting as a function of margin of victory (electoral district)

Figure 7.3 shows that these medical caravans systematically targeted poorer census districts ($p < .05$). In fact, moving from a district one standard deviation below the median wealth index to one above substantially reduced the predicted caravan activity. This, notably, completely reversed the relationship identified between the Brotherhood's brick-and-mortar facilities and markaz/qism wealth in chapter 5. Whereas the IMA's Mubarak-era brick-and-mortar facilities were more likely to be located in wealthier markaz/qism, the opposite was true for where the Brotherhood's mobile caravans were heading in early 2013.

While the Brotherhood lacked the preexisting brick-and-mortar social service infrastructure in poorer areas that it could rely upon to mobilize voters, it did have a large, wealthy, and committed organization. Leveraging internal resources like volunteer labor and member contributions, the Brotherhood flooded these poorer areas with revocable medical caravans in an attempt to boost its prospects in the upcoming parliamentary elections. But the fact that these were relatively new voting blocs limited the Brotherhood's ability to make "reasonable predictions about voters' behavior" (Hicken 2011, 293). Instead, it had relatively poor information about how these citizens thought about the movement. How did the Brotherhood cope with this uncertainty?

One part of the answer lies in the transitory nature of the medical caravans and their particular ability to hold out the prospect of electoral gain while hedging against the possibility that these locales would gratefully accept the Brotherhood's largesse yet defect to a competitor on election day. Figure 7.4 provides another part of the answer: more medical caravans clustered in electoral districts where the margins between the Brotherhood and their closest competitor had been slimmest, while avoiding places where the Brotherhood had either won (or lost) in blowouts ($p < .01$). Given the overall strategic dilemma, this makes sense: in these swing districts, the smallest outlays would likely produce the largest effect on election day.[28]

One reading of these results is that the Brotherhood was attempting to replace the NDP as the patron of Egypt's poorer voters. There is some evidence in the press coverage of the Together We Build Egypt campaign that these similarities went beyond the theoretical and encompassed concrete interactions with the same local notables who had once been part of the NDP's networks (Menza 2013, 143; Masoud 2014a, 167). For example, in May 2013 (at the height of the Together We Build Egypt campaign) the Egyptian newspaper *al-Masry al-Youm* published a purported dossier of high-level funders of the Brotherhood's charitable efforts. Prominent on the list was a series of wealthy individuals connected to the erstwhile National Democratic Party. The Brotherhood, for its part, claimed that these figures' participation in the Together We Build Egypt campaign was natural. As the Brotherhood responded to the report, "There is nothing shameful about this."[29]

It is worth confronting again the issue of an ecological fallacy: spatial evidence shows that in early 2013 the Muslim Brotherhood flooded Egypt's poorer areas with medical caravans, contrasting with its reliance on brick-and-mortar provision in wealthier locales. But even at these fairly disaggregated levels of analysis, these data do not tell us *who* visited the facilities. One could fairly object that the caravans might actually have been targeting wealthier citizens who lived in generally poorer districts, perhaps in an attempt to tide them over until more permanent structures could be established.

There is qualitative evidence that these caravan efforts were specifically targeted at the poor, including the Brotherhood's own statements and the fact that these caravans were usually offered for free or nothing more than a "symbolic price," but it is possible to probe deeper. Recall that the survey, discussed in prior chapters, was structured in such a way as to gather information about respondents' prior experiences with the Brotherhood's social service efforts, including separate questions about whether they or their families had used brick-and-mortar and/or caravan-based manifestations (the results of this question vis-à-vis the brick and mortar facilities was briefly discussed in chapter 5). Figure 7.5 cross-references these usage statistics for both brick-and-mortar and mobile medical caravans with socioeconomic status of the respondents to identify, at an individual level, how audiences for these two types of provision map onto the socioeconomic cleavages identified above.

These data provide independent confirmation that there was a decided anti-poor bias in Egyptians' usage of brick-and-mortar facilities: poor Egyptians were significantly less likely to report having direct experience with the Brotherhood's

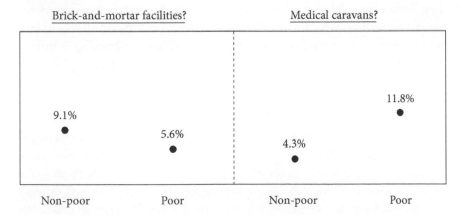

FIGURE 7.5. Microlevel usage: Brick-and-mortar facilities vs. medical caravans. Question: "Have you or a member of your family ever used the Brotherhood's . . . ?" (percentage answering yes)

brick-and-mortar medical facilities than their non-poor counterparts ($p < .05$). But the caravan usage data completely reverse the socioeconomic dynamic present in the brick-and-mortar facilities. In doing so, they support the above ecological analysis showing that the caravans disproportionately targeted poor areas: poor respondents were systematically *more* likely to have experience with the Brotherhood's medical caravans than were their wealthier countrymen and women ($p < .01$). We cannot definitively conclude whether or not these caravan visits would have yielded the hoped-for electoral benefits, as Egypt's military ended preparations for parliamentary elections when it seized power in July 2013.[30] But it is plausible that the Together We Build Egypt campaign marked the Brotherhood's emergence as a "do everything" party in which clientelism would staple newly available poorer voters to the Brotherhood's powerful and preexisting middle-class core (Singer and Kitschelt 2011; Wyatt 2013; Thachil 2014a, 2014b).

Prior chapters show how the Brotherhood's ability to use social service provision to drive political mobilization stemmed more from good fortune than from adroit strategizing. But these results show that when it came to the use of medical caravans during the Together We Build Egypt campaign, the Brotherhood's social service strategy was quite calculated and embedded in the logic of electoral competition. The Together We Build Egypt campaign was smart politics, adeptly executed.

The Inevitable Pull of Politics

This chapter has carried the investigation through the end of Egypt's democratic transition. The 2011 collapse of the National Democratic Party opened up Egypt's poorer areas for politicking. Through a massive outlay of organizational resources the Brotherhood went after these voters, deploying medical caravans to disproportionately target less affluent Egyptians clustered in swing districts.

The Together We Build Egypt campaign differed in both form and content from the Brotherhood's prior efforts and thus highlights the different linkages that emerged from these divergent modes of social service provision. Under Mubarak, the Brotherhood strove to keep social service provision and electoral politics realms at arm's length—not only because allowing them to mix would be legally fatal but also because of a realization that a firewall between social activism and electoral politics *heightened* the ability of the former to speak to the latter. The Together We Build Egypt campaign, in contrast, punched through this firewall by blatantly politicizing social service provision, emphasizing the transactional linkages between party and voter rather than the reputational ones that mattered under Mubarak.

THE POLITICS OF SOCIAL SERVICE PROVISION

In this book I have argued that autocrats can use nonstate providers to navigate out of moments of economic crisis, but in doing so they lay the foundation for a future challenge. The reason some providers can use social service provision to generate political mobilization has less to do with their internal characteristics or ability to deftly evade state monitoring than with their initial decisions of *whom* to target. Providing paying care to middle-class customers engages a series of mechanisms that build reputation-based linkages with those voters who can most afford to support the opposition. Providing services to the poor, in contrast, tends to squander valuable resources on those least able to reciprocate with political support.

This book has also provided an important empirical contribution about the specific case of Islamist groups' provision of social services. Over the past few decades it has become a matter of faith that groups like the Muslim Brotherhood derive significant political support from their activities in the social sphere, yet the subject has largely resisted sustained empirical investigation. An in-depth case study of the Egyptian Muslim Brotherhood not only reveals how this network functions but also pushes the relationship between social service provision and electoral mobilization beyond simple "just so" stories and into the realm of falsifiable and generalizable theory.

After reviewing the key claims of the theory developed in the first chapter about social service provision in nondemocratic environments, in this chapter I provide a brief discussion of the fate of the Islamic Medical Association since the

July 3, 2013, military coup. In addition to bringing the narrative up to the present, I discuss how the large-scale crackdown on the Brotherhood's social service network following the coup highlights the risks of suddenly closing services upon which millions of citizens rely. I conclude the chapter by examining implications of the theory for literatures on democratization, authoritarian survival strategies, the dynamics of regime and opposition, the sources of the Islamist advantage, and how social movements interact with political parties.

Revisiting Key Claims

In this book I have sought to answer three intertwined questions. First, why do nondemocratic regimes allow their oppositions to operate large networks of social service provision? Second, under what conditions can these groups use this activism to lodge an electoral challenge against the regime? And finally, what is the character of the linkage between party and voter that is forged by social service provision?

Prior researchers have tended to answer these three questions by focusing on either state debility, the assumed advantage possessed by ideological organizations, or the time-tested ability of parties to mobilize voters through material exchange. While each of these explanations holds a kernel of truth, none fully explain the specific case of the Egyptian Muslim Brotherhood. For example, the Egyptian state played a seminal role in encouraging the growth of nonstate providers—the Brotherhood included—and remained able to monitor and disrupt their activities through the end of the Mubarak era. And while in other cases organizations able to draw on the labor of devoted cadres have often realized an advantage over their less ideological counterparts, the Islamic Medical Association eschewed movement resources and functioned essentially as a business. Finally, this emphasis on paying customers troubles the quid pro quo at the heart of the clientelist-style exchange that many see connecting the Brotherhood's social service provision to its political success.

Instead, I have theorized that devolving social service provision to nonstate actors can be a smart strategy for autocrats seeking to mitigate the immediate consequences of economic reform. But this initial decision generates its own momentum that, over time, becomes difficult to reverse. As nonstate providers become integrated into the daily lives of citizens, regimes lose the ability to credibly threaten these provider organizations with sanction or closure. Autocrats who embark on this strategy effectively bargain away their future for their present.

The authoritarian political economy defines which organizations are able to make political hay out of this social service provision. This is because levels of competition in nondemocratic elections often vary according to the underlying social and economic geography. Specifically, while poorer districts tend to succumb to proregime monopolies built on clientelist linkages, wealthier areas suggest the possibility of more open competition. This has considerable implications for the tie between social service provision and electoral mobilization: organizations that provide social services to the poor will be targeting a voting bloc that is least free to support an opposition party. In contrast, organizations that provide social services to middle-class citizens, using a pay-for-service model, are interfacing with exactly those voters who are most likely to reject clientelist linkages and instead support the opposition.

A decision to operate on a business model helps shape the quality of provision in important ways. First, it incentivizes the provider organization to devote attention to the quality of care as much as its simple presence. Second, it imposes structure on the internal organization and operation of the facility, allowing managers to hire and promote (or fire) employees on the basis of attitude and technical competence rather than the simple availability of volunteer labor. Third, it reduces the need to politicize the provision, which would not only alienate middle-class voters but also risk triggering a response from a wary regime. The cumulative effect is to generate an impression of honesty, reliability, and modesty that adheres to the party as well as the movement, and resonates particularly deeply with those more affluent voters who are most likely to use this type of information when casting a ballot.

Evidence to support the theory came from an in-depth examination of Egypt with a particular focus on the Muslim Brotherhood. This is the archetypical organization that combines social service provision and electoral mobilization. A variety of new historical evidence shows how Anwar al-Sadat, shaken by the bread riots of 1977, increasingly used nonstate providers to blunt the cutting edge of economic reforms. Among the many organizations empowered by his decision was the Egyptian Muslim Brotherhood, who registered the Islamic Medical Association with the state in late 1977. This organization, which grew into the largest organized sector of the Brotherhood's vaunted social service network, was founded specifically to provide depoliticized, high-quality care at affordable prices to Egyptians caught between a failing public sector and unaffordable private one.

This initial decision put the Islamic Medical Association in daily contact with millions of Egyptians for reasons quite divorced from electoral politics. In fact, the Brotherhood went to great extent to distance its social activism from its political ambitions. But as Egypt's authoritarian electoral system congealed following a change in electoral laws in 1990, those electoral districts that saw the highest levels competition, including frequent entry of candidates from the

Muslim Brotherhood, also happened to be the districts in which the IMA's facilities were physically located. In those neighborhoods and towns, wealthier voters' interactions with the IMA convinced them that the honest and competent care they witnessed was a reliable indicator of what the Brotherhood's candidates for elected office truly stood for.

Egypt's brief democratic interlude confirmed the extent to which political institutions influenced the Brotherhood's style of social service provision. Specifically, the collapse of proregime clientelist networks in 2011 opened less affluent neighborhoods and villages for political competition. Through a massive campaign of social service provision in early 2013, the Brotherhood poured contingent resources into these areas to establish linkages with a new bloc of voters. But instead of the reputation-based relationships that had buoyed the group under authoritarianism, the Brotherhood used mobile resources in an attempt to forge essentially clientelist relationships with Egypt's less affluent.

The IMA under Abdel Fattah El-Sisi

In a 2006 study of Islamic groups' social service provision, Imad Siyam speculated that this type of activism forges connections between the Islamist movement and the population that are "impossible to uproot through campaigns of liquidation or siege" (2006, 79). Egypt's post-2013 military regime is currently testing Siyam's assertion by fiercely targeting the Muslim Brotherhood's social institutions as it seeks to consolidate around Abdel Fattah El-Sisi (Brooke 2017a).

A September 2013 court case established the legal basis for the regime to crack down on the Muslim Brotherhood's social service network. In that ruling (Judgment 2315 of 2013) the Cairo Court for Urgent Matters ruled that the Muslim Brotherhood was a terrorist organization. The court simultaneously established a committee to investigate and assess the possibilities for seizure of the Brotherhood's physical and financial assets.[1] At the end of December 2013 the committee completed its preliminary investigation of the Brotherhood's assets, and the lists of social organizations allegedly linked to the Muslim Brotherhood soon leaked to the Egyptian press. Prominent on the list was the Islamic Medical Association, which soon found its bank accounts frozen.[2]

The IMA responded with a front page ad in the state daily *al-Ahram* pleading with the regime to allow it to continue operations "on behalf of two million sick and tens of thousands of those who receive kidney dialysis on a continuing basis, and premature infants, and those unable to pay for their treatment, as well as those who visit the hospitals."[3] Except for the dialysis centers (which, as chapter 4 discussed, were reliant on state reimbursements for part of their operating budget), it is not clear how much the freeze actually affected the IMA's ability to function. Because the IMA operated on a cash-in, cash-out basis, it was somewhat protected from the freeze (Brooke 2013). In an interview after the freeze, one IMA manager emphasized the organization's history of cooperation with the government and expressed hope that the conflict would pass. He even claimed that three new hospitals were close to entering service.[4]

This optimism was misplaced. The regime clamped down suddenly in early 2015, formally assuming control of the IMA and seizing its assets. The IMA reacted with shock: "Not only has the Ministry of Social Affairs not recorded a violation over the past year," the IMA's director of public relations argued, "but it has praised the IMA!"[5] The management teams of the individual hospitals were dissolved and reconstituted with proregime figures. Driving home the change in orientation, the IMA's new chairman is the staunchly proregime religious figure 'Ali Gum'a, the former grand mufti of Egypt (Warren 2017).[6] Gum'a is notorious for his anti-Brotherhood attitudes, including a postcoup sermon in which, speaking about pro-Morsi protests, he urged members of the military and police to "shoot them in the heart. . . . We must cleanse our Egypt from these riffraff."[7] In the aftermath of the decision to nominate Gum'a, one patient at an IMA facility lamented that "the wolf now guards the sheep."[8]

With its speed and comprehensiveness, Egypt's current military regime has gone further than the governments of Anwar al-Sadat or Hosni Mubarak in its efforts against the Brotherhood's social services. As chapter 3 noted, toward the end of their terms in power, in late 1981 and 2010, respectively, both Sadat and Mubarak began to crack down on the Brotherhood's social services. But neither managed to get as far as the current government (in fact, in both al-Sadat's and Mubarak's cases the crackdowns were a prelude to the disintegration of the regime). Now Abdel Fattah El-Sisi and his regime are attempting to navigate between securing their rule and risking mass unrest by depriving significant chunks of the citizenry of access to basic services. Amid the crackdown, for instance, one patient at a Brotherhood hospital voiced frustration with the regime: "The government neither provides us with hospitals suitable for human beings, nor do they allow the hospitals that treat us well to continue operating!"[9]

Perhaps aware of the potential for mass unrest, the regime has made efforts to compensate the citizenry for its renewed hardship. As security services forced out the management teams of hospital after hospital, regime officials stressed that the facilities would not close and that their quality would not suffer.[10] And as part of the attempt to blunt the effect of the closures, state actors, including the various state-owned and affiliated funds (Misr al-Khayr, Jam'iyyat Urman, Bayt Zakat) have been ramping up their efforts at social service provision.[11] Even the military and security services—Egypt's institutions of last resort—have also become directly involved in social provisioning, distributing boxes of food and organizing medical caravans.[12]

With most forms of activism off the table, the Brotherhood has reoriented its social service provision networks to providing for the families of those imprisoned or killed in the regime's ongoing crackdown (Fayed 2017, 254).[13] And in exile, some in the Brotherhood are reconsidering the mistakes of the post-Mubarak period, including how the group allowed its social services to become obvious tools of political mobilization in the spring of 2013. The next sections use this criticism to begin to isolate the theory's implications for democratization, political party–social movement relations, authoritarian survival strategies, the evolution of niche parties, and the Islamist political advantage.

Scuttling Democratic Transitions

A common explanation for the failure of Egypt's democratic transition is that the Brotherhood's bumbling and autocratic style alienated the Egyptian population, prompting mass mobilization and, eventually, military intervention (Trager 2016). Patrick Haenni, for example, suggests that the Brotherhood's failed because it "neglected the game of party politics" (2016, 19). The implication is that, if the members of the Brotherhood had been better politicians or more attuned to public opinion, they might have been able to preserve their political standing and forestall the polarization that set the stage for the military coup.

The preceding chapters outline an alternative explanation with broader implications. At the time of its ouster, the Brotherhood had spent months crafting a potent political machine on the back of its social service activism. In particular, while the Brotherhood's brick-and-mortar facilities generated reputation-based linkages with wealthier voters, the group's caravans were hard at work establishing more contingent, episodic connections to poorer ones. As a result, on the eve of the July 3, 2013, coup, the Muslim Brotherhood was seemingly on the verge of assembling the type of cross-cutting electoral coalition that had produced powerful political hegemonies in Mexico and Argentina (Gibson 1997). In effect, the story of Egypt in early 2013 was one of a dominant party being born.

Sheri Berman (1997) suggests that, under certain conditions, extensive civil society activism can gnaw at the foundations of even the most consolidated democracies. Weimar Germany's sclerotic and elitist political parties and weakly responsive governing institutions drove citizens into civil society activism, which both cleared the field for the rise of the Nazi party and created a convenient pool of highly socialized and professional citizens from which it could draw. One uncomfortable extension of this book is that such robust civil society activity can scuttle democratic transitions before they even reach the relatively consolidated state of Weimar Germany.

Democracy provides stability only if the competing political groups "believe that the institutional framework that organizes the democratic competition will permit them to advance their interests in the future" (Przeworski 1991, 19). In post-Mubarak Egypt, the "institutional framework" theoretically permitted opponents to assume future power. On the ground, however, the Brotherhood's decades-long history of civic and social activism had generated an incredible amount of both social capital and reserve capacity that put a stranglehold on the country's institutional politics. Especially coupled with the Brotherhood's extant social service infrastructure, the "mobilizational asymmetry" on display during the Together We Build Egypt campaign showed the group's opponents that attempting to dislodge the group via elections was likely to fail (Angrist 2011).[14] Egypt's non-Islamists assumed—probably correctly—that so long as the Brotherhood was able to call upon its extensive personal and material resources, new elections would do no more than entrench the Brotherhood-dominated political order (Masoud 2014b).[15] Ahmed Maher, leader of the opposition April 6 Movement, told a journalist at the height of the TWBE campaign that "the big problem with the opposition is that we don't have grassroots. We need time."[16] Shortly before the coup another veteran activist with the opposition Tagammuʻ Party flatly noted, "We can't compete [with the Brotherhood] because of our lack of capacities."[17] In a retrospective, one member of the opposition noted that he and his colleagues were "taken aback by the fact that the Brotherhood's Freedom and Justice Party could single-handedly swallow them" which led to the realization that even trying to oppose the group at the ballot box "wasn't worth the effort." Instead, he continued, the activists "began to collect signatures in support of Abdel Fattah al-Sisi, which later became the *tamarrud* [rebellion] campaign [demanding an end to Morsi's rule]."[18]

The result of Egypt's non-Islamists' disenchantment with the electoral process was a military coup. Analyzing the process by which the military decides whether or not to intervene in politics, Alfred Stepan famously observed that "the capacity of the military as a complex institution to develop a consensus for intervention is greatly aided to the extent that civil society 'knocks on the doors' of the barracks" (1988, 128). Egypt's military had a history of opposition to the Brotherhood and certainly relished any opportunity to get out from under the thumb of its long-time foe. But what changed in early 2013 was the orientation of those civilian politicians who "recurrently appeal to the armed forces for solutions" (O'Donnell and Schmitter 1986, 31). After a run of Brotherhood victories in elections and referendums that showed no sign of abating, these non-Islamist figures realized that the Brotherhood's seemingly built-in civil society–based advantages—at that time the group was engaged in a nationwide effort at voter mobilization—presaged for the opposition an extended period in the political wilderness. So instead of committing to the electoral process, Egypt's non-Islamist politicians repeatedly probed the exit option (Hirschman 1970). During this time, for example, the de facto leader of the opposition Mohammed El-Baradei spurned repeated requests to meet with Morsi while frequently beating a trail to the defense ministry to meet with Abdel Fattah El-Sisi (Ashour 2015, 14). Faced with the difficulties of countering the Brotherhood's mobilization, Egypt's civilian politicians were quite literally knocking on the barracks door. The military, for its part, was happy to oblige them (Ketchley 2017).

Research has suggested that politicians who build on authoritarian-era civil society formations—for instance, unions—can create the durable parties arrayed over stable cleavages that augur well for democratic transitions (LeBas 2011). But the Egyptian case suggests that if these resources are not equally distributed among the opposition parties, the consequences can be disastrous for democratic transition. At multiple points Egypt's transition might have fulfilled Dankwart Rustow's necessary initial conditions for democracy: "a prolonged and inconclusive political struggle" eventually leading to inclusion and compromise (1970, 352). Instead, the Brotherhood's reserve of social capital meant that it could at every point muscle through its preferred policies at the ballot box. For example, after El-Baradei suggested boycotting parliamentary elections in the spring of 2013, the Brotherhood leader 'Isam al-'Ariyan dismissed his concerns, claiming that "we've never yet known [the opposition] to face any election or serious test."[19] Of course, it is ironic that the Brotherhood—an organization that had for decades been forced to fend off charges that its commitment to elections was only skin deep—was the actor most committed to the ballot box. Yet the tragedy was that this affinity and skill for electoral mobilization, built on the back of a considerable reserve of civic and social activism, led not to democratic consolidation but to collapse.

Separating Party and Movement

The Brotherhood's "relentless electoralism" (Ketchley 2017, 81), and specifically its explicit use of social services for politicking helped convince the opposition that its best chance for a seat at the table came on the back of military intervention. Was this outcome inevitable? Was there any way the Brotherhood could have "credibly committed" to separate its social service activism from politics and thus keep the opposition engaged in the electoral process (Powell 2006)?

In the spring of 2011 the Brotherhood formally separated the social movement (the Muslim Brotherhood) from the political party (the Freedom and Justice

Party). Soon after the party was founded, then-party head Mohammed Morsi explained the division of labor to a group of Turkish academics: "the party represents the political wing of the [Brotherhood], and the [movement] focuses on religious and community outreach projects."[20] This formal separation was an attempt to make such a commitment to not leverage their social institutions, although it ultimately failed because the stakes during this period of "founding elections" rose dramatically (O'Donnell and Schmitter 1986). Early election winners would have disproportionate power to shape the institutions—such as by writing the new constitution—and thus the future direction of the country. So while in the heady days after Tahrir Square, the Brotherhood may have felt confident it could maintain the same separation between party and movement that it had under decades of authoritarian rule, these promises dissolved once no-holds-barred electoral competition began. Given how "the party acts as a bridge between society and government," Diarmuid Maguire tells us, "and it is a bridge that movement strategists cannot resist attempting to cross" it might have been more surprising if the Brotherhood had not politicized its services (1995, 202).

The exigencies of politics soon overflowed the party-movement barrier—something most conspicuous in the realm of social service provision. In that post-Mubarak period one Brotherhood activist, clearly discomfited by the ambiguity of the supposed separation, told Marie Vannetzel that "the [Freedom and Justice Party] deals with everything but religion; the [Muslim Brotherhood Movement] with everything but politics . . . but both do social work" (2016, 47). In my own interviews as well, veteran Brotherhood service providers, men who had for years little or no involvement with politics, were clearly uncomfortable with the increasing politicization of their work and were doing as much as they could to stop the contamination (for example, the letter of reprimand). But during the Together We Build Egypt campaign, for all intents and purposes, party and movement merged into a single entity.

It is unclear whether there exists a universe in which the Brotherhood *could* have maintained a strict separation between movement and party amid the pressures to win elections. Had it been able to do so, such a clean separation might have reduced the group's political prowess and thus incentivized it to compromise with the opposition, preserving Rustow's deadlock and compromise, rather than a run of electoral victories muscled through by movement resources. And the opposition, for its part, might have then remained committed to an electoral process in which it was conceivable to make gains. A brief comparison with Tunisia is illustrative on this point. That country's founding elections returned a victory for Ennahda, an Islamist movement akin in many ways to the Egyptian Muslim Brotherhood. One of the key differences, however, was that at potential crisis points Ennahda was willing to accommodate the non-Islamist opposition's demands rather than use its social power to push ahead at the ballot box. One important concession was on precisely the issue of movement-party divide: in 2016 Ennahda leaders proposed—and resoundingly passed—a stark separation of political work and social activism at their party congress.[21]

Other Islamist parties, such as the PJD in Morocco and the IAF in Jordan, have also attempted to formalize the relationship between party and movement, with varying degrees of success (Schwedler 2006; Wegner and Pellicer 2009; Clark and Dalmasso 2015). Ennahda's example is worth following precisely because Tunisia is currently in the midst of a democratic consolidation. But Ennahda's case might be singular. Most obviously, the Egyptian Brotherhood built up an expansive network of social services over decades. By the time Mubarak fell, it was difficult for the organization to keep these activities depoliticized, even though it tried. In contrast, it was difficult for Ennahda to even exist under Ben Ali—let alone build up a network comparable to what its Egyptian compatriots possessed. After Ben Ali fell, the lack of a substantive Muslim Brotherhood-style social movement dramatically eased the decision to enforce a (largely hypothetical) separation. Still, Ennahda's party-movement divide exists only on paper. Whether or not it will hold up under the rough and tumble of a political campaign remains to be seen. As the party's Egyptian counterparts discovered, in these situations the temptation to leverage every bit of one's assets to win an election will be huge. So when Tunisians head to the polls for future elections, it will be instructive to see if Ennahda's touted barrier between party and movement remains rigid and impermeable or collapses under the weight of the party's electoral ambitions.

The difficulty of maintaining the party-movement divide bodes ill for democratic transitions in which one contestant has a distinct advantage in terms of an affiliated social movement. The broader implication is that civil society–based parties that exit authoritarianism—particularly in cases where outside actors retain the capability to scuttle the transition—must find a way to credibly commit to avoid using these advantages to overrun their opponents. Yet the above dynamics show that this is easier said than done, especially in the high-stakes contests of founding elections: expecting a party to *not* rely on the resources of its social movement affiliates when the stakes are highest is akin to expecting a boxer to enter a title bout with one hand tied behind his or her back.

There is another dimension to the party-movement divide that is particularly pronounced for religious organizations: the way that blatant engagement in partisan political competition jeopardizes other aspects of the social and cultural mission. Authors have found that religious organizations, defined broadly, assume significant risks when they delve directly into "petty politics" (Grzymała-Busse 2015, 2). In a cross-national study, David Buckley concludes that direct religious influence in politics "carries risks for religious communities themselves, from the taint of corruption to defeat of political allies to sowing dissension within congregations" (2016, 359). This dilemma may be underlined for Islamist movements, which explicitly present themselves as engaged in a transformative sociocultural project that goes far beyond the narrow question of electoral participation. Nathan Brown suggests Islamists are well aware of this, fearing "that they will be sucked into emphasizing politics too exclusively and lose sight of the broader mission" (2012, 9). Quinn Mecham and Julie Chernov Hwang argue that Islamist political parties may be particularly susceptible to these tensions. These parties, they suggest, "may find themselves at odds with the nonpolitical goals of the movement regarding religious, social, or economic issues, and be constrained in their political behavior due to their organizational ties to an Islamist movement with a broader set of objectives and incentives" (2014a, 5).

The Muslim Brotherhood understood that segregating its social service project protected it from the inevitable failures of politics: losing elections, pursuing failed policies, and compromising with ideological opponents. But two factors make it difficult to determine how much of their ability to separate politics was due to their own self-control rather than the hard external constraint on depoliticization provided by authoritarian rule. The first was legal necessity: Egyptian law forbade politicization of the civic and social sector, a stricture that was backed by the coercive power of the authoritarian regimes of Anwar al-Sadat and Hosni Mubarak. Even if the Brotherhood had wanted to politicize its endeavors, doing so would likely have triggered a regime crackdown. Accommodating this reality was eased by a second factor: in the highly circumscribed system that obtained under Sadat and Mubarak, elections were not the be-all and end-all of politics (Brown 2012). "Rational party leaders," Mainwaring explains, "will not make vote maximizing their first priority if votes are not the primary currency of politics" (2003, 18). Under these conditions the pressures to fully deploy one's arsenal to win an election were relatively minimal, a contrast that is especially visible in light of how dramatically this calculus changed in early 2013.

Regardless of whether it was externally imposed or internally generated, maintaining the divide between party and movement served the Brotherhood well for decades. This recognition of the dangers of cross-contamination challenges much of the current thinking on the relationship between political party and social movement. In other contexts, a close relationship can be beneficial—for instance when parties cleverly leverage the resources of the social movement to reach out to new audiences, forge new alliances, and establish robust electoral coalitions (Van Cott 2005; Thachil 2011; Anria 2013). Stathis Kalyvas, for example, explains how Catholic clubs, organizations, and social associations magnified the power of pro-Church electoral coalitions in nineteenth- and early twentieth-century Europe because they "were able to reach voters whom the church and its priests alone could only reach with difficulty, if at all" (1996, 101). These types of interactions are both unidirectional (movement to party) and positive (they help the party).

But the intense politicization that the Brotherhood experienced in 2013 shows how the work of the party—in this case electoral participation—can contaminate the movement in the way alluded to above. "It was mistake," the longtime Brotherhood parliamentarian and board member of the IMA Gamal Hishmat conceded when I asked him about allowing the activities of the movement and the party to intertwine during the Together We Build Egypt campaign.[22] Amr Darrag, former minister in Morsi's government, elaborated in an interview that "it is clearly impossible for the [Brotherhood] to compete politically against a large segment of the population but at the same time work alongside them socially. This is simply not achievable, and this is the largest mistake that took place."[23] The Muslim Brotherhood activist Ammar Fayed concurs, noting that "in hindsight, it appears that the Brotherhood's direct participation in competitive politics has done substantial damage to decades of social and religious institution building" (2017, 250–51). The solution, as these figures now argue, is to redouble their efforts to keep the two sides of the organization separate. As Hishmat explained in a statement in 2016, "The whole group is determined to keep the competitive partisan side away from the educational and reform side and activities."[24]

Escaping the Niche Party Trap

The Brotherhood's success under authoritarian rule suggests another implication for the study of nondemocratic regimes. In his study of the Partido Revolucionario Institucional, which dominated Mexican politics for over seventy years, Ken Greene (2007) identifies a particularly crippling affliction that besets opposition parties. Because they cannot compete against the dominant party's resource advantage, the opposition must lean ever more heavily on specialized and single-issue platforms to attract voters. And while this facilitates electoral mobilization in the short term, in the long term a reliance on strident ideological appeals renders these parties unable to appeal beyond a "niche" of committed activists.

This argument certainly seems to explain what happened to Egypt's non-Islamist opposition parties, which continually fractured and struggled to broaden their electoral coalitions throughout the Mubarak years (Stacher 2004; Albrecht 2013). The Brotherhood, which *began* in the 1970s as a niche party dedicated to implementing Islamic law (the sharia) above all else, would seem a prime candidate to follow this trajectory. As Shadi Hamid notes, "It is worth recalling that most Islamist groups were founded as *niche parties*, a term used to describe 'single issue' parties whose raison d'être is to inject a particular issue—one neglected by mainstream parties—into the public discourse" (2014, 47).

In fact, when the bread riots shook Sadat's hold on power, most analysts downplayed the risk of Islamists and instead focused on how the Wafd party's supposedly broad base and foothold in electoral politics positioned it to challenge Sadat. A CIA analysis from 1979 suggested that the Wafd was best positioned to "rapidly grow into the majority party in Egypt... and [threaten] Sadat with a specter of true political opposition."[25] A 1977 British Foreign Office document reported the same.[26] But instead of flourishing as Sadat foundered, the Wafd party crumbled into a niche party in the same way Mexico's opposition did under PRI rule. The Brotherhood, in contrast, escaped the niche party trap and managed to steadily grow its electoral coalition so that, during the waning years of the Mubarak era, it sat atop a broad electoral coalition of leftists, revolutionaries, Islamists, labor, and activist youth. Figure 8.1 charts these two organizations' divergent fates.

Why did the Wafd party shrivel? How did the Brotherhood reverse the niche party trajectory, "transform[ing] itself from a fringe phenomenon in the early

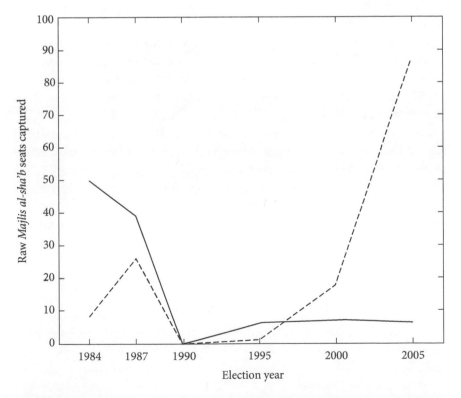

FIGURE 8.1. Electoral performance: Muslim Brotherhood (dashed) vs. Wafd (solid)

1970s to the largest opposition force in the country by the first decade of the twenty-first century" (Naguib 2009, 104)?

It would be tempting to attribute the two organizations' differing fates to ideological factors: as Egypt's electorate Islamized, the argument goes, Islamist groups would be a natural beneficiary. In contrast, groups that affiliated themselves to non-Islamic ideologies—like the nationalist Wafd—would correspondingly suffer. But if the Brotherhood's success was a product of its proximity to Egypt's theoretically conservative median voter, then why were other parties unable to capture more voters by shifting rightward (Downs 1957)? We know that they tried: the aforementioned CIA report from the 1970s noted how leftist parties were attempting to bolster their religious bona fides: "The leftists even attempted to woo the religious right by peppering their published statements with liberal quotes from the Koran and, on a less elevated plane, by bribing religious groups."[27] Hamid also describes the transformation of Wafd party along similar lines: "In [Wafd's] original 1977 program, there was only one passing mention of sharia as the 'original' (aṣīl) source of legislation. The 1984 program, in contrast, included an entire section devoted to the application of Islamic law (ṭatbīq al-sharia), in which Wafd stated that Islam was both 'dīn wa dawla' (religion and state) and that the sharia was the principal source of legislation" (2014, 86).

If all organizations (including the Egyptian government) were puffing up their Islamic credentials, what made the Brotherhood different (Skovgaard-Petersen 1997; Masoud 2014a)? This book's emphasis on the tie between political and social activism suggests an answer: social service activism can help opposition parties mobilize voters with minimal reference to ideology. The Brotherhood used social service provision to supplement its ideological core with voters attracted by the group's reputation for probity and competence. It effectively escaped the niche party trap by becoming a "do everything" party (Singer and Kitschelt 2011).

This suggests two extensions to the literature on political mobilization and movement-party relationships. First, nearly all of these studies have examined politics in democratic settings. Shifting the institutional context to Mubarak's electoral authoritarian regime shows a different face of the interaction (Clark and Dalmasso 2015). In particular, it raises the possibility that the way out of the niche party trap—which has ensnared many an opponent of authoritarianism— lies in the ability of organizations to subtly and indirectly leverage the support of affiliated movements to reach *beyond* what Robert Michels referred to as the "ideal world" of party cadre ([1915] 1966, 219). This supports Nathan Brown's contention that, in the Arab World, "those [parties] who focus exclusively on elections have little to show for themselves and therefore have withered into small shells with few supporters" (2012, 25). But it is also important not to lose sight of the fact that the Brotherhood's success in this regard was as much the result of path-dependent decisions and fortuitous convergences as it was a cunning and forward-looking strategy. Future investigations may find it profitable to extend this argument to other contexts, in the process refining the argument.

Second, much of this literature on party-movement relations takes as the unit of analysis the *organization*. This book extends the focus to the individual, showing the precise nature of the linkages that emerge as voters transverse the party-movement divide. Particularly among middle-class voters, those who might be repelled by a more instrumental exchange of goods for political support, the quality of interaction with the social movement forms the basis for relatively sophisticated political inferences about the party. This implies that much of the Islamist advantage lies in decidedly worldly factors that indeed may translate into a diverse set of comparative cases.

The Islamist Advantage

The Muslim Brotherhood was able to politically profit from its social service provision because it provided consistent and relationally enjoyable service that spoke to the concerns of Egypt's wealthier citizens. But, as should be apparent, the mechanism appears to have very little to do with the particular identity of the provider organization, in this case the Brotherhood's "Islamism." What this suggests is that the "Islamist advantage" (Pepinsky, Liddle, and Mujani 2012; Cammett and Jones Luong 2014; Masoud 2014a; Brooke 2017b) owes as much to particular historical circumstances and patterns of path-dependent development as it does to the uncommon foresight or particular ideological qualities of Islamists themselves.

Islamist groups wrung political benefits from their social service provision neither due to their religious identity nor because of their supposed ability to operate in spaces where the state was weak or absent. Instead, Islamists grounded their provision on an overwhelmingly paying customer base, which enabled them to sustain high-quality care. Other providers prioritized free or low-cost social service provision, deployed as either charity or clientelism. Not only did this decision force them into futile competition with proregime networks, but it robbed them of the ability to consistently generate the type of provision that would resonate with those middle-class voters most likely to be able to vote for them. This emphasis on heavy doses of serendipity suggests tempering our tendency to view Islamist groups as especially cunning, strategic, or forward-looking, and instead focus on more worldly sources of success.

My argument that Islam—or ideology more generally—has little to do with the vaunted Islamist advantage dovetails with the above implication that attracting nonideological voters is critical for any party seeking to avoid collapsing into a niche party. Islamists succeeded because of their "dual constituency," the division between those who support the group for ideological or religious reasons and those who are attracted for more quotidian ones (Mecham 2014, 21). Other Islamist parties have seemingly managed to assemble broad coalitions by emphasizing non-ideological factors. Prior to the 2004 elections, for example, the Islamist PKS in Indonesia explicitly focused on buttressing its core by attracting voters through an image of compassion and clean government. As Saiful Mujani and R. William Liddle explain, "After the party's weak showing in 1999 . . . the party also decided at this time to adopt a second-track strategy, the projection of a non-Islamic image to the larger society. In 2004, the party's campaign themes were *bersih* (clean, meaning non-corrupt, government) and *peduli* (caring, meaning concern for social welfare). In the event, PKS received more than eight million votes" (2009, 582).

This insight has the additional benefit of explaining swings in Islamist support, from highs under authoritarianism through early transition periods, then dropping under the weight of observed political setbacks. This volatility suggests that non-Islamists are indeed vital to the Islamist electoral coalition. We would expect, in other words, that those who support Islamist groups for ideological reasons would generally continue to do so amid the various downturns and failures that are part and parcel of politics. Those who are attracted to these groups for nonideological reasons, however, would seemingly more carefully condition their support on events on the ground (Mecham and Hwang 2014b, 190). Indeed, Melani Cammett and Pauline Jones Luong hypothesize that voters punish Islamists *more* for failing to live up to the particularly lofty expectations bred by their activities outside the electoral realm (2014, 189).

Investing the Opposition

One of the most vibrant research agendas in comparative politics has been the investigation of how autocratic and dominant party regimes hold power. Authors have identified a number of mechanisms, including political parties (Geddes 2005; Brownlee 2007; Greene 2007), elections (Magaloni 2006; Blaydes 2011), regime institutions (Lust-Okar 2005; Gandhi 2008; Stacher 2012a), and strategic political liberalization (Brumberg 1992; Robinson 1998). The prior pages isolate a new mechanism these regimes use to maintain and perpetuate themselves: the use of nonstate providers in order to alleviate weighty distributive burdens.

This is, superficially, a question of economic reform: autocrats worry more about the immediate consequences of massive street protest or swift internal coup sparked by distributive changes than about the risk that they may be empowering a political opponent years down the road. In these conditions, reducing citizen disenchantment by off-loading social welfare functions to these actors is a best response. The drawback, however, is that as these nonstate providers become more important in helping citizens meet their daily needs, regimes will find their ability to circumscribe these providers' political ambitions in the future limited.

But there is another, more subtle, pathway through which this strategy may help an autocrat endure. For any regime—and especially autocracies—the challenge is to funnel activism out of the streets and into institutions, and there to render it visible, predictable, and ultimately controllable (Huntington 1968). This logic underpins the interaction between the regime and nonstate providers. Regimes acquiesce to the opposition's social service activism so long as it occurs in spaces that they can monitor, and in exchange the provider reduces its own risk of operating extralegally (Wiktorowicz 2000). This was the very bargain that the Brotherhood struck in the late 1970s, when it decided to eschew underground activism and instead operate its social service provision legally, in full view of the regime.

This same logic extends to the electoral realm, which is why authoritarian regimes that invest potential and current opponents into the existing political system—such as by allowing the opposition to achieve limited gains in elections or progress through the ranks of hierarchies—tend to last longer than more exclusionary types of nondemocracy (Geddes 1999; Brownlee 2007). Viewed through this prism, opposition movements that take up social service provision and begin to realize electoral support from that endeavor may *doubly* enhance regime longevity. Not only do they alleviate the initial distributive consequences of economic reform, but they end up channeling whatever popular support they gain in society into the realm of institutional politics, where it is more easily monitored and controlled than had it remained in civil society (Albrecht 2005). In cases like this, Ira Zartman observed, opposition can support the state: "Both government and opposition have interests to pursue within the political system, and this complementarity of pursuit reinforces the state" (1990, 221).

Beyond the theoretical implications for the study of nondemocratic regimes, this emphasis is also particularly relevant for the study of Islamist parties. As discussed in the first chapter, authors have tended to examine Islamists' social activism as a Gramscian strategy of passive revolution, of "bypassing the state" (Davis and Robinson 2012). This was, according to one knowledgeable observer, a success: "The Muslim Brothers' commitment to socioreligious change through da'wa and associational work wrested much of urban society from state control" (Bayat 2007a, 137).

The picture that emerges in this book is more complicated. The Brotherhood's activism was conspicuous for how it adhered to the ground rules established by the regime across both the political and civic sectors. This is normalization: "the process by which Islamist parties increasingly accommodate themselves to the rules of the political regimes in which they operate" (Mecham and Hwang 2014a, 7). But this raises a paradox: actors' increasing habituation to institutional competition ("moderation") usually has the effect of entrenching, rather than weakening, nondemocratic regimes (Tezcür 2010, Brownlee 2010b). 'Abboud al-Zumur, one of the leaders of the notorious al-Jihad, the group that assassinated Anwar al-Sadat, condemned the Brotherhood's strategy on exactly these grounds: "The aim [of the regime] in allowing Islamists to contest parliamentary elections was an attempt to pull a wide segment of the youth into these efforts, in the process causing them to lose their way and transform their goals. The Islamists' presence in the parliament legitimizes the regime beyond its wildest dreams, and orienting the Islamists toward participating in the elections was the way to realize that goal" (quoted in Mubarak 1995, 355). It is telling that, as the regime shook in late 2010 and early 2011, the Brotherhood's first instinct was not to flood Tahrir square and publicly press for greater political emancipation. Instead, it sought to advance its interests by negotiating for more political space—reportedly gaining legal recognition as a political party and a civic association—within the regime as it stood (Tadros 2012, 35–37).

The prior pages knit the story of social service provision into this larger narrative of institutional domestication. Instead of stoking revolutionary fires on the frontiers of regime control, the Muslim Brotherhood was more or less operating within limits defined and policed by Egypt's rulers. Egyptian state institutions profoundly shaped the Brotherhood's provision of social services, just as these types of institutional environments have exercised similar influence over the developments of Islamist parties elsewhere (Wiktorowicz 2001; Brown 2012; Hwang 2012; Yadav 2013; Mecham 2017). The "normalization" extends beyond the shape of the Brotherhood's provision to its effects: if the population reacted to the Brotherhood's social service provision by heading to the polls—rather than rioting in the street or withdrawing the legitimacy they bestowed on the regime—then very little of the Brotherhood's activism can truly be categorized as revolutionary. Instead, by dampening citizen discontent through social service provision and further by channeling those citizens back into the easily managed domain of institutionalized politics, the Brotherhood was, to a considerable extent, defending the authoritarian status quo.

Future Research

Two issues raised by this book seem particularly fruitful for additional study. First, the theoretical pathway identified and tested over prior pages suggests a number of implications that are best assessed in different country contexts.

Second, the investigation has cast doubt upon the prominent role played by provider ideology in the provision of services. Yet there remains much more that can be done to investigate, and potentially revise, this conclusion.

A consistent problem stalking research into nonstate social service provision under conditions of authoritarianism has been the lack of in-depth empirical data with which to establish and test hypotheses. This is doubly true when it comes to the universe of Islamist providers. This book has begun to surmount this difficulty by assembling an array of original material drawn from a variety of disparate sources on a single-country case. But this required a conscious trade-off between breadth and depth. Leveraging subnational and over-time variation in a single case study, with shorter focused comparisons with other providers, provided a better chance to understand causal mechanisms and derive broader yet ultimately untested theoretical insights than a more superficial multicountry comparison.

In light of this, a natural extension of this research agenda is to systematically explore how social service provision functions in other nondemocratic contexts. What, for example, are the implications for the reputation-based mechanisms in countries with cross-cutting ethnic and religious cleavages (Cammett 2014; Corstange 2016)? How does citizen perception of quality change when public services are in a comparatively better state than Egypt's? Given that the medical profession may be particularly well-suited to display the types of positive traits that citizens value in their political representatives, what are the implications for other types of social service provision (Boas 2014)? Would a study of education, for example, run through alternative pathways or produce different effects than those charted in this book?

The prior chapter suggests an implication for democratic competition. In democracies, social service provision can be an especially effective tool to mobilize *poor* voters, albeit through different mechanisms than the reputational one specified here (Thachil 2014a). Chapter 7 shows how the Muslim Brotherhood reacted to the liberalization of electoral competition by deploying a fleet of mobile medical caravans to do just that. An outstanding question, however, is whether this is best thought of as a case of conversion, of complete reorientation of the network, to focus on poor voters. Or is it rather an instance of layering, where a new component—in this case, outreach to the poor—coexists alongside the existing network of pay-for-service–based care (Mahoney and Thelen 2010)? And if it is a case of layering, can a party or movement simultaneously use social service provision to establish both reputation-based linkages to the wealthy and clientelist-based ones to the poor? Can these two linkage styles exist separately, or must they eventually bleed together?[28]

Researchers should also disentangle the precise interaction between religion and the theorized reputation-based mechanism. As noted above, while Islamist parties like the Muslim Brotherhood benefited from this effect, there seems little reason to suggest that the mechanism is solely the province of *Islamic* organizations or, for that matter, religious ones. The Muslim Brotherhood was able to use social services to generate political mobilization because it alone was able to generate high-quality social services. Rather than religious atmospherics or ideological commitment, the Muslim Brotherhood produced this effect by crafting its social service outreach around paying customers and running the facilities in a modern, efficient, and businesslike manner. We could, for example, envision an avowedly secular political party using pay-for-service provision to generate the type of reputational effect envisioned here.

Yet it may also be the case that there *is* an Islamist advantage, in that high-quality and compassionate social service provision effectively confirms the (positive) traits that individuals already associate with religious—or Islamic—groups. Thomas Pepinsky and his coauthors refer to this as a "conditional" advantage: though policies may be the same, voters may "reward Islamic parties with popular policies more [or punish them less] than they do non-Islamic parties" (2012, 587). Anecdotally, at least, there is ample evidence that people do try to tap into a general religious "brand" because they believe it gives them an edge in politics or business. As one business owner told Asef Bayat, "Islamic names bring *baraka* (grace), raise people's trust, and attract them to business." This led Bayat to conclude that "many private schools and clinics chose Islamic tags even though they differed little from non-Islamic institutions of the same type" (2007a, 149). Suheir Morsy calls this "the placebo effect provided by religious symbolism" (1988, 366). This raises the possibility that Islamists' self-styled identity as representatives of the faith serves to magnify and elevate an essentially run-of-the-mill social service into something more. Customers may *perceive* the service offered by Islamists to be better, or believe that it says something about Islamists that it does not say about non-Islamists, thus generating a unique political effect despite technical similarities across different provider organizations.

This possibility speaks to the need to further disentangle and measure the different—and potentially divergent—technical and interpersonal facets of social service provision. I simply lack the technical knowledge to judge certain aspects of medical care such as doctor knowledge or appropriateness of diagnostic techniques, for instance. But another reason that I did not spend an extensive amount of time studying the technical aspects of care is that this is less important to most patients, and more difficult to assess, than the interpersonal experience (Ginsburg and Hammons 1988). But this seems a ripe area for future research: not only to explore how technical capacity varies across different providers but to identify how the perception of care, technical skill, and potential political effects vary across religious and nonreligious provider organizations (Cammett and Şaşmaz 2017).

The Political Effects of Social Service Provision

For decades the Muslim Brotherhood's social service networks spread across the Egyptian political landscape, driven neither by gushing flows of oil money nor by the single-minded determination of ideologically committed cadres. They grew because they offered Egyptians help in navigating the exigencies of daily life in a state that was struggling to meet the basic needs of its citizens. The Brotherhood did not offer charity to the penniless, nor did it supplement the aid it provided with a heavy dose of religious indoctrination. Instead, the group offered reliable, honest, and compassionate care at a fair price, which in turn helped those exposed to it form an impression of what the Brotherhood stood for politically. That this was such a valuable service to so many Egyptians reflects the failures of the Egyptian government as much as it does the successes of the Muslim Brotherhood.

Nearly every study or piece of commentary on the Muslim Brotherhood contains some version of the phrase "a vast network of social services, including kindergartens, schools, clinics, hospitals, job training programs, marriage programs, and housing services." Yet for such a ubiquitous and ostensibly powerful network, there has been remarkably little empirical material with which to understand how it works. This book has used historical, qualitative, spatial, and experimental data to try to flesh out the Brotherhood's social apparatus and, in the process, give those who are interested in learning more a place to begin their own investigation.

But this book is about more than the Muslim Brotherhood. It is a story of how, in nondemocratic regimes, social service provision can credibly convey an image of probity and compassion about the provider organization. As these vague impressions interact with electoral institutions and socioeconomic geography, they translate into concrete political mobilization. When these services benefit the middle class, they are reaching those who are most likely to integrate those experiences into their decision calculus on election day. Against other parties locked into a hopeless battle against the regime for the votes of the poor, this provides organizations whose social service provision ties them to the middle class a considerable political advantage.

This appendix provides more detail about the calculations reported in the previous chapters. Data and related .do files are available at www.steventbrooke.com.

Materials Relevant to Chapter 5

The empirical analysis of chapter 5 centered on estimating patterns of general electoral competition, patterns of specific competition by Muslim Brotherhood candidates, and the locations of IMA medical facilities, all as a function of underlying socioeconomic data.

Variation in District-Level Competition (Overall)

What accounts for district-by-district variation in patterns of electoral competition during the multidecade rule of Hosni Mubarak (r. 1981–2011)? The dependent variable in the following analysis, competition, is the median number of candidates who entered a race in that district across five parliamentary election years: 1990, 1995, 2000, 2005, and 2010.[1]

The independent variables in the following model (as well as in all following models) are drawn from a version of the 2006 Egyptian census, downloaded from the IPUMS.org website.[2] The variables include the following:

A. Wealth (wealth index). Respondents were asked how many of these eleven common household items they owned: an automobile, a landline phone, a mobile phone, an internet connection, a computer, an automatic washing machine, a freezer, a refrigerator, a TV, a VCR, or a radio. A principal component factor analysis reveals that these items load on a common underlying factor ($\alpha = .8983$). I thus produce a wealth index by first coding all respondents according to whether they own (1) or do not own (0) the specific item. I then sum to the level of the electoral district the number of owned items, divided by (11^* respondents in the district). Thus in a district where all respondents owned each of the items, the wealth index would be equal to one.

B. Density (log crowding). Following Masoud (2014a), I produce a measure of population density by first summing the number of persons per dwelling as well as the number of rooms per dwelling. I then divide the number of rooms in the dwelling by the number of residents per dwelling at the district level. To normalize the distribution I take the natural log of the result.

C. Infrastructure (electrified). As a measure of infrastructure availability, I generate for each dwelling a dummy variable consisting of one if the dwelling is connected to the electrical grid and zero if it is not. I then sum the number of electrical hookups and the number of dwellings, dividing to generate a percentage of dwellings with access to electricity.

D. Sectarian balance (percentage Muslim). Because there is potentially a sectarian dimension to NGO-based welfare provision, I also include a variable accounting for the percentage of Muslims. I code each Muslim respondent a one and all others (for all intents and purposes Christians) a zero. I sum the number of Muslims and divide by the total number of residents.

As described in the body of the book, electoral district-level statistics were produced by assigning residents of specific census districts (markaz or qism), which were given in the 2006 census data set, to specific electoral districts. This was accomplished manually, by matching the name of the markaz or qism in the census data set to the electoral district by reference to the relevant Egyptian law, 206 of 1990 (Majlis al-Sha'b 1990). In many cases this process was straightforward. But in a number of cases electoral districts were carved out of portions of multiple markaz or qism that were already assigned to other electoral districts. Because I cannot disaggregate the markaz or qism into smaller units, these electoral districts drop from the district-level analysis in chapter 5 (table A.1) (hence the n of 204 rather than 222).

TABLE A.1. Determinants of electoral district-level competition (general)

	(1)
	MEDIAN CANDIDATE ENTRY, 1990–2010
Wealth index	37.86***
	(6.931)
Percentage Muslim	7.844
	(6.972)
Crowding (log)	−2.998
	(2.631)
Percentage electrified	−20.68
	(13.65)
Constant	18.82
	(14.22)
Observations	204
Adjusted R^2	0.137

Note: Standard errors in parentheses.
+ p < 0.1, * p < 0.05, ** p < 0.01, *** p < 0.001.

Table A.1 presents the results of an OLS regression model estimating levels of competition (median candidate entry) in a given electoral district, as a function of the above variables.

Variation in District-Level Competition (Muslim Brotherhood)

What accounts for district-by-district variation in patterns of Muslim Brotherhood electoral competition during the multidecade rule of Hosni Mubarak (r. 1981–2011)? The independent variables in the following analysis are identical to the ones above: wealth, density, infrastructure, and sectarian balance.

The dependent variable in the following analysis is the percentage of times a candidate from the Muslim Brotherhood entered a race in that district across four parliamentary election years: 1995, 2000, 2005, and 2010.[3] Because the dependent variable is a proportion (proportion of times a Muslim Brotherhood candidate has contested the seat, min = 0, max = 1), table A.2 presents the results of a fractional logit model to estimate levels of Muslim Brotherhood competition in a given electoral district as a function of the same right-hand side variables as listed above.

TABLE A.2. Determinants of electoral district-level competition (Muslim Brotherhood)

	(1)
	MUSLIM BROTHERHOOD CONTESTATION, 1995–2010
Wealth index	5.519***
	(1.202)
Percentage Muslim	3.120*
	(1.449)
Crowding (log)	0.449
	(0.603)
Percentage electrified	15.01**
	(5.644)
Constant	−20.73***
	(5.482)
Observations	204
Pseudo R^2	0.048

Note: Robust standard errors in parentheses.
+ p < 0.1, * p < 0.05, ** p < 0.01, *** p < 0.001.

IMA Placement

Under what conditions does the Muslim Brotherhood establish an IMA medical facility? The dependent variable in the following regression model is the existence (1) or nonexistence (0) of an IMA medical facility in a given markaz/qism during the rule of Hosni Mubarak.

The independent variables are identical to the ones above: wealth, density, infrastructure, and sectarian balance. There is one key difference. Here they are aggregated/calculated at the level of the census district (markaz/qism) rather than the electoral district (as in tables A.1 and A.2). The structure of the data in this analysis is also hierarchical: specifically, markaz/qism are nested inside a larger electoral district, although disjunctures created by the difficulties of assigning markaz/qism to electoral districts, as described above, reduces the number of cases slightly.

Because of the inclusion of electoral districts in the analysis, I produce a new independent variable in this model:

- Brotherhood electoral competition. This is the same as the dependent variable in table A.2: the percentage of times a candidate from the Muslim Brotherhood appeared in that electoral district over the four elections 1995, 2000, 2005, and 2010.

Table A.3 presents the results of a logistic regression estimating the probability of an IMA facility's existing in a given markaz/qism nested in a given electoral district. Cluster robust standard errors are entered at the electoral district.

TABLE A.3. Predictors of IMA facility existence (markaz/qism [MQ] nested in electoral district [ED])

	(1)
	IMA FACILITY
MQ: wealth index	10.44***
	(3.021)
MQ: percentage Muslim	−2.238
	(2.953)
MQ: crowding (log)	−1.018
	(1.692)
MQ: percentage electrified	7.605
	(13.05)
ED: Muslim Brotherhood contestation, 1995–2010	2.387+
	(1.285)
Constant	−12.21
	(12.33)
Observations	295
Pseudo R^2	0.1871

Note: Cluster robust standard errors in parentheses.
+ p < 0.1, * p < 0.05, ** p < 0.01, *** p < 0.001.

Precinct Analysis

Does proximity to an IMA facility influence pro-Brotherhood turnout? The dependent variable in the below calculation is the percentage of registered voters at that precinct who voted for Mohammed Morsi. While the fine-grained nature of the investigation prevents a more extensive analysis, I am able to produce two independent variables with the available data:

- Proximity. I use the QGIS software package to draw concentric circles around each precinct of 500, 750, and 1000 m radii. If an IMA facility falls inside one of those circles, then the precinct is marked with a dummy variable at that buffer distance.
- Number of boxes. Because precincts contain multiple colocated boxes, I am able to control for the possibility that the number of boxes at that precinct is related to voting outcomes there.

Because the dependent variable is a proportion, the percentage of the registered voters per precinct turned out by the Mohammed Morsi campaign (min =.026, max =.407), table A.4 presents the results of a fractional logit model to estimate levels of pro-Morsi turnout in a given precinct.

TABLE A.4. Ballot box analysis

	(1)	(2)	(3)
	PRO-MORSI TURNOUT	PRO-MORSI TURNOUT	PRO-MORSI TURNOUT
Boxes per precinct	−0.00248	−0.00428	−0.00471
	(0.0154)	(0.0154)	(0.0155)
500 m buffer	0.176**		
	(0.0569)		
750 m buffer		0.0845+	
		(0.0481)	
1,000 m buffer			0.0351
			(0.0374)
Constant	−1.207***	−1.201***	−1.197***
	(0.0479)	(0.0481)	(0.0487)
Observations	497	497	497
Pseudo R^2	0.000	0.000	0.000

Note: Robust standard errors in parentheses.
+ p < 0.1, * p < 0.05, ** p < 0.01, *** p < 0.001.

Materials Relevant to Chapter 6

Chapter 6 contains the analysis of a survey experiment designed to identify the microlevel relationship between social service provision, perception of

Brotherhood candidates for elected office, and likelihood of voting for the Brotherhood's candidates. The Egyptian Center for Public Opinion Research (Baseera) executed this survey experiment by telephone over seven days, from May 14 to May 20, 2014. The survey response rate was 50.8 percent.[4]

External Validity

The survey queried Egyptians aged eighteen to ninety-one over both landline (48.21 percent of the sample) and mobile phones (51.79 percent). All respondents were selected by simple random sampling (mobile customers were selected through random digit dialing, while landline customers were selected from a database of all Egyptian landlines). For purposes of external validity, table A.5 compares the survey sample against the version of the 2006 Egyptian census used in the prior calculations. Note that "urban governorates" encompasses five governorates traditionally categorized as such by the Egyptian government: Cairo, Giza, Alexandria, Port Said, and Suez.

TABLE A.5.   Survey and population characteristics

	SURVEY SAMPLE (2014)	2006 CENSUS (AGE 18 AND UP)
Mean age	39.88 years	36.76 years
Percentage female	47.52	49.14
Percentage Christian	5.51	5.65
Percentage unemployed	9.40	4.48
Percentage living in urban governorates	32.34	28.57

The categories either are broadly similar (age, sex, religion) or have differences that are likely attributable to the gap between the 2006 census and the 2014 survey. It seems plausible, for example, that there is more unemployment and more rural-urban migration in 2014 than in 2006.

Randomization

For purposes of internal validity, table A.6 shows the differences in means of key population variables, as well as enumerator gender (Benstead 2014), across treatment and control groups with p values represented by asterisks.

Although in substantive terms the difference is small, the treatment group (those receiving the battery of Muslim Brotherhood questions) was significantly more rural than the control group (those receiving the battery of Ministry of Health questions), and those in the treatment group were substantially more likely to have been contacted by mobile phone.

TABLE A.6. Distribution of key variables, treatment vs. control

	TREATMENT MEAN	CONTROL MEAN
Mean age	39.912	39.851
	−0.401	−0.409
Percentage poor	0.413	0.401
	−0.014	−0.013
Percentage rural	0.379	0.312***
	−0.014	−0.013
Percentage female	0.477	0.474
	−0.014	−0.014
Percentage Christians	0.048	0.062
	−0.006	−0.007
Percentage unemployed	0.095	0.092
	−0.008	−0.092
Percentage anti-Brotherhood	0.195	0.175
	−0.011	−0.011
Mean years of formal schooling	12.737	12.799
	−0.162	−0.158
Percentage contacted via mobile	0.561	0.502**
	−0.014	−0.014
Percentage receiving a male enumerator	0.282	0.288
	−0.013	−0.013

+ p < 0.1, * p < 0.05, ** p < 0.01, *** p < 0.001.

As a robustness check on whether or not the unbalance is driving the results, table A.7 models individual responses to the two variables of interest: how likely you are to vote for the Brotherhood ("vote choice") and how you perceive the Brotherhood candidates' traits ("reputation"). These outcomes are analyzed as a function of the various socioeconomic predictors in table A.6 as well as a dummy variable representing whether or not an individual is assigned to the treatment or the control. In table A.7 models one and two predict respondent electoral choice and respondent perception of candidate traits solely as a function of assignment to the treatment or the control, respectively. Models three and four also include the relevant socioeconomic variables to examine how this affects the coefficient on the treatment/ control dummy. If the treatment was not driving the observed differences in vote choice and likability, one indication would be a notable shift in the coefficient on the treatment dummy when all the socioeconomic variables are added to the model.

The lack of a substantive change in the coefficient estimates for the treatment dummy when these other variables are included suggests that the differences in underlying sample composition do not substantively influence the analysis: exposure to the treatment remains a significant predictor of both individual vote choice and perception of Brotherhood candidates.

TABLE A.7. Predictors of vote choice and reputation, with and without full controls

	(1)	(2)	(3)	(4)
	VOTE CHOICE	**VOTE CHOICE**	**REPUTATION**	**REPUTATION**
Treatment	0.0926*	0.0965**	0.136***	0.136***
	(0.0362)	(0.0360)	(0.0402)	(0.0396)
Age		−0.00284*		−0.00532***
		(0.00137)		(0.00150)
Poor		0.0407		0.0270
		(0.0399)		(0.0442)
Urban		−0.126**		−0.157***
		(0.0399)		(0.0443)
Female		−0.0428		−0.104*
		(0.0386)		(0.0427)
Christian		−0.131+		−0.278**
		(0.0792)		(0.0858)
Unemployed		−0.0652		−0.154*
		(0.0639)		(0.0698)
MB opponent		−0.361***		−0.386***
		(0.0455)		(0.0489)
Male enumerator		−0.00926		0.0517
		(0.0404)		(0.0440)
Contacted via mobile		−0.0103		−0.0211
		(0.0398)		(0.0436)
Years of formal education		0.00725*		0.0157***
		(0.00356)		(0.00404)
Constant	0.453***	0.649***	0.682***	0.935***
	(0.0255)	(0.101)	(0.0281)	(0.111)
Observations	2224	2195	1921	1892
Adjusted R^2	0.002	0.039	0.005	0.064

Note: Standard errors in parentheses.
+ $p < 0.1$, * $p < 0.05$, ** $p < 0.01$, *** $p < 0.001$.

Correction Table

The repetitive t-tests across different subgroups (full, poor, non-poor) reported in chapter 6 raise the problem of multiple comparisons. Briefly, repeated hypothesis testing increases the chance of incorrectly rejecting the null hypothesis of no relationship, a false positive or "type 1 error." Put in terms of this specific experiment, it increases the possibility that there may be no relationship between the treatment and control means, but applying the standard value for α (.95) would lead one to conclude the difference was significant. To mitigate this possibility, the statistical tests here report Bonferroni corrected values for α alongside the uncorrected value (.05). Table A.8 illustrates this process and notes the results of comparisons following the correction.

TABLE A.8.   Bonferroni correction table

QUESTION	SUBGROUP	P VALUE	CORRECTED α	NEW RESULT
Vote propensity	Non-poor	0.0062	.0167	Remains significant
Vote propensity	Full	0.0106	.0167	Remains significant
Vote propensity	Poor	0.4541	.0167	Remains insignificant
Reputation index	Full	0.0008	.0167	Remains significant
Reputation index	Non-poor	0.0051	.0167	Remains significant
Reputation index	Poor	0.0581	.0167	Remains insignificant

Alternative Measure of Socioeconomic Class

The analysis of socioeconomic class-based differential effects in the survey experiment was based on an asset index. As a robustness check, in figures A.1 and A.2 I reproduce the analysis yet use educational attainment to proxy for socioeconomic class, breaking the sample between those who finished high school and those who did not.

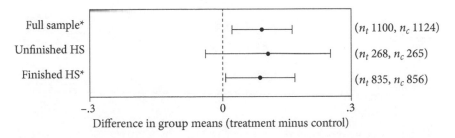

FIGURE A.1.   Propensity to vote for the Muslim Brotherhood

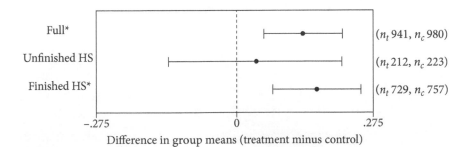

FIGURE A.2.   Reputation of Muslim Brotherhood candidates and deputies

Causal Mediation Analysis

Table A.9 presents the results of the causal mediation analysis.

The causal mediation analysis rests on an assumption of sequential ignorability that cannot be directly tested (Imai et al. 2011). However the *mediation* package for Stata also allows iterative violations of the assumption by allowing the error terms of the two regression models (mediator and outcome) to correlate more and more strongly. As this sensitivity parameter (ρ) approaches complete correlation (1 or −1), the value of ρ when the average causal mediation effect (ACME) reaches zero provides a rough metric of the validity of the causal mediation analysis. Figure A.3 presents the relationship graphically.

In this case, the ACME reached zero at $\rho = .6341$. As Kosuke Imai and his colleagues point out, there exists no baseline standard for judging the acceptable value of ρ. Instead, they suggest comparing the value of ρ in the analysis under

TABLE A.9. Mediation results, effect of "reputation" on propensity to vote for Brotherhood candidates

	MEAN	95% CONFIDENCE INTERVALS	
Average causal mediation Effect (ACME)	0.08275	0.02953	0.13299
Direct effect	0.00458	−0.05832	0.06252
Total effect	0.08733	0.00561	0.16346

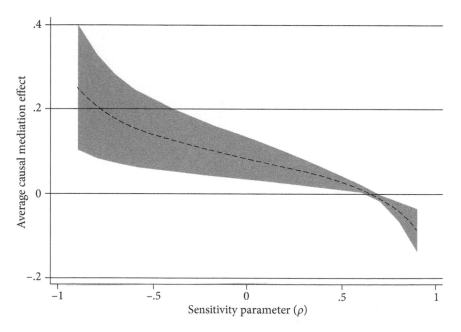

FIGURE A.3. Sequential ignorability (ρ)

examination with the value of ρ as observed in other examples of mediation analysis in the literature (2011, 776). For instance, in a separate article, Imai, Keele, and Yamamoto (2010) note a value of ρ = .48 for a study of media framing (Nelson and Kinder 1996). Again, while a substantive explanation of the value of ρ as observed in the above causal mediation analysis is not possible, it is possible to say that it is notably stronger than in this example, and robust to fairly significant violations of the sequential ignorability assumption (ρ = 0).

Materials Relevant to Chapter 7

Chapter 7 introduced a new data set to examine the effects of social service provision during the spring of 2013. Specifically, it includes an analysis of medical caravan distribution, based on a data set I constructed from open-source Arabic language research. Here I describe two validity checks I conducted on this data set.

Caravan Activity vs. Internet Penetration

Because my data set is constructed entirely from online sources, it is possible that the distribution of caravans is related to differential rates of internet usage rather than reports of caravan visits. In other words, caravans visiting locales with high levels of internet usage would be disproportionately more likely to be logged in online media and thus more likely to appear in my data set. It is possible to tentatively assess this relationship with off-the-shelf survey data.

The dependent variable in the below analysis is a count of the number of caravans appearing in the markaz/qism. This variable has a min of 0 and a max of 14. I produce the independent variable of interest, markaz/qism—level rates of internet usage, from the third round of the Arab Barometer survey (n = 1,200). Fortuitously, this survey was carried out in Egypt in the middle of the Together We Build Egypt campaign (specifically in the first week of April 2013). I code all respondents as either users or nonusers of the internet, according to their answer to the question "Do you use the internet?" Respondents who answered "daily or almost daily," "at least once a week," "at least once a month," or "a few times a year" were coded as a one, and those who answered "I do not use the internet" or "I do not know" were coded a zero. This allowed me to produce a measure of the percentage of respondents in that markaz/qism who use the internet (min = 0, max = 1).

Unfortunately, the Arab Barometer is representative only at the national level, so the markaz/qism data here cannot be treated as representative.[5] Furthermore,

TABLE A.10. Caravan activity vs. internet usage (markaz/qism)

	(1)
	CARAVAN VISIT
Internet penetration	−1.286
	(0.983)
Constant	1.095**
	(0.341)
Observations	64
Pseudo R^2	0.007

Note: Standard errors in parentheses.
+ p < 0.1, * p < 0.05, ** p < 0.01, *** p < 0.001.

only a portion of Egypt's markaz/qism was covered by the Arab Barometer enumerators, which reduces the sample size. However, the sixty-four markaz/qism for which I have data were effectively chosen at random from the universe of Egyptian markaz/qism, reducing concerns of skewed data.

I use a negative binomial regression to model the relationship between caravan activity in a given markaz/qism as a function of this statistic on internet usage; table A.10 presents the results.

The relationship between internet penetration (measured by usage) and medical caravan visits was not statistically significant. This bolsters confidence that the spatial distribution of the medical caravans charted in my data set is not simply an artifact of internet penetration.

Accuracy of the Caravan Data Set

A complete listing of the Brotherhood's medical caravan activity is not available, and the 488 caravans I located may not be representative of the overall effort. However, on May 20, 2013, the Brotherhood's official Arabic-language news portal in Alexandria, *Amal al-Umma*, published a list of to-date statistics on the campaign, including mention of 2,039 medical caravans (the last caravan in my data set occurred over a month after this list was published, on June 26). Although the article lacked specific date and geographic information on the caravans, it did note how many had appeared in each of Egypt's governorates to date.[6] The article includes caravan data for all governorates, although it treats the two Sinai governorates (North and South) as a single entity. In this comparison I do the same.

I use OLS to model the relationship between caravan activity in a given governorate in my data set (Caravan Data Set) and official statistics on caravan activity released by the Brotherhood via the *Amal al-Umma* news service (Brotherhood Data Set). Table A.11 presents the results.

TABLE A.11.   "Ground truth" comparison (governorate)

	(1)
	CARAVAN VISIT
Brotherhood caravan tally	0.106**
	(0.031)
Constant	10.23**
	(3.409)
Observations	26
Adjusted R^2	0.307

Note: Standard errors in parentheses.
+ p < 0.1, * p < 0.05, ** p < 0.01, *** p < 0.001.

Activity in the Brotherhood's data set and that in my own are positively and significantly correlated at $p < .01$. While the aggregated level of the comparison and, relatedly, the small n should be kept in mind, the fact that both my assembled data set and the official Brotherhood statistics for caravan activity are so closely correlated should ease concerns that my assembled data set substantially misrepresents the ground truth.

Caravan Targeting Analysis

Under what conditions does the Muslim Brotherhood target a location with medical caravans? The dependent variable in the following model is the number of caravans that appeared in a given markaz/qism during the Together We Build Egypt campaign.

The independent variables are identical to the ones introduced in chapter 5—wealth, density, infrastructure, and sectarian balance—aggregated/calculated at the level of the markaz/qism. The structure of this data is hierarchical: specifically, every markaz/qism is nested inside a larger electoral district.[7] Because of this, I include two electoral district-level independent variables in this model:

- Absolute margin. Because these elections would be essentially a rerun of the 2011–12 contests, I return to that data and generate a district-level statistic measuring how closely contested (from the Muslim Brotherhood's point of view) that earlier race was. Specifically, I subtract the vote percentage won by the Muslim Brotherhood/Freedom and Justice Party from its nearest competitor, then take the absolute value of the result to identify those districts where the margins were slimmest, i.e. "swing districts."
- Prior Brotherhood candidate. Although competition in these districts was based on a PR/List system, I attempted to match candidates on those lists with my data set of Muslim Brotherhood candidates under Mubarak

(1995–2010). If a list contained a candidate from pre-2011 (i.e., someone who might be better known), I indicate it with a one; otherwise the value is zero.

Table A.12 reports the results of a mixed-effects negative binomial regression to estimate caravan targeting in a given markaz/qism nested in a given electoral district.

TABLE A.12.   Determinants of caravan activity (markaz/qism [MQ] nested in electoral district [ED])

	(1)
	CARAVAN VISIT
MQ: IMA facility (dummy)	0.591+
	(0.328)
MQ: Wealth index	−3.100*
	(1.353)
MQ: Percent Muslim	1.235
	(1.612)
MQ: Crowding (log)	0.488
	(0.438)
MQ: Percent electrified	5.230*
	(2.250)
ED: 2011/2012 vote margin	−6.622**
	(2.113)
ED: Prior Brotherhood candidate (dummy)	−0.259
	(0.239)
Constant	−4.413
	(2.748)
Random intercept (ED)	.2976871*
	(.131058)
Markaz/qism observations	308
Electoral district observations	46

Note: Standard errors in parentheses.

+ p < 0.1, * p < 0.05, ** p < 0.01, *** p < 0.001.

Notes

1. SOCIAL SERVICES AND POLITICAL MOBILIZATION IN NONDEMOCRATIC REGIMES

1. Lisa Blaydes, for instance, calls Mubarak-era Egypt "the modal authoritarian regime that exists in the world today" (2011, 21), while Marina Ottaway dubs it a "perfect model" (2003, 31) of these types of regimes.

2. For instance, one author asserts that the Brotherhood operates "more than 20,000 clinics" throughout Egypt yet provides no source for the claim (Ibrahim 1988, 642–43). Nancy Davis and Robert Robinson state that the Muslim Brotherhood operates one thousand medical clinics throughout Egypt and three hundred in Cairo alone (2012, 55). Yet the article they cite as evidence actually mentions *Islamic* medical clinics, not *Brotherhood* ones (Talhami 2001, 317). Further illustrating the point, even those claims are suspect. The raw numbers (one thousand Islamic medical clinics in Egypt and three hundred in Cairo) originated in an unsourced column in an Egyptian newspaper in the late 1980s, which Suheir Morsy cited in her article "Islamic Medical Clinics in Egypt: The Cultural Elaboration of Biomedical Hegemony" (1988). Janine Clark (1995) cited both Morsy's academic article and the newspaper column in her own academic article, although she wisely included a disclaimer about the original source, the newspaper column. Talhami, in turn, cited Clark's article for the thousand/three hundred figure but dropped Clark's important disclaimer. Davis and Robinson then cited Talhami's article. Thus a weakly sourced and dubious claim about Islamic clinics *in general* became a specific statement about the Brotherhood's medical empire.

3. The idea of operating outside state control is exemplified in the language authors use to describe the Brotherhood's network of social and civic activities as a "state within a state" (Esposito 2003, 71) or an "alternative" to the existing state (Springborg 1989, 225).

4. "Qarar Raqm 2348 li-l-Sana 1978" [Decision No. 2348 for Year 1978], *al-Waqa'i' al-Misriyya*, January 1979, 2.

5. Author interview, IMA executive A, January 23, 2013.

6. Note that this essay was written in response to a work by the author (Brooke 2017a).

7. Thachil (2011), for instance, shows how the BJP's long-term and intensive engagement in these communities actually shifts the underlying preferences of voters, making them more amenable to the BJP.

8. Letter dated April 26, 2012. Copy in author's possession.

9. Ed Husain, "Is The Muslim Brotherhood Bribing Voters in Egypt?" *The Arab Street* (blog), November 9, 2011, http://blogs.cfr.org/husain/2011/11/09/is-the-muslim-brotherhood-bribing-voters-in-egypt; Eric Trager, "The Muslim Brotherhood Won an Election, but Is It Really Democratic?" *New Republic*, June 26, 2012, http://www.new republic.com/article/104412/eric-trager-muslim-brotherhood-won-election-it-really-democratic.

10. 'Abd Allah Dif, "Ta'yid Sha'bi Wasi' li-Murashshahi al-Wafd bi-Hayy al-Arba'in bi-l-Suwis" [Wide popular support for the Wafd's candidates in the Arba'in neighborhood of Suez], *al-Wafd*, November 16, 2011, http://goo.gl/ToSV21.

11. See Ahmad Amin 'Arafat, "Al-Qawafil al-Tibbiyya: Rishwa Siyasiyya!" [Medical caravans: Political bribery!], *al-Ahram*, December 21, 2013, http://digital.ahram.org.eg/articles.aspx?Serial=1495761&eid=19.

12. After Anwar al-Sadat's assassination *al-Daʻwa* moved operations to Geneva (and later Pakistan). It also shifted from a generally Egypt-centric magazine to a bulletin covering the broader Muslim World. I have found no mention of the IMA in these issues.

13. I also found an advertisement for the Islamic Medical Association in the Egyptian Islamist magazine *Liwaʾ al-Islam*. See issue for May 17, 1988, 58. IMA founder Ahmad al-Malt also had a regular column in *Liwaʾ al-Islam,* and parts of these were later compiled into his 1993 book, *Risalati ila al-Shabab* [My message to the youth].

14. See the inside cover advertisements in *al-Daʻwa* issues for January 1981 and February 1981. There was also an article discussing the charitable efforts of the Brotherhood-leaning industrialist ʻUthman Ahmad ʻUthman (whom Kepel calls the "Egyptian Rockefeller" [2003, 109]). See "'Ashrat min Dawr al-ʻIbada wa-l-ʻIlm Tuqam li-Iʻla' Kalimat al-Haqq wa-l-Din" [Tens of places of worship and learning are created to uphold the word of truth and religion], *al-Daʻwa,* May 1977, 44.

15. Author interview, IMA executive A, January 15, 2013.

16. Ibrahim Qasim, Nurhan Hasan, and Muhammad al-ʻAlim, "Baʻd Qarar al-Tahaffuz 'ala Amwal wa-Mumtalakat al-Jamʻiyya al-Tibbiyya al-Islamiyya: 'Hasr Amwal al-Ikhwan': Thani Akbar Masdar Tamwil li-l-Jamʻa bi-Qima 300 Milyun Guinea." [Follow-up to the decision to take control of the accounts and assets of the Islamic Medical Association . . . inventorying the Brotherhood's accounts: the second-largest source of funding for the group is valued at 300 million pounds], *al-Watan,* January 14, 2015, http://goo.gl/DuvdTw; "Seized Properties of Egypt's Banned Muslim Brotherhood worth $ 1.1 Bln," *al-Ahram,* January 24, 2016, http://english.ahram.org.eg/News/185791.aspx.

17. See Robert F. Worth, "Egypt's Human Bellwether," *New York Times,* January 19, 2012, http://www.nytimes.com/2012/01/22/magazine/mohamed-beltagy-future-of-egypt.html?pagewanted=all&_r=0.

18. On the Muwasat Association, see Ahmad al-Sukkari, "Al-Sadat Yatarid 'ala Hall Jamʻiyyat 'al-Muwasat'" [Al-Sadat disagrees with the dissolution of the "Muwasat Association"], *al-Wafd,* December 22, 2010, http://goo.gl/rpkTv9; Mohammed Essawy, "260 Muwazzafan wa-Maridan bi-Mustashfa al-Muwasat bi-l-Manufiyya Yatathahirun Ihtijajan 'ala Qarar Hall al-Jamʻiyya" [260 employees and patients of the Muwasat Hospital in Manufiyya rally to protest the decision to dissolve the (Muwasat) Association], *al-Ahram,* December 21, 2010, http://digital.ahram.org.eg/articles.aspx?Serial=379034&eid=715.

19. After Mohammed Morsi's election, for instance, a number of prominent IMA members were appointed to the Ministry of Health. Saad Zaghloul and Ibrahim Mustapha became Assistant Ministers of Health for Curative Care (al-ṭibb al-ʻilājī) and Health Insurance, respectively. Another member became the health minister's official spokesperson. See Mustafa al-Marsafawi, Ayat al-Jabal, and ʻUmar ʻAbd al-ʻAziz, "Hukumat al-Muqattam, fi Wizarat Qandil" [The government of Muqattam (where the Brotherhood's headquarters was located), in Qandil's Ministry]," *al-Masry al-Youm,* February 15, 2013, http://today.almasryalyoum.com/article2.aspx?ArticleID=371220. "Al-Jamʻiyya al-Islamiyya Tunazim Qafila Tibbiyya bi-Aswan fi Nihayat Nufimbir [Islamic association organizes a medical caravan in Aswan at the end of November]," *al-Mashhad,* September 20, 2011, http://goo.gl/wZouQ3.

20. Khaled Fahmy, "Giulio, the Islands, and National Security," *Mada Masr,* April 23, 2016, https://www.madamasr.com/en/2016/04/23/opinion/u/giulio-the-islands-and-national-security.

21. The survey was conducted in collaboration with Jason Brownlee of the University of Texas at Austin.

22. "Egypt: Raba Killings Likely Crimes against Humanity," *Human Rights Watch,* August 12, 2014, https://www.hrw.org/news/2014/08/12/egypt-raba-killings-likely-crimes-against-humanity.

2. MIDDLE-CLASS PROVISION, REPUTATION, AND ELECTORAL SUCCESS

1. In his study of the Peronist party in Argentina, Steven Levitsky also notes how increasing reliance on clientelism raises the issue of corruption, leaving the party vulnerable to challengers able to make a "clean government" critique (2003, 210).

2. One reason they do not probe further is that, as they go on to say, "many of the functions of the machine have been taken over by governmental bureaucracies" (Stokes et al. 2013, 14), which reduces the need for these types of intercessions. The implication is that this type of linkage may be more consequential in weaker states than in stronger ones.

3. Thomas Pepinsky, "Social Services and Political Islam in Southeast Asia: Two Failures," *Project on Middle East Political Science*, September 23, 2014, http://pomeps. org/2014/09/26/social-services-and-political-islam-in-southeast-asia-two-failures.

3. REBUILDING THE BROTHERHOOD BRAND

1. W. Morris, "Summary: On First Looking at Sadat's Egypt," February 9, 1976, NFE 014/2 (FCO 93/847[1]).

2. *Middle East Economic Digest*, January 21, 1977, 18.

3. "Sadat's Liberalization Policy: A Research Paper," PA 79-10245, Central Intelligence Agency/National Foreign Assessment Center, June 1979, 10.

4. T. C. Quinlan to Wheeler and Tomkins, "Cairo Dispatch of 31 January: The Disturbances of 18/19 January," February 8, 1977, NFE 015/2 (FCO 93/1045); "DCO Diplomatic Report No. 128/77: The Disturbances of 18/19 January in Egypt," January 31, 1977, NFE 015/2 (FCO 93/1045).

5. "Sadat Faces Mounting Religious Tension," *Arab Report and Record*, October 1977, 827; *Middle East Economic Digest*, September 30, 1977, 19.

6. "Misr al-'Ariqa Lan Takun Abadan Ard al-Farqa wa-l-Inqisam" [Honorable Egypt will never be a land of factionalism and division], *al-Ahram*, October 12, 1977.

7. Ezzat 'Abdel Mo'neim, "22 Milyon Guinea Li-l-Khata al-Jadida Li-l-Da'wa al-Islamiyya: Insha' Wahdat Mutakamila Li-Khidmat al-Mujtama' bi-l-Masajid al-Jadida" [22 million guineas for a new plan for Islamic outreach: Establishing comprehensive units for social services in new mosques], *al-Ahram*, April 10, 1979.

8. Khamis al-Bakri, "The Comprehensive Mosque: An Overall Plan Aimed at Turning 40,000 Mosques into Integrated Cultural Centers," *al-Liwa' al-Islami*, July 6, 1981. Reprinted and translated in FBIS/Near East Report.

9. Bakri, "The Comprehensive Mosque."

10. "Ifta'," *al-Itisam*, May–June 1980, 37. I appreciate Aaron Rock-Singer's bringing this source to my attention and clarifying how the fatwa requests usually functioned.

11. Bakri, "The Comprehensive Mosque." Coincidentally or not, one month prior to being singled out for praise by the government, the Rightly Guided Caliphs Association had officially changed its name (essentially dropping the word "Mosque" from the title) and mission to emphasize a broader role, shifting from a rather narrow focus on mosque operation and eldercare (*riāyat shaykhūkha*) to a broader social service umbrella. See "Qarar Shahr Ta'dil Raqm 36 li-l-Sana 1981 [Registration emendation decision no. 36 for year 1981]," *al-Waqa'i' al-Misriyya*, June 3, 1981, 20–21.

12. Ibrahim Misbah, "Jam'iyyat al-Khulafa' al-Rashidin li-l-Ta'lim . . . wa-l-Din" [The Rightly Guided Caliphs Association for education . . . and Islam], *Uktubir*, March 25, 1979, 70.

13. Itimad 'Abd al-Aziz and Zaynab 'Abd al-Mu'nim, "'Awdat al-Ruh ila Qahirat al-Alaf Mi'dhana" [Return of the spirit to Cairo, (city of) 1,000 minarets], *Uktubir*, August 3, 1980, 44–45.

14. Sadat had sought to rehabilitate the Brotherhood as early as 1971, when the Saudi king Faysal had brokered a meeting between Said Ramadan (Hasan al-Banna's

son-in-law) and Sadat, although the reconciliation remained at arm's length until the intercession of 'Uthman Ahmad 'Uthman (see below) (Haykal 1983, 116–18).

15. Ahmed al-Malt died in May 1995, in the midst of a pilgrimage to Mecca. His obituary appeared in multiple Arab newspapers, including *al-Ahram* (May 15, 1995, 22); *al-Hayat* (Muhammad Salah, "Wafat Na'ib al-Murshid al-'Am li-l-Ikhwan al-Muslimin fi Misr" [Death of the Deputy General Guide of the Muslim Brotherhood in Cairo], *al-Hayat*, May 15, 1995, 7); and *al-Ahrar* ("Wafat al-Duktur al-Malt Na'ib al-Murshid al-'Am li-l-Ikhwan al-Muslimin" [Death of Doctor Ahmad al-Malt, Deputy General Guide of the Muslim Brotherhood], *al-Ahrar*, May 15, 1993, 3.)

16. This short biography is based on a number of sources, including "al-Duktur Ahmad al-Malt," *Ikhwanwiki*, n.d., http://goo.gl/D0y8w; 'Abduh Mustafa Dasuqi, "Dr. Ahmad al-Malt: Khidmat al-Din wa-l-Mujtama'" [Dr. Ahmad al-Malt: Serving religion and society], *Ikhwanonline*, May 8, 2008, http://goo.gl/RCDLn8; Muhyi al-Din al-Zayit, "Rajul min al-Khalidin bi-'Amalihi" [An immortal man through his work], *Ikhwanwiki*, n.d., http://goo.gl/SNDmUv; Rida 'Abd al-Wadud, "Safahat Khalida min Hayat al-Tabib al-Mujahid Duktur Ahmad al-Malt" [Immortal pages from the life of the *mujahid* doctor, Dr. Ahmad al-Malt], *al-Hikma*, July 2012, 24–29; and "The Egyptian Muslim Brotherhood Building Bases of Support: A Research Paper," NESA 86-10025, Central Intelligence Agency/Directorate of Intelligence, May 1986, 13. It also includes information from Muhammad Habib's memoirs (2012, 437–42).

17. Wadud, "Safahat Khalida," 29.

18. The Brotherhood possessed a formidable pre-Nasir network of clinics and dispensaries, of which Muhammad Zaki reproduces a list for Cairo and Giza (1980, 229). These seem to have been completely taken over or shuttered during the Nasir years. Because some street names changed in the 1952 revolution, I used historical maps to identify the addresses Zaki mentioned and mapped them onto contemporary streets but did not find any evidence of Brotherhood operations at those locations in 2012–13. It seems that the Brotherhood was starting from scratch in the mid-1970s.

19. 'Abd al-Mun'im Abu al-Futuh briefly discusses the episode in his memoirs (2012, 36). A more comprehensive account is available in Zayit, "Rajul min al-Khalidin."

20. "Awwal Jam'iyya Tibbiyya Islamiyya Tukawwan fi Misr: La Budda min Ijad al-Tabib al-Muslim al-Mutamayyiz bi-Shakhsiyyatihi" [The first Islamic medical association established in Egypt: The exceptional Muslim doctor is distinguished by his character], *al-Da'wa*, January 1978, 60.

21. "Al-Jam'iyya al-Tibbiyya al-Islamiyya" [The Islamic Medical Association], *al-Da'wa*, November 1977, inside front cover.

22. "Al-Jam'iyya al-Tibbiyya al-Islamiyya," inside front cover.

23. "Takwin al-Jam'iyya al-Tibbiyya al-Islamiyya" [The formation of the Islamic Medical Association], *al-Da'wa*, May 1977, 37.

24. Author interview, January 23, 2013.

25. "Tasa'ulat hawla: Al-Jam'iyya al-Tibbiyya al-Islamiyya" [Questions about the Islamic Medical Association], *al-Da'wa*, October 1978, 42.

26. "Takwin al-Jam'iyya al-Tibbiyya al-Islamiyya," 37.

27. See also Malt's argument against violence as a means of change in Salah 'Abd al-Maqsud, "'Ashara Ittihamat Muwajaha ila al-Jama'a" [Ten charges facing the Brotherhood], *Liwa' al-Islam*, February 7, 1989, 12–15.

28. See issue of October 25, 1977, 12.

29. *Al-Da'wa*, December 1977, 76.

30. "Takwin al-Jam'iyya al-Tibbiyya al-Islamiyya," 37.

31. Ahmad al-Malt, "Nida' ila al-Muslimin: Mashru' al-Mustashfa al-Islami" [Call to the Muslims: the Islamic Hospital project], *al-Da'wa*, March 1980, 63; Ahmad al-Malt,

"al-Jam'iyya al-Tibbiyya al-Islamiyya: al-Mustashfa al-Islami al-Markazi" [The Islamic Medical Association: The Islamic Central Hospital], *al-Da'wa,* January 1981, 56.

32. 'Abd al-'Aziz and 'Abd al-Mu'nim, "'Awdat al-Ruh ila Qahirat al-Alaf Mi'dhana," 44–45.

33. The Badr Association itself was founded in 1974 under the auspices of Law 32 of 1964 to provide cultural, scientific, and religious services, as well as welfare and other social services. Registration documents appear in "Qarar Shahr Raqm 1971 li-l-Sana 1974" [Registration decision number 1971 for the Year 1974], *al-Waqa'i' al-Misriyya*, January 11, 1975, 5.

34. Malt, "Al-Jam'iyya al-Tibbiyya al-Islamiyya: al-Mustashfa al-Islami al-Markazi," 57. 'Uthman also served as a type of intermediary between Sadat and the Muslim Brotherhood's leadership, including Malt. See Wadud, "Safahat Khalida," 28.

35. Ahmad al-Malt, "Al-Mustashfa al-Islami al-Markazi [Islamic Central Hospital]," *al-Da'wa*, June 1981, 28. 'Abd al-'Aziz and 'Abd al-Mu'nim, "'Awdat al-Ruh ila Qahirat al-Alaf Mi'dhana," 44–45.

36. 'Abd al-'Aziz and 'Abd al-Mu'nim, "'Awdat al-Ruh ila Qahirat al-Alaf Mi'dhana," 44–45.

37. *Al-Mustashfa al-Khayri al-Markazi*, advertising brochure, n.d. I appreciate Tarek Masoud's sharing this material with me. Masoud also discusses this episode in *Counting Islam* (2014a, 77).

38. Malt, "Nida' ila al-Muslimin," 63; Ahmad al-Malt, "Nida' min al-Jam'iyya al-Tibbiyya al-Islamiyya bi-l-Qahira: Ya Muslimun! [A call from the Islamic Medical Association in Cairo: O Muslims!]," *al-Da'wa*, February 1978, 56.

39. Advertisement in *al-Da'wa*, August 1979, 23; Malt, "Al-Jam'iyya al-Tibbiyya al-Islamiyya," 57. See also the announcement of the bank account opening in *al-Da'wa*, April 1978, 51.

40. *Al-Da'wa*, June 1981, 29.

41. Malt, "Al-Jam'iyya al-Tibbiyya al-Islamiyya," 57.

42. Malt, "Al-Mustashfa al-Islami al-Markazi," 28.

43. Qarar Ra'is Jumhuriyyat Misr al-'Arabiyya Raqm 492 li-l-Sana 1981, reproduced in Hamid and 'Arab (2002, 634–35).

44. Al-Idara al-'Ama li-l-Jam'iyyat wa-l-Ittihadat, "Qarar Raqm 2 li-l-Sana 1981" [Decision Number 2 for the Year 1981], *al-Waqa'i' al-Misriyya*, November 11, 1981, 17.

45. In a contemporary cable, however, U.S. ambassador to Egypt Herman Eilts noted that Sadat's strategy to empower Islamist groups was akin to "playing with fire." See "Muslim Resurgence: Fanatic and Mainstream," U.S. Embassy Cairo, Cable No. 1976CAIRO16440_b, November 26, 1976, https://search.wikileaks.org/plusd/cables/1976CAIRO16440_b.html.

46. Author interview, IMA employee A, February 2, 2013.

47. Author interview, IMA facility manager A, May 11, 2013.

48. Author interview, IMA executive B, May 16, 2013.

49. The clinic plays a small but critical role in the history of modern Islamic militancy. In his memoirs, the current al-Qa'ida leader, Dr. Ayman al-Zawahiri, recounts that he was working in the Sayyida Zaynab clinic in 1980 when the clinic's director convinced him to go to Afghanistan as part of a medical relief effort. It was in Afghanistan that he met Usama bin Ladin and joined al-Qa'ida (2001, 59). The director Zawahiri mentions was probably Malt, who was quite active in medical relief efforts in Afghanistan (Malt 1993, 215–45).

50. Muhammad 'Abd al-Salam, "Surur Yuhasim al-Fi'a . . . wa-Thalatha 'ala Maqa'id al-'Ummal fi al-Sayyida Zaynab" [Surour clinches the professional's seat, while three contest the worker's seat in Sayyida Zaynab], *al-Ahram*, September 21, 2010, http://digital.ahram.org.eg/articles.aspx?Serial=266470&eid=2555.

51. Author interview, IMA executive A, January 15, 2013.

52. Author interview, IMA facility manager C, January 19, 2013. See also "Mubarak Yaftatih Ahdath Mustashfa 'Askari wa-Yazur Darihay al-Sadat wa-l-Jundi al-Majhul fi 'Id Tahrir Sina'" [Mubarak inaugurates the latest military hospital and visits the two tombs of Anwar al-Sadat and the Unknown Soldier on the occasion of Sinai Liberation Day], *al-Ahram*, April 24, 1992.

53. "Al-Jam'iyya al-Tibbiyya al-Islamiyya" [The Islamic Medical Association], Dar al-Salam Hospital Website, n.d., http://goo.gl/qpNVni.

54. "Al-Hasuma al-Fajira: Hadm Mustashfa Khayri Dakhm 'ala Ra's al-Marid wa-l-Atibba' li-anna Muhasib 'ala al-Ikhwan" [The ridiculous rivalry: Destroying a charity hospital over the head of patients and doctors because of its relationship to the Brotherhood], *Nafidhat Misr*, December 7, 2009, http://www.egyptwindow.net/news_Details. aspx?News_ID=5941.

55. "Al-Ikhwan: al-Mushawarat al-Mukathifa Tamhidan li-'Aqd al-Intikhabat al-Ra'isiyya al-Misriyya" [The Brotherhood: Intense discussions in advance of the upcoming Egyptian presidential elections], *Islamonline*, December 11, 2009, http://islamonline.com/ news/articles/25/vdi582b8ueuknyvi.html.

56. Video clips of the demolition attempts in the author's possession, both dated December 14, 2009.

57. Author interview, IMA executive B, May 16, 2013.

58. Video clip: "Al-Jam'iyya al-Tibbiyya al-Islamiyya: Qidaya Mukhalifat Idariyya am Qidaya Siyasiyya?" [The Islamic Medical Association: An administrative case or a political one?], https://www.youtube.com/watch?v=j0zHrB39r1o.

59. "Al-Hasuma al-Fajira."

60. "Hukm Tarikhi didd Wazir bi-Man' Hadm Mustashfa al-Jam'iyya al-Tibbiyya ba'd Hadmiha bi-Shakl Hamji" [Historic judgment against the governor forbidding the destruction of the (Islamic) Medical Association's hospital following its brutal destruction], *Nafidhat Misr*, December 18, 2009, http://www.egyptwindow.net/news_Details. aspx?News_ID=6126.

61. Author interview, IMA employee A, February 2, 2013. See also "Taqrir Mustashfa al-Sharabiyya" [Report on the Sharabiyya Hospital], *Murasilun*, n.d., http://www.youtube. com/watch?v=BB9Ef5KXtmI.

62. Author interview, IMA employee B, May 1, 2013.

63. Author interviews, IMA facility manager A, May 11, 2013; IMA employee C, May 9, 2013; IMA employee D, May 11, 2013; IMA facility manager C, January 19, 2013.

64. Author interview, IMA employee E, November 11, 2012.

65. Ahmad al-Sukkari, "Al-Sadat Yatarid 'ala Hall Jam'iyyat 'al-Muwasat'" [Al-Sadat disagrees with the dissolution of the "Muwasat Association"], *al-Wafd*, December 22, 2010, http://goo.gl/rpkTv9; Mohammed Essawy, "260 Muwazzafan wa-Maridan bi-Mustashfa al-Muwasat bi-l-Manufiyya Yatathahirun Ihtijajan 'ala Qarar Hall al-Jam'iyya" [260 employees and patients of Muwasat Hospital in Manufiyya rally to protest the decision to dissolve the (Muwasat) Association], *al-Ahram*, December 21, 2010, http://digital. ahram.org.eg/articles.aspx?Serial=379034&eid=715.

66. "Li-Madha al-Musharika fi al-Intikhabat" [Why participate in the elections]? *Ikhwanonline*, October 10, 2013, http://goo.gl/13a6SU. See also "Al-Jihaz al-Khidmi li-l-Jama'a Yahtazz" [The (Brotherhood's) service organization is shaken], *al-Mal*, October 26, 2010, http://www.almalnews.com/Pages/StoryDetails.aspx?ID=13708.

4. INSIDE THE ISLAMIST ADVANTAGE

1. In Egypt, the term "middle class" encompasses both an objective statement of one's material conditions and a more diffuse and perception-based categorization of social status (Wickham 2002, 36–37). Both sides of this definition are important to the argument

here. On the one hand, the role of material conditions ties into the fact that visitors to the IMA are not in search of charity; they do not expect—nor do they generally receive—free care. They have a certain amount of surplus income, through a government or private-sector job, that allows them to patronize fee-based services rather than proceeding hat in hand to the various free and discounted public or charity options. On the other hand, the formation of a distinct "middle-class status" exercises an important effect on decision making. The growth of consumerist lifestyles during the infitāḥ created a situation whereby "lower class" became synonymous with "uses public services," while an ability to avoid these ignominies was the mark of more advanced social status. In the sense that the IMA allowed those who could not afford the private "investment" or "international" hospitals another way to avoid public facilities, it knitted into this broader understanding of what it meant to be a "middle-class" Egyptian.

2. "Sadat Vows Protection against Want, Senility, and Death," May 7, 1980, NFE 014/1 (FCO 93/2370).

3. For example, even Egypt's poor began to increasingly visit private clinics, even at tremendous expense, because of a desire to avoid public facilities (Nandakumar, Chawla, and Khan 2000). This caused significant inequalities because of the lower classes' much lower discretionary income. I appreciate Melani Cammett's articulating this point to me.

4. Author interview, January 23, 2013.

5. Among the questions included in the index were these: In your opinion did the physician spend enough time with you? How long did you wait to be examined? Was the examination room clean?

6. Yasmine Fathi, "Egypt's Public Hospitals: From Bad to Worse," al-Ahram, November 25, 2012, http://english.ahram.org.eg/NewsContent/1/64/58686/Egypt/Politics-/Egypts-public-hospitals-From-bad-to-worse.aspx.

7. Amr Adly, "Objective Notes on Hesham Geneina's Corruption Report," Mada Masr, July 12, 2016, http://www.madamasr.com/en/2016/07/12/opinion/economy/objective-notes-on-hesham-geneinas-corruption-report.

8. Three hundred eighty-seven respondents reported not having to pay a bribe; 214 reported having to pay "once or twice"; 133 reported having to pay "a few times"; and 75 reported having to pay "often."

9. Global Corruption Barometer, https://www.transparency.org/gcb2013/country?country=egypt.

10. "Awwal Jam'iyya Tibbiyya Islamiyya Tukawwan fi Misr: La Budda min Ijad al-Tabib al-Muslim al-Mutamayyiz bi-Shakhsiyyatihi" [The first Islamic medical association established in Egypt: The exceptional Muslim doctor is distinguished by his character], al-Da'wa, January 1978, 61.

11. Author interview, January 23, 2013. In his memoirs, Futuh cites Malt as one of the Brothers who introduced him to the movement in the early 1970s (2012, 78).

12. "Al-Jam'iyya al-Tibbiyya al-Islamiyya [The Islamic Medical Association]," al-Da'wa, November 1977, inside front cover.

13. Author interviews, IMA facility manager A, May 11, 2013; IMA employee C, May 9, 2013.

14. Author interview, IMA employee F, October 31, 2012.

15. Author interview, IMA executive A, January 15, 2013.

16. "The Egyptian Muslim Brotherhood Building Bases of Support: A Research Paper," NESA 86–10025, Central Intelligence Agency/Directorate of Intelligence, May 1986, 13.

17. Author interviews, IMA facility manager D, February 2, 2013; IMA employee A, February 2, 2013.

18. Author interview, IMA employee C, May 9, 2013. Some hospitals reported problems with patients reselling free or subsidized medicine on the black market,

requiring the facility to be more stringent with investigations and taking protective measures—for instance, distributing smaller amounts or removing the labels from the medicine.

19. Author interview, IMA employee D, May 11, 2013.

20. But because *al-Hikma* is not approved by the national press council, it must be distributed for free (for instance, at the IMA's hospitals); this method tends to reach mostly those already in the IMA's orbit.

21. Muhammad Taha, "D. 'Ali Abu Sayf: Basus wa-l-Khalil wa-Bani Suwayf Mustashfayat Jadida Tadkhul al-Khidma Qariban" [Dr. 'Ali Abu Sayf: Basus, al-Khalil, and Bani Suwayf Hospitals are entering service soon], *al-Jam'iyya al-Tibbiyya al-Islamiyya*, August 15, 2014, http://ima-egy.net/2013-09-24-14-31-06/497-2014-08-15-00-57-03.

22. Author interview, IMA executive B, May 16, 2013.

23. Author interview, IMA facility manager B, May 9, 2013.

24. Author interview, IMA employee B, May 1, 2013.

25. Author interview, IMA facility manager B, May 9, 2013.

26. Author interview, IMA employee E, November 11, 2012.

27. Author interview, IMA employee C, May 9, 2013.

28. Author interview, IMA employee B, May 1, 2013.

29. Author interview, IMA employee C, May 9, 2013.

30. Author interview, IMA employee E, November 11, 2012.

31. Author interview, IMA employee E, November 11, 2012.

32. Author interview, IMA hospital manager A, May 11, 2013.

33. Author interview, IMA executive B, November 8, 2012.

34. "Al-Faruq Tukrim 18 'Amila Mithaliyya min al-'Amilat bi-l-Mustashfa" [Al-Faruq (Hospital) Recognizes 18 as Exemplary (Female) Hospital Employees], *al-Jam'iyya al-Tibbiyya al-Islamiyya*, November 2, 2013, http://ima-egy.net/branche/183-18; "Al-Hadi Yukrim Abna' al-'Amilin al-Mutafawwiqin" [Al-Hadi (Hospital) Honors the Children of Outstanding Employees], *al-Jam'iyya al-Tibbiyya al-Islamiyya*, February 21, 2014, http://ima-egy.net/message/312-2014-02-21-02-27-15.

35. The historical record of the Brotherhood's provision of medical services prior to the formation of the IMA also yielded little evidence that discrimination was prevalent. In certain issues of the Muslim Brotherhood's newspapers from the interwar period, one doctor (Ibrahim Abu Sunna) advertised a 50 percent discount for members of the Brotherhood at his clinic (see, for instance, *Jaridat al-Ikhwan al-Muslimin*, February 28, 1935, 15, and *Jaridat al-Ikhwan al-Muslimin*, May 21, 1935, 39). But even in these cases it is not clear that the effort was anything more than one doctor's marketing strategy. 'Abduh Mustafa Dasuqi and al-Sayyid Ramadan al-'Abadi open their discussion of the founding of the Brotherhood's official medical section in 1944 by mentioning that "therefore the Brotherhood decided to establish a general charity clinic, opening their doors to all social trends [*kull tawaif al-sha'b*]" (2013, 19). Finally, in his valuable account of the Brotherhood's social service activity during that same period, Muhammad Zaki specifically dispels the rumor that these facilities discriminate: "It is worth mentioning that every one of these facilities is for all, Egyptians and foreigners, Muslim and non-Muslim. One should not think that these are services for the Brotherhood only" (1980, 216).

36. Rida 'Abd al-Wadud, "Safahat Khalida min Hayat al-Tabib al-Mujahid Duktur Ahmad al-Malt," [Immortal pages from the life of the *mujahid* doctor, Dr. Ahmad al-Malt]," *al-Hikma,* July 2012, 26.

37. Ahmad al-Malt, "Nida' ila al-Muslimin: Mashru' al-Mustashfa al-Islami" [Call to the Muslims: The Islamic Hospital project], *al-Da'wa*, March 1980, 63. See also "Tasa'ulat

hawla: al-Jamaiyya al-Tibbiyya al-Islamiyya" [Questions about the Islamic Medical Association], *al-Da'wa*, October 1978, 42.

38. See also the short video "Muqaddimat al-Jam'iyya al-Tibbiyya al-Islamiyya" [Introducing the Islamic Medical Association]," n.d., https://www.youtube.com/watch?v=6PKj51Kgt-I&feature=youtube_gdata.

39. Author interview, IMA executive A, January 15, 2013.

40. Author interview, January 23, 2013.

41. The effect was similar to what Steve Negus charted fifteen years earlier, when he wrote, "Posters in Brotherhood-influenced hospitals might exhort Muslims to pray, women to wear the *hegab* [headscarf]," but "there is never a quid pro quo for services rendered, Brotherhood observers say. No one was ever told 'You are receiving this operation courtesy of the Muslim Brotherhood.'" See Steve Negus, "Down but Not Out: The Muslim Brotherhood Keeps a Low Profile but Their Main Activity, Charity Work, Still Goes On," *Cairo Times*, April 3, 1997.

42. "Hadith Dhikrayat ma'a Khalid 'Abd al-Qadir 'Awda . . . 1" [Discussing the Memories with Dr. Khaled 'Abd al-Qadir 'Awda . . . 1], *IkhwanTube*, February 7, 2010, https://goo.gl/wxbuZm. I appreciate Aaron Rock-Singer's bringing this source to my attention.

43. Brotherhood periodicals during the period printed the names of those who contributed money to the publishing efforts. See, for example, *Jaridat al-Ikhwan al-Muslimin*, February 2–7, 1934, 15–18.

44. Author interview, January 23, 2013.

45. Author interview, IMA executive A, January 15, 2013.

46. Author interview, January 23, 2013.

47. Author interview, IMA employee G, October 31, 2012.

48. Author interview, IMA executive A, January 15, 2013.

49. Author interview, Hizb al-Asala Doctor A, April 25, 2013.

50. As Janine Clark argues, in Egypt the poor tend to visit specific *doctors*, while the middle class visit *facilities* (2004, 72–73).

51. Author interviews, al-Jam'iyya al-Shar'iyya facility manager A, December 10, 2012; al-Jam'iyya al-Shar'iyya facility manager B, December 10, 2012.

52. A handbook from the organization lists 332 mosques (al-Jam'iyya al-Shar'iyya, n.d., 10), but in a 2005 interview, the organization's leader claimed that it controlled twenty times that, over six thousand mosques). See Humam 'Abd al-Mabud, "Rais al-Jam'iyya al-Shar'iyya bi-Misr: Nushrif 'ala 6000 Masjid" [President of al-Jam'iyya al-Shar'iyya in Egypt: We Supervise 6000 Mosques]," *almoslim.net*, April 4, 2005, http://www.almoslim.net/node/86714.

53. Amro Hassan, "Egypt: Islamic Charity Spending Is Also an Economic Pillar, Figures Show," *Los Angeles Times*, February 21, 2010, http://latimesblogs.latimes.com/babylonbeyond/2010/09/egypt-islamic-charity-spending-is-also-an-economic-pillar-figures-show.html.

54. Author interview, al-Jam'iyya al-Shar'iyya Doctor A, April 21, 2013.

55. Sarah Childress, "Muslim Brotherhood Spokesman Detained in Cairo," *PBS Frontline*, September 17, 2013, http://www.pbs.org/wgbh/frontline/article/muslim-brotherhood-spokesman-detained-in-cairo.

56. I appreciate Tarek Masoud's bringing this source to my attention.

57. "Awqaf Minister on Mosque Extremism Controls," *al-Musawwar*, September 23, 1994. Translated in FBIS Daily Report, Near East & South Asia, FBIS-NES-94-190, September 30, 1994.

58. Shortly after the military coup, Egypt's new rulers fired a shot across al-Jam'iyya al-Shar'iyya's bow, placing the group under investigation for supporting the Brotherhood

and moving to strip it of its responsibilities in the country's religious sector. After a brief period they reconciled, the message apparently having been delivered.

5. THE POLITICAL GEOGRAPHY OF ISLAMIST SOCIAL SERVICE PROVISION

1. "Qarar Ra'is Jumhuriyyat Misr al-'Arabiyya bi-l-Qanun Raqm 206 li-l-Sana 1990 fi Shan Tahdid al-Dawa'ir al-Intikhabiyya li-Majlis al-Sha'b" [Decision by law of the president of the Egyptian Arab Republic regarding constituting the borders of the electoral districts for the People's Assembly], *al-Jarida al-Rasmiyya*, October 6, 1990.

2. "What SIGINT Revealed about the Egyptian Election" October 5, 2005, https://theintercept.com/snowden-sidtoday/4389789-what-sigint-revealed-about-the-egyptian-election. I appreciate Elizabeth Nugent's bringing this to my attention.

3. Blaydes discusses the reverse of this assumption: citizens understand that if they elect opposition parliamentarians, the regime will retaliate by reducing public funding to that district (2011, 64–76).

4. The al-Ahram Center compiled the candidate numbers in its study of the 1990 elections (Din 1991, 39–44).

5. *Al-Ahram*, November 27, 1995, 38–44.

6. It is not clear if a full pre-election list was ever published, although a first-round list did appear in *al-Jumhuriyya*, October 11, 2000, 17–19. As a proxy for these elections, I use the number of candidates who registered for them in the first twenty-four hours after the registration period opened. See "Ha'ula' Qadamu Awraqahum . . . li-l-Barlaman al-Amal . . . fi 24 Sa'a" [Here are those who've submitted their paperwork . . . (to contest) the parliamentary elections . . . in (the first) 24 hours], *al-Jumhuriyya*, September 23, 2000, 3–5.

7. I appreciate Tarek Masoud for discussing this idea and sharing the candidate entry data for the 2005 and 2010 elections with me.

8. Technically I used a large-scale pretest of the 2006 census, which also—unlike the census itself—asked a respondent's religion (Muslim, Christian, or "other"), which is crucial for the analysis. For more details, see the appendix.

9. An unfortunate characteristic of Egyptian electoral law during this period (1990–2010) was that in some cases the districts were not coterminous with the underlying qism or markaz. In those cases, the electoral district was described in the law as consisting of "All villages [*shiyākhāt*] of *Markaz* [name] but with some villages from *Markaz* [other name]." As a map of these shiyākhāt does not exist with the census data that I use available at the qism and markaz level, I use my best judgement to assign the entire qism or markaz to the appropriate electoral district or drop it if the assignment cannot be made with a degree of confidence. Note also that the nature of the 2006 census subsample aggregates smaller qism and markaz in governorates, which also contributes to missing data. Using the markaz and qism as the level of analysis does have the benefit, however, of easing comparisons in the post-Mubarak period, during which the electoral map was redrawn (discussed in chapter 7).

10. Respondents were asked which of the following they owned: an automobile, a landline phone, a mobile phone, an internet connection, a computer, an automatic clothes washing machine, a freezer, a refrigerator, a TV, a VCR, or a radio.

11. These plots are drawn from an OLS regression model, with included variables to control for sectarian balance (percentage Muslim), density (a logged measure of persons per rooms), and available infrastructure (percentage of electrified dwellings). Full information, including traditional regression table, is available in the appendix.

12. In fact, it could tell us the exact opposite—areas of strong Brotherhood local networks might have been *more* likely to trigger outcome-altering interference because the regime could prearrange rigging efforts. In these cases, coding on candidate success might overweight those districts in which the Brotherhood was comparatively weaker, which

allowed it to take advantage of an under-the-radar surge in turnout to catch the regime by surprise.

13. The Brotherhood boycotted the 1990 elections in protest over the abrupt change in electoral system.

14. An online appendix contains a detailed discussion of how this data set was created: http://www.steventbrooke.com.

15. Because the outcome variable is a percentage (i.e., bounded between zero and one), I rely on a fractional logit model, as opposed to the OLS regression above. The same control variables are also included. See the appendix for more details.

16. Ben Hubbard, "Muslim Brotherhood's Machine Helps in Egypt Vote," Associated Press, November 30, 2011, http://goo.gl/wO2Qcy.

17. "Egypt's Muslim Brotherhood Flexes Potent Political Force," *PBS Newshour*, September 14, 2011, http://www.pbs.org/newshour/bb/world-july-dec11-egypt_09-14.

18. Author interview, IMA employee D, May 11, 2013.

19. Author interviews, IMA executive B, November 8, 2012; IMA employee A, February 2, 2013.

20. Author interview, IMA employee C, May 9, 2013.

21. Author interviews, IMA executive A, January 15, 2013; ʿAbd al-Muʿnim Abu al-Futuh, January 23, 2013.

22. Author interview, IMA executive A, January 15, 2013.

23. Author interview, IMA executive A, January 15, 2013.

24. Author interview, IMA employee G, October 31, 2012.

25. Author interview, IMA executive B, May 16, 2013.

26. Author interview, IMA executive A, January 15, 2013.

27. Author interviews, IMA executive A, January 7, 2014; IMA facility manager B, November 8, 2012. See also Jad al-Mawli Muhammad, "Marakiz al-Kuli bi-l-Jamʿiyya al-Tibbiyya al-Islamiyya . . . Khidmat Insaniyya bi-Haja li-l-Damm" [Dialysis centers of the Islamic Medical Association . . . humanitarian services in need of support], *al-Jamʿiyya al-Tibbiyya al-Islamiyya*, January 2, 2014, http://ima-egy.net/2013-09-24-14-31-06/269-2014-01-19-14-34-44; Ahmad Hasan, "Markaz Naʾima li-l-Ghasil al-Kulwi Yuʿalij 3500 Marid Sanawiyyan" [The Mercy Center for dialysis cares for 3,500 patients yearly]," *al-Jamʿiyya al-Tibbiyya al-Islamiyya*, November 2, 2014, http://ima-egy.net/programs/578-3500.

28. Muhyi al-Din al-Zayit, "Rajul min al-Khalidin bi-ʿAmalihi" [An immortal man through his work], *Ikhwanwiki*, n.d, http://goo.gl/SNDmUv.

29. Author interview, IMA executive A, January 15, 2013.

30. Author interview, ʿAbd al-Muʿnim Abu al-Futuh, January 23, 2013.

31. Available at http://www.imaegy.com/l3.php?id=36.

32. Available at http://http://wikimapia.org.

33. I use a dummy, rather than a count, because the IMA would occasionally use nearby but physically separate buildings to expand capacity or add new services such as a dialysis center to an existing hospital facility (for example, see figure 5.7).

34. The same control variables as above—percentage Muslim, percentage dwellings electrified, and the logged crowding variable—are also included. Cluster robust standard errors also included at the electoral district. Discussion in the appendix.

35. Muhyi al-Din al-Zayit, "Rajul min al-Khalidin."

36. "Al-Murshid al-ʿAm Yaʿni Dr. Lutfi Shahwan" [The General Guide mourns Dr. Lutfi Shahwan], *Ikhwanonline*, August 7, 2008, http://www.ikhwanonline.com/new/Article.aspx?ArtID=30863&SecID=0. See also Masoud 2014a, 77.

37. Al-ʿAriyan won, and al-Gazar lost. See "Asmaʾ al-Murashshahin ʿala Qawaim Hizb al-ʿAmal" [Names of candidates on the Labor Party's list], *al-Shaʿb*, March 10, 1987, 7.

38. Picture available online at http://goo.gl/YEbxlp.

39. Campaign biography of Muhammad Gamal Hishmat, 2000 elections, http://albehira 2000.faithweb.com/Pages/heshmat.htm.

40. "Muhandis Ashraf Badr al-Din: Faris Lajnat al-Muwazana bi-l-Barlaman al-Misri" [Engineer Ashraf Badr al-Din, a knight of the budget committee in the Egyptian parliament], Facebook, October 5, 2010, https://goo.gl/u3Y1UK.

41. Campaign biography of Muhammad 'Ali Bishr, http://www.ikhwanonline.net/data/baralman2005/ikhwan3.htm. Bishr was also the group's candidate in 1987 (Siyam 2006, 106).

42. "Ta'arruf 'ala Dr. Hisham al-Suli, Murash Hizb al-Hurriya wa-l-'Adala Fardi" [Get to know Dr. Hisham al-Suli, Freedom and Justice Party candidate for the individual seat], Ismailiyya Online, November 19, 2011, https://www.facebook.com/freedom.justice. ismailia/posts/319474861414439.

43. "Al-Marhala al-Ula" [Stage One], Ikhwanwiki, n.d., http://goo.gl/sDqMbe.

44. "Al-Marhala al-Ula."

45. "Al-Marhala al-Ula."

46. Author interview, IMA facility manager D, February 2, 2013.

47. "Al-Marhala al-Ula."

48. Ahmad Hasan, "Al-Duktur Abu 'Ila Qarni . . . Rihlat 'Ata' ma'a Mustashfa al-Hawamdiyya" [Doctor Abu 'Ila Qarni . . . a voyage of giving with the Hawamdiyya Hospital], al-Jam'iyya al-Tibbiyya al-Islamiyya, December 27, 2014, http://ima-egy.net/media-assembly/596-2014-12-27-00-15-09.

49. Yasir Hadi, "Abu 'Ila Qarni Yad'u li-Intikhab Dr. Gamal bi-l-Hawamdiyya" [Abu 'Ila Qarni campaigns for the election of Dr. Gamal (Qarni) in Hawamdiyya], Ikhwanwiki, n.d., http://goo.gl/qmo6cF; Shayma' Galal, "Al-Na'ib Gamal Qarni . . . Khidmat ma'a al-Dawr al-Riqabi wa-l-Tashri'i" [Parliamentary deputy Gamal Qarni . . . services along with a legislative and oversight role], Ikhwanonline, October 24, 2010, http://www.ikhwanonline. com/new/Article.aspx?ArtID=72655&SecID=0.

50. Author interview, May 9, 2013.

51. Author interview, January 23, 2013.

52. "Qanun Raqm 38 li-l-Sana 1972" [Law 38 of 1972], al-Jarida al-Rasmiyya, September 28, 1972, 550–54.

53. "Qanun Raqm 114 li-l-Sana 1983" [Law 114 of 1983], al-Jarida al-Rasmiyya, August 11, 1983, 1864–82.

54. "Qanun Raqm 188 li-l-Sana 1986" [Law 188 of 1986], al-Jarida al-Rasmiyya, December 31, 1986, 3-8.

55. "Qanun Raqm 68 li-l-Sana 2010" [Law 68 of 2010], al-Jarida al-Rasmiyya, May 18, 2010, 2–201.

56. "Marsum bi-Qanun Raqm 121 li-l-Sana 2011 bi-Tadil Ahkam al-Qanun Raqm 206 li-l-Sana 1990" [Decree/ law 121 for 2011 amending some judgments of Law 206 of 1990], al-Jarida al-Rasmiyya, September 26, 2011, 8–82.

57. Muhammad Taha, "Dirasa: 'al-Jam'iyya al-Tibbiyya' Tu'alij nahwa 7 Milyun Marid khilal 4 Sanawat" [Study: "(Islamic) Medical Association" treats approximately seven million sick over four years], al-Jam'iyya al-Tibbiyya al-Islamiyya, January 2, 2015, http://www.ima-egy.net/2013-09-24-14-31-06/607-7-4.

58. The anti-Brotherhood attitude at the time this survey was conducted (post-coup) potentially underreports the actual value by establishing significant incentives to downplay one's involvement with the organization.

59. Data for four boxes are missing. A number of boxes were often colocated because of the necessity to have separate polling stations for men and women. On the assumption that the errors of colocated individual boxes are correlated, in the below analysis I collapse

the results of all colocated boxes into a single precinct at that one location. This yields 497 precincts, the unit of analysis. I am particularly indebted to Bernard Rougier and Hala Bayoumi for providing these data.

60. I follow the rough approach of Braun (2016) by comparing buffers of various distances to compensate for the fact that threshold distances are not immediately obvious.

61. Ballot box icon in figure 5.7 by Nevit Dilmen, CC BY-SA 3.0, https://commons.wikimedia.org/w/index.php?curid=31922999.

6. ELECTING TO SERVE

1. All quotes and information come from Mohammed Galal's testimony at https://www.youtube.com/watch?v=rHi4ciTzyr8(posted May 29, 2014). Note that the video is an official release from the Islamic Medical Association and thus should be considered in that light, although there is no evidence he was falsifying or exaggerating his experience. See also the patient testimonials at https://www.youtube.com/watch?v=_dazTLBjQCE and https://www.youtube.com/watch?v=wd8m1oSSkqk.

2. Brochures in author's possession.

3. The cartoons in figures 6.1 and 6.2 are reproduced from Zayd (2006).

4. "Al-Jam'iyya al-Tibbiyya al-Islamiyya" [The Islamic Medical Association], al-Da'wa, November 1977, inside front cover.

5. "Awwal Jam'iyya Tibbiyya Islamiyya Tukawwan fi Misr: La Budda min Ijad al-Tabib al-Muslim al-Mutamayyiz bi-Shakhsiyyatihi" [The first Islamic medical association established in Egypt: The exceptional Muslim doctor is distinguished by his character], al-Da'wa, January 1978, 20–21.

6. Author interview, IMA employee A, February 2, 2013.

7. Author interview, IMA executive A, January 13, 2013.

8. Author interview, IMA executive B, November 8, 2012.

9. Author interview, IMA facility manager B, November 8, 2012.

10. Author interviews, IMA employee A, February 2, 2013; IMA facility manager D, February 2, 2013.

11. Author interview, IMA employee B, May 1, 2013.

12. Author interview, former Muslim Brotherhood member A, September 18, 2012. In his study of the Jordanian Muslim Brotherhood, Quintan Wiktorowicz found a similar arrangement: one member of the Brotherhood described how beneficiaries "voluntarily find themselves morally indebted to the movement. . . . When the movement is in elections or needs support, they repay the debt" (2001, 109). This approximates research on clientelism that focuses less on the instrumental exchange and strict monitoring of the interaction than on the ways that a sense of reciprocity or inherent "fair play" for receiving benefits compels recipients to support the provider organization (Auyero 1999; Finan and Schechter 2012; Lawson and Greene 2014). While it is likely that those who visited the Brotherhood's social services felt some degree of attachment to the organization for providing them care, this pathway is distinct from the reputation-based argument I have articulated. Briefly, in this conception recipients feel that they *have* to support the provider organization politically, whereas I argue that they *want* to.

13. Futuh's use of "bastards" (*awlād al-zinā*) was to underscore the difference between what he saw as the Brotherhood's method of connecting with Egyptians and the behavior of other parties, who used social services in a classically clientelist fashion, which meant that they (supposedly) did not care about the recipients of their services beyond what their votes meant on election day.

14. Author interview, January 23, 2013.

15. The Cairo-based Egyptian Center for Public Opinion Research (Baseera) carried out the survey using Computer-Aided Telephone Interviewing (CATI) in May 2014. The

survey was conducted with Jason Brownlee of the University of Texas at Austin. Further details on the survey are available in the appendix.

16. One potential comparison could be the Salafi Nur party, yet this party emerged only after February 2011, and its social service network was almost completely informal.

17. The questions did not list specific candidates by name. In the parliamentary elections that most closely preceded the survey experiment (November 2011–January 2012), the Brotherhood fielded candidates in every electoral district.

18. This hypothetical framing ("If the Brotherhood did participate . . .") was also adopted in order to suggest that the regime had acquiesced to the Brotherhood's political participation, giving respondents cover to oppose the regime's current position.

19. Because cases with a missing value for one of the three trait assessments (honest, capable, modest) were dropped, the size of the treatment and control groups is smaller in figure 6.4 than in figure 6.3.

20. Multiple measures of socioeconomic status were considered, including more subjective measures of satisfaction with one's economic situation as well as direct queries on levels of income. In the pilot surveys these questions generated confusion, and an asset index was ultimately chosen based on the survey company's expertise with the Egyptian case, the space and cognitive demands of a telephone survey, and the available literature (Filmer and Pritchett 2001; Sahn and Stifel 2003). The appendix reproduces the experimental manipulation with what is assumed to be the closest available proxy for socioeconomic status—educational attainment—and finds substantively similar results.

21. The appendix reports a variety of robustness checks and different presentations of the data, including presentation via a traditional regression table instead of the difference-of-means style in this chapter. It also contains a correction table to account for the issue of multiple comparisons (the corrected levels of α do not change the results here).

22. Full output available in the appendix.

23. It is important to note that the results here are valid so long as the sequential ignorability assumption obtains. This is not directly testable; however, the appendix reports the results of an analysis showing that the above procedure is robust to fairly significant violations of this critical assumption ($\rho = .6341$).

24. Word cloud created by wordle (www.wordle.net). For presentation purposes, those descriptive terms mentioned fewer than five times are not included in the word cloud.

7. MOHAMMED MORSI'S MACHINE

1. David D. Kirkpatrick, "Blow to Transition as Court Dissolves Egypt's Parliament," *New York Times*, June 14, 2012, https://www.nytimes.com/2012/06/15/world/middleeast/new-political-showdown-in-egypt-as-court-invalidates-parliament.html.

2. Ziad al-Ali, "The Constitutional Court's Mark on Egypt's Elections," *Foreign Policy*, June 6, 2013, http://foreignpolicy.com/2013/06/06/the-constitutional-courts-mark-on-egypts-elections.

3. See, for instance, Hisham al-Miyani, "'Ajil . . . al-Ri'asa: Ba'd Ijra'at Intikhabat Majlis al-Nuwwab 25 Fabrayir" [Breaking . . . the presidency: Preparations for the lower house parliamentary elections begin February 25], *Bawabat al-Ahram*, January 9, 2013, http://gate.ahram.org.eg/NewsContentPrint/13/70/293358.aspx; Adam Makary, "Egypt to Hold Parliamentary Elections in April," *CNN*, February 22, 2013, http://www.cnn.com/2013/02/21/world/meast/egypt-elections.

4. Neil MacFarquhar, "In Egypt, Fears of Mubarak's Outlawed Party, 'the Remnant,' Loom over Vote, *New York Times*, November 14, 2011, http://www.nytimes.com/2011/11/15/world/middleeast/in-egypt-mubarak-loyalists-are-ousted-but-still-feared.html; "Nus Fatwa al-Shaykh 'Emad 'Effat bi-Tahrim Intikhab al-Felul" [Text of

Shaykh 'Emad 'Effat's fatwa prohibiting voting for remnants (of the National Democratic Party)], May 29, 2012, https://old.egyptwindow.net/news_Details.aspx?News_ID=19702.

5. No other party, including Nur, mobilized its cadres for these contests. Nur, in particular, claimed that it was waiting to begin outreach efforts until a specific date for elections was set. Author interview, Nur party official A, February 3, 2013.

6. "Hamlat 'Ma'an Nabni Misr' bi-l-Arqam" [The "Together We Build Egypt" campaign by the numbers], Amal al-Umma, May 20, 2013, http://www.amlalommah.net/new/wap.php?id=34769&mod=article.

7. See, for example, 'Adil al-Sha'ir, "Al-Hurriya wa-l-'Adala Yunazzim Qafila Tibbiyya bi-l-Sharqiyya dimna Fa'iliyyat Hamlat Bina'" [Freedom and Justice organizes a medical caravan in Sharqiyya as part of the "building" campaign events], al-Ahram, January 24, 2013, http://gate.ahram.org.eg/NewsContentPrint/5/35/299795.aspx.

8. The flyer is available online at https://goo.gl/mC3MXS.

9. For instance, a May 1988 story in the Islamist magazine Liwa' al-Islam that reported on a Brotherhood deputy from the 1987 parliament in his home district relayed that he had organized a blood donation campaign. Accompanying the story was a photo of the event, prominently displaying an "Islam Is the Solution" banner looming over the enterprise. See "Hamlat li-l-Tabarru' bi-l-Dam taht Shi'ar 'al-Islam Huwa al-Hall'" [Blood donation drive under the slogan "Islam Is the Solution"], Liwa al-Islam, May 17, 1988, 36. Earlier in Egypt's transition period (i.e., prior to the Together We Build Egypt campaign), the Brotherhood had come under fire for providing at least one medical caravan that offered female genital mutilation. I appreciate Vickie Langohr for bringing this episode to my attention and providing a copy of that flyer.

10. Muhammad al-Tuhami, "Al-Ighatha al-Insaniyya Tajri 300 'Amaliyyat fi al-'Uyun Majjanan bi-Wahat Siwa" [Humanitarian relief effort carries out 300 free eye surgeries in Siwa Oasis], Ikhwanonline, May 5, 2013, http://ikhwanonline.com/Article.aspx?ArtID=148331&SecID=480.

11. Khayr Allah Fuad, "Ghadan: Qafila Tibbiyya li-l-Hurriya wa-l-'Adala bi-Kafr al-Shaykh" [Tomorrow: Freedom and Justice Party medical caravan in Kafr al-Shaykh], Fitu [Veto] Yawm, March 7, 2013, http://www.masress.com/veto/153701.

12. Muhammad Abu 'Ila, "Hizb al-Hurriya wa-l-'Adala bi-Itay al-Barud Yudashshin Hamlat al-Iktishaf al-Mubakkir bi-Amrad Saratan al-Thady" [Freedom and Justice Party in Itay al-Barud campaigns for the early detection of breast cancer], Ikhwan Beheira, February 9, 2013, http://elbehira.net/elbehira/nd_shnws.php?shart=28273.

13. "FJP Woos Voters with Charity Drives ahead of Elections," al-Masry al-Youm (English), March 4, 2013, http://www.egyptindependent.com//news/fjp-woos-voters-charity-drives-ahead-elections.

14. "Ikhwan: La 'Alaqa li-Hamlat 'Ma'an Nabni Misr' bi-Maw'id al-Intikhabat" [Brotherhood: There is no relation between the "Together We Build Egypt" campaign and the date of the elections], Akhbar al-Yawm, January 22, 2013, http://akhbarelyom.com/news/newdetails/121766/1/0.html#.U5C5L5RdVSr; "Muslim Brotherhood: Services for Egyptian Public Regular, Unrelated to Any Election," Ikhwanweb, January 20, 2013, http://www.ikhwanweb.com/article.php?id=30582; "Al-Hurriya wa-l-'Adala: Sha'biyyat al-Ikhwan Taraja'at, wa-Nu'alij bi-Ma'arid al-Sila'" [Freedom and Justice: The Brotherhood's popularity dropped (but) we can cure it with charity fairs], al-Fajr, http://new.elfagr.org//Detail.aspx?nwsId=276466&secid=1&vid=2#.

15. 'Umar 'Uways, "Al-Hurriya wa-l-Adala Yakhud al-Intikhabat bi-Shiar 'Ma'an Nabni Misr'" [Freedom and Justice run in the elections under the slogan "Together We Build Egypt"], Moheet.com, March 6, 2013, http://www.masress.com/moheet/601039.

16. From its earliest days the Brotherhood had struggled to make inroads into these areas, tending instead to establish an organizational presence in areas with higher

percentages of literate citizens and lower levels of participation in the agricultural economy (Brooke and Ketchley 2018). Hussam Tammam, however, argues that the Brotherhood was undergoing what he calls a "ruralization" (*taryyīf*) during the Mubarak period, although he frames it largely as a process by which rural practices and behaviors (for instance, forms of address) became more prevalent inside the group (2012, 71–83).

17. Anwar 'Abduh, "Bi-Ri'ayat al-Hurriya wa-l-'Adala: 300 Mustafid fi al-Qafila al-Tibbiyya al-Majjaniyya bi-Kubri Diyab bi-Idku" [Under the authority of the Freedom and Justice Party: 300 beneficiaries from a free medical caravan in (the area of) the Diyab Bridge, in Idku (province)], *el-Beheira.com*, June 8, 2013, http://elbehira.net/elbehira/nd_shnws.php?shart=32680.

18. Mustafa Mahmud, "2500 Mustafid min Qafila Tibbiyya li-l-Ikhwan wa-l-Hurriya wa-l-'Adala bi-l-Suwis" [2,500 benefit from a Brotherhood/Freedom and Justice medical caravan in Suez], *Ikhwanonline*, March 16, 2013, http://ikhwanonline.com/Article.aspx?ArtID=142270&SecID=250.

19. Angie Hiba, "Akhir al-Mustaqilin min 'al-Hurriya wa-l-'Adala: al-Hizb 'Kartuni' wa-Qararat 'al-Shatir' Nafidha" [Latest to resign from Freedom and Justice: The party is (nothing more than) a cartoon (i.e., fake), and a window into (Khayrat al-) Shatir's decisions]," *al-Watan*, February 24, 2013, http://www.elwatannews.com/news/details/136522.

20. Ahmad 'Abdel 'Azim 'Aamir, "Bawabat al-Ahram Tanfarid Bi-Nashir 'al-Qa'ima al-Kamila' li-Asma' al-Mutahafiz ala Amwalhum" [Ahram Gate publishes the "complete list" of those Brothers whose accounts have been frozen], *al-Ahram*, January 7, 2014, http://gate.ahram.org.eg/News/439966.aspx.

21. Ahmad al-'Ajuz, "Hamlat 'Ma'an Nabni Misr' Tughatti Kafat Qura wa-Mudun al-Manufiyya" [The "Together We Build Egypt" campaign blankets Manufiyya's villages and cities], *Bawabat al-Hurriya wa-l-Adala*, January 25, 2013, http://www.masress.com/fjp/42379; Mahmud, "2500 Mustafid."

22. The appendix reports two checks on the data set, first showing no correlation between district-level rates of reported internet usage in the 2013 Arab Barometer and caravan activity, the second showing a strong correlation between my data set and official statistics released by the Muslim Brotherhood at the governorate level.

23. All source URLs are provided in the data set, and .pdf copies of each of the 488 source web pages are also available from the author.

24. In larger cities and towns the source material would mention a specific landmark, street, or facility, allowing a very high degree of accuracy. Accuracy was lower in rural areas, where rarely more than the village's name was available. In most cases, however, the village was small enough to make the location academic.

25. The minimum number of caravan visits per district was zero, while the maximum was 14.

26. In my fieldwork during this time I noticed at some IMA facilities banners denoting their participation in or hosting of a Together We Build Egypt caravan. This was also noted in some of the articles about specific caravans. See, for instance, "Al-Qafila al-Tibbiyya bi-Mustashfa al-Rahma taht Ri'ayat Hizb al-Hurriya wa-l-'Adala bi-Shibin" [Medical caravan at the Rahma Hospital under the authority of the Freedom and Justice Party in Shibin], Facebook, June 23, 2013, https://goo.gl/HxKdhQ.

27. Happily, unlike the Mubarak-era electoral districts, the electoral districts for the 2011–12 parliamentary elections (and proposed for the 2013 redo) were coterminous with the borders of the underlying markaz/qism.

28. This notably conflicts with Michael Albertus's (2012) finding that parties should direct durable goods to swing voters while using more contingent transfers to interact with core voters. The Brotherhood was doing the opposite: using revocable benefits to reach out to unaligned voters but minimizing the loss if the beneficiaries defected on election day.

29. Yasir ʿAli, "Rijal al-Watani Yumawwilun Hamlat Ikhwaniyya li-l-Tabarruʿat, wa-l-Jamaʿa: "Mish ʿAyb [Ex-NDP members fund the Brotherhood's charity campaigns with donations. . . . The Brotherhood says there is nothing shameful about this], al-Masry al-Youm, May 14, 2013, http://www.almasryalyoum.com/news/details/316357.

30. In addition to evidence from outside Egypt that suggests that these forms of outreach are highly successful (Thachil 2014a), experimental evidence from a separate survey conducted in the Spring of 2013 shows that those Egyptians more recently exposed to the Brotherhood's Together We Build Egypt initiatives reported themselves more likely to vote for the group than those exposed less recently (Brooke 2018).

8. THE POLITICS OF SOCIAL SERVICE PROVISION

1. David D. Kirkpatrick, "Egyptian Court Bans the Muslim Brotherhood," New York Times, September 23, 2013, http://www.nytimes.com/2013/09/24/world/middleeast/egyptian-court-bans-muslim-brotherhood.html?_r=0.

2. Muhammad al-Saʿdani, "Al-Masry al-Youm Tanshir Qaʾima bi-Asmaʾ Jamʿiyyat ʿal-Ikhwanʾ al-Mujammada" [Al-Masry al-Youm publishes a list with names of the Brotherhood community associations whose funds are frozen], al-Masry al-Youm, December 24, 2014, http://www.almasryalyoum.com/news/details/363611.

3. Al-Ahram, December 28, 2013, 1.

4. Muhammad Taha, "D. ʿAli Abu Sayf: Basus wa-l-Khalil wa-Bani Suwayf Mustashfayat Jadida Tadkhul al-Khidma Qariban" [Dr. ʿAli Abu Sayf: Basus, al-Khalil, and Bani Suwayf Hospitals are entering service soon], al-Jamʿiyya al-Tibbiyya al-Islamiyya, August 15, 2014, http://ima-egy.net/2013-09-24-14-31-06/497-2014-08-15-00-57-03.

5. Said ʿAbd al-Rahim, "Misr Tatahaffaz ʿala al-Mustashfayat al-Islamiyya" [Egypt "seizes" Islamic hospitals], al-Arabi al-Jadid, January 19, 2015, http://goo.gl/2odzY8.

6. "Al-Tahaffuz ʿala Amwal al-Jamʿiyya al-Tibbiyya al-Islamiyya" [Seizure of the Islamic Medical Association's funds], Hizb al-Hurriya wa-l-Adala, January 14, 2015, http://www.fj-p.com/Our_news_Details.aspx?News_ID=61304; A. Sh. A., "Lajnat Idarat Amwal al-Ikhwan Tatahaffaz ʿala al-Jamʿiyya al-Tibbiyya al-Islamiyya" [Committee managing the Brotherhood's funds seizes the Islamic Medical Association], al-Masry al-Youm, January 14, 2015, http://www.almasryalyoum.com/news/details/629557; and ʿAli Ghanim, "Al-Inqilab Yasriq al-Jamʿiyya al-Tibbiyya al-Islamiyya . . . al-Harb ʿala Milayin al-Marda" [The coup regime steals the Islamic Medical Association: War on millions of patients], Ikhwanonline, January 14, 2015, http://ikhwanonline.com/Article.aspx?ArtID=218310&SecID=230.

7. Amr Osman, "Ali Gomaa: Kill them, They Stink," Middle East Monitor, January 27, 2014, https://www.middleeastmonitor.com/20140127-ali-gomaa-kill-them-they-stink.

8. "Mudir Mustashfa al-Rahma ʿAqiba al-Istilaʾ ʿalayha: Al-Inqilab Faqad ʿAqlahu" [The director of the Rahma (Mercy) Hospital following its seizure: The coup regime has lost its mind), al-Rasad, January 14, 2015, http://rassd.com/15-128042.htm.

9. "Mudir Mustashfa al-Rahma ʿAqiba al-Istilaʾ ʿalayha:

10. Bahiyya Makki, "Bi-l-Suwar . . . Amn al-Qalyubiyya Yatahaffaz ʿala Mustashfayat al-Ikhwan bi-l-Khanka" [In pictures: Security forces in Qalyubiyya seize the Brotherhood's hospitals in Khanka), Bawabat al-Qahira, January 14, 2015, http://goo.gl/V3a0YQ; Islam Abu al-Wafa, "Tafasil al-Tahaffuz ʿala Mustashfa Dar al-Salam al-Tabiʿa li-l-Ikhwan bi-l-Buhayra" [Details of the seizure of the Brotherhood's Dar al-Salam Hospital in Buhayra], Ruz al-Yusuf, January 14, 2015, http://goo.gl/nG2WZQ; Karim al-Bakri, "Al-Sihha: La Niyya Ladayna li-Ighlaq Mustashfayat al-Ikhwan" [Ministry of Health: We have no intention of closing the Brotherhood's hospitals], al-Shuruq, January 14, 2015, http://www.shorouknews.com/mobile/news/view.aspx?cdate=14012015&id=3f8b4507-8ef4-40ba-8ac1-bc6674e59c3d.

11. Husam Rabi', "Al-Quwwat al-Musallaha al-Misriyya Tuhawil al-Ta'wid 'an Dawr Jam'iyyat al-Ikhwan al-Khayriyya" [The Egyptian armed forces are attempting to substitute for the role of the Brotherhood's charity associations], *Rasif 22*, July 22, 2015, http://goo.gl/U5hngm.

12. Maha Salim, "Al-Quwwat al-Musallaha Tuwazzi' Milyunan wa-Nisf al-Milyun Kartuna Aghdhiya bi-l-Manatiq al-Akthar Ihtiyajan" [The armed forces distribute 1.5 million boxes of food in areas with the greatest need], *al-Ahram*, July 15, 2015, http://gate.ahram.org.eg/News/698177.aspx; "Qafila Tibbiyya min al-Quwwat al-Musallaha li-Ahali Bi'r al-'Abd fi Shamal Sina'" [Medical caravan from the armed forces for the people of Bi'r al-'Abd in North Sinai], *Dot Misr*, February 7, 2016, http://goo.gl/QDH7ks; "Al-Quwwat al-Musallaha Tursil Qafila Tibbiyya ila al-Wadi al-Jadid" [The Armed Forces send a medical caravan to Wadi Jadid (Governorate)]," *Dot Misr*, March 1, 2016, http://goo.gl/xc7a72; "al-Jaysh Yuwazzi' 'Milyun wa-Nisf' Hissa Ghidha'iyya 'ala al-Muwatinin bi-Munasabat Ramadan" [Egyptian Army distributes 1.5 million boxes of food to the citizens on the occasion of Ramadan]," *al-Masry al-Youm*, June 4, 2016, http://www.almasryalyoum.com/news/details/959443; "General Intelligence Service Hands Out Subsidized Food in Bani Swaif," *Egypt Independent*, June 4, 2016, http://www.egyptindependent.com//news/general-intelligence-service-hands-out-subsidized-food-bani-swaif.

13. Abdelrahman Youssef, "The Brotherhood's Changing Approach," *Sada*, June 4, 2015, http://carnegieendowment.org/sada/60317.

14. I appreciate Tarek Masoud's bringing this source to my attention.

15. Elizabeth Arrott, "Morsi Critics Demand Early Elections," Voice of America News, June 19, 2013, http://www.voanews.com/content/morsi-critics-demand-early-egypt-elections/1684744.html.

16. Nancy A. Youssef, "Egyptians Don't Like Morsi's Presidency, but Opposition Flounders Anyways," McClatchy Newspapers, May 20, 2013, http://www.mcclatchydc.com/2013/05/20/191739/egyptians-dont-like-morsis-presidency.html.

17. Tom Perry and Abdel Rahman Youssef, "Special Report: Egypt's Brotherhood Turns to Flour Power," Reuters, June 13, 2013, http://www.reuters.com/article/2013/06/13/us-egypt-brotherhood-bread-specialreport-idUSBRE95C07P20130613.

18. "Questions about June 30: Who Were We and What Were We Thinking? Part 1," *Mada Masr*, July 8, 2016, http://www.madamasr.com/sections/politics/questions-about-june-30-who-were-we-and-what-were-we-thinking-part-1.

19. "Egypt Opposition Leader Calls for Election Boycott," Associated Press, February 23, 2013, https://www.usatoday.com/story/news/nation/2013/02/23/egypt-opposition-leader-calls-for-election-boycott/1941513.

20. Morsi Discusses FJP Structure with Turkish Academics," *Ikhwanweb*, July 10, 2011, http://www.ikhwanweb.com/article.php?id=28808.

21. Monica Marks, "How Big Were the Changes Tunisia's Ennahda Just Made at Its National Congress?" The Monkey Cage, *Washington Post*, May 25, 2016, https://www.washingtonpost.com/news/monkey-cage/wp/2016/05/25/how-big-were-the-changes-made-at-tunisias-ennahda-just-made-at-its-national-congress; Carlotta Gall, "Tunisian Islamist Party Re-Elects Moderate Leader," *New York Times*, May 23, 2016, https://www.nytimes.com/2016/05/24/world/africa/tunisia-rachid-ghannouchi-ennahda.html.

22. Author interview, April 25, 2016.

23. Abdelrahman Youssef, "Egyptian Brotherhood Leader Reflects on Group's Fate, Future," *al-Monitor*, May 22, 2016, http://www.al-monitor.com/pulse/originals/2016/05/egypt-brotherhood-leader-interview-sisi-mistakes-future.html#.

24. Talaat Fahmy, "Muslim Brotherhood Press Statement," *Ikhwanweb*, May 25, 2016, http://www.ikhwanweb.com/article.php?id=32544.

25. "Sadat's Liberalization Policy: A Research Paper," PA 79-10245, Central Intelligence Agency/National Foreign Assessment Center, June 1979, 11.

26. W. Morris to W. R. Tomkins, "The Wafd Reborn," September 10, 1977, NFE 011/1 (FCO 93/1040).

27. "Sadat's Liberalization Policy," 9. See also "Islam in Egypt," December 6, 1979, NFE 226/1 (FCO 93/1965)c

28. Melani Cammett and Pauline Jones Luong hypothesize that these modes cannot coexist: "Real or perceived vote-buying, for example, can tarnish the images of Islamist parties, undercutting their relatively clean reputations and diminishing their claims to authenticity, which in turn can lead to reduced vote shares in subsequent elections" (2014, 202). Indeed, this seems to have happened—at least in the assessment of some in the Muslim Brotherhood—regarding the TWBE campaign.

APPENDIX

1. The 1984 and 1987 elections were held under different electoral systems across differently compiled districts and are therefore excluded from the analysis.

2. Technically the IPUMS data are an approximately 10 percent sample of Egyptians drawn by the Egyptian Center for Public Mobilization and Statistics. There are drawbacks to these data, including lack of full coverage, mainly that small markaz/qism in each governorate are aggregated into a single category that, unfortunately, has to be dropped from the analysis. The data are also not disaggregated below the markaz/qism level, which would have been ideal for proper electoral district assignment. But this partial sample does have a singular and significant advantage over the official census: it includes a question on religious affiliation, which is a critical variable for this type of research. A description of the data is available on the IPUMS website at https://international.ipums.org/international-action/sample_details/country/eg#eg2006a.

3. The Muslim Brotherhood boycotted the 1990 elections.

4. I conducted the survey with Jason Brownlee of the University of Texas at Austin.

5. I appreciate Michael Robbins for clarifying this point to me and for sharing the disaggregated Arab Barometer data.

6. "Hamlat 'Ma'an Nabni Misr' bi-l-Arqam" [The "Together We Build Egypt" campaign by the numbers], *Amal al-Umma*, May 20, 2013, http://www.amlalommah.net/new/wap.php?id=34769&mod=article.

7. Note that these electoral districts (from 2011–12) are not the same as in chapter 5's electoral districts (from 1990 to 2010) because of a shifting electoral map (electoral borders were significantly redrawn in 2011). Because the 2011–12 districts were effectively coterminous with markaz/qism—in other words, markaz/qism were not split across multiple electoral districts in the 2011 changes—the analysis gains roughly a dozen cases.

Works Cited

Abdelrahman, Banan. 2013. "Navigating State Lines: The Muslim Brotherhood's Social Welfare System under Hosni Mubarak." BA honors thesis, Rutgers University.

Abdelrahman, Maha M. 2004. *Civil Society Exposed: The Politics of NGOs in Egypt.* London: IB Tauris.

Abed-Kotob, Sana. 1995. "The Accommodationists Speak: Goals and Strategies of the Muslim Brotherhood of Egypt." *International Journal of Middle East Studies* 27 (3): 321–39.

Agati, Mohamed. 2006. "Undermining Standards of Good Governance: Egypt's NGO Law and Its Impact on the Transparency and Accountability of CSOs." *International Journal of Not-for-Profit Law* 9 (2): 52–83.

Agnew, John A. 2014. *Place and Politics: The Geographical Mediation of State and Society.* London: Routledge.

Akin, John S., Nancy Birdsall, and David deFerranti. 1987. *Financing Health Services in Developing Countries: An Agenda for Reform.* Washington, DC: World Bank.

Anani, Khalil al-. 2007. *Al-Ikhwan al-Muslimum Fi Misr: Shaykhukha Tusariʿ al-Zaman* [The Muslim Brotherhood in Egypt: Gerontocracy fighting time]. Cairo: Dar al-Shuruq.

——. 2016. *Inside the Muslim Brotherhood: Religion, Identity, and Politics.* Oxford: Oxford University Press.

Arian, Abdullah al-. 2014. *Answering the Call: Popular Islamic Activism in Egypt.* Oxford: Oxford University Press.

Awadi, Hesham al-. 2004. *In Pursuit of Legitimacy: The Muslim Brothers and Mubarak, 1982–2000.* London: IB Tauris.

——. 2005. "Mubarak and the Islamists: Why Did the 'Honeymoon' End?" *Middle East Journal* 59 (1): 62–80.

Albertus, Michael. 2012. "Vote Buying with Multiple Distributive Goods." *Comparative Political Studies* 46 (9): 1082–1111.

Albrecht, Holger. 2005. "How Can Opposition Support Authoritarianism? Lessons from Egypt." *Democratization* 12 (3): 378–97.

——. 2013. *Raging against the Machine: Political Opposition under Authoritarianism in Egypt.* Syracuse, NY: Syracuse University Press.

Alesina, Alberto, Reza Baqir, and William Easterly. 1999. "Public Goods and Ethnic Divisions." *Quarterly Journal of Economics* 114:1243–84.

Amin, Galal. 2001. *Whatever Happened to the Egyptians? Changes in Egyptian Society from 1850 to the Present.* Oxford: Oxford University Press.

——. 2011. *Egypt in the Era of Hosni Mubarak.* Oxford: Oxford University Press.

Anderson, Lisa. 1997. "Fulfilling Prophecies: State Policy and Islamist Radicalism." In *Political Islam: Revolution, Radicalism, or Reform?*, edited by John L. Esposito, 17–32. Boulder, CO: Lynn Reinner.

Angrist, Michele Penner. 2011. *Party Building in the Modern Middle East.* Seattle: University of Washington Press.

Anria, Santiago. 2013. "Social Movements, Party Organization, and Populism: Insights from the Bolivian MAS." *Latin American Politics and Society* 55 (3): 19–46.

Arafat, Alaa al-Din. 2009. *The Mubarak Leadership and the Future of Democracy in Egypt*. New York: Palgrave Macmillan.

Arendt, Hannah. 1973. *The Origins of Totalitarianism*. New York: Houghton Mifflin Harcourt.

Arthur, W. Brian. 1989. "Competing Technologies, Increasing Returns, and Lock-in by Historical Events." *Economic Journal* 99 (394): 116–31.

Ashour, Omar. 2015. *Collusion to Crackdown: Islamist-Military Relations in Egypt*. Washington, DC: Brookings Institution.

Atia, Mona. 2013. *Building a House in Heaven: Pious Neoliberalism and Islamic Charity in Egypt*. Minneapolis: University of Minnesota Press.

Attallah, May. 2017. "The Determinants of Voting for Islamists in Egypt's First Post-Revolution Elections 2011–2012." *Middle East Development Journal* 9 (2): 184–97.

Auyero, Javier. 1999. "From the Client's Point(s) of View: How Poor People Perceive and Evaluate Political Clientelism." *Theory and Society* 28 (2): 297–334.

——. 2001. *Poor People's Politics: Peronist Survival Networks and the Legacy of Evita*. Durham, NC: Duke University Press.

Ayubi, Nazih. 1991. *The State and Public Policies in Egypt since Sadat*. Reading, UK: Ithaca Press.

——. 1996. *Over-Stating the Arab State: Politics and Society in the Middle East*. London: IB Tauris.

Badrawi, Husam, and Muhsin Yusuf. 2007. *Al-Shaffafiyya Wa-Muharabat al-Fasad Fi Qita al-Sihha* [Transparency and the fight against corruption in the health sector]. Alexandria, Egypt: Maktabat al-Iskandariyya.

Baker, Raymond William. 1990. *Sadat and After: Struggles for Egypt's Political Soul*. Cambridge, MA: Harvard University Press.

Banerjee, Abhijit, Lakshmi Iyer, and Rohini Somanathan. 2005. "History, Social Divisions, and Public Goods in Rural India." *Journal of the European Economic Association* 3 (2–3): 639–47.

Banfield, Edward C., and James Q. Wilson. 1966. *City Politics*. New York: Vintage Books.

Barkey, Henri J. 1992. Introduction to *The Politics of Economic Reform in the Middle East*, edited by Henri J. Barkey, 1–10. New York: St. Martin's.

Bartels, Larry M. 2002. "The Impact of Candidate Traits in American Presidential Elections." In *Leaders' Personalities and the Outcomes of Democratic Elections*, edited by Anthony King, 44–69. Oxford: Oxford University Press.

Bates, Robert H. (1981) 2005. *Markets and States in Tropical Africa: The Political Basis of Agricultural Policies*. 2nd ed., Berkeley: University of California Press.

Bayat, Asef. 2006. "The Political Economy of Social Policy in Egypt." In *Social Policy in the Middle East*, edited by Masoud Karshenas and Valentine M. Moghadam, 135–55. New York: Palgrave.

——. 2007a. *Making Islam Democratic: Social Movements and the Post-Islamist Turn*. Stanford: Stanford University Press.

——. 2007b. "Radical Religion and the Habitus of the Dispossessed: Does Islamic Militancy Have an Urban Ecology?" *International Journal of Urban and Regional Research* 31 (3): 579–90.

Baylouny, Anne Marie. 2006. "Creating Kin: New Family Associations as Welfare Providers in Liberalizing Jordan." *International Journal of Middle East Studies* 38 (3): 349–68.

Beattie, Kirk J. 2000. *Egypt during the Sadat Years*. New York: Macmillan.

Behrend, Jacqueline. 2011. "The Unevenness of Democracy at the Subnational Level: Provincial Closed Games in Argentina." *Latin American Research Review* 46 (1): 150–76.

Beinin, Joel. 2009. "Workers' Struggles under 'Socialism' and 'Neoliberalism.'" In *Egypt: Moment of Change*, edited by Rabab El-Mahdi and Philip Marfleet, 68–88. London: Zed Books.

Bellin, Eva. 2000. "Contingent Democrats: Industrialists, Labor, and Democratization in Late-Developing Countries." *World Politics* 52 (2): 175–205.

Ben Néfissa, Sarah. 2002. "Citoyenneté morale en Egypte: Une association entre état et Frères Musulmans" [Moral citizenship in Egypt: An association between the state and the Muslim Brothers]. In *Pouvoirs et associations dans le monde Arabe*, edited by Sarah Ben Néfissa, 148–79. Paris: CNRS Editions.

Ben Néfissa, Sarah, and 'Ala' al-Din 'Arafat. 2005. *Al-Intikhabat Wa-l-Zaba'iniyya al-Siyasiyya Fi Misr: Tajdid al-Wusata' Wa-'Awdat al-Nakhib* [Elections and political clientelism in Egypt: Renewal of intermediaries and the return of the voter]. Cairo: Markaz al-Qahira li-Huquq al-Insan.

Benstead, Lindsay J. 2014. "Effects of Interviewer–Respondent Gender Interaction on Attitudes toward Women and Politics: Findings from Morocco." *International Journal of Public Opinion Research* 26 (3): 369–83.

Berger, Morroe. 1970. *Islam in Egypt Today: Social and Political Aspects of Popular Religion*. Princeton: Princeton University Press.

Berman, Sheri. 1997. "Civil Society and the Collapse of the Weimar Republic." *World Politics* 49 (3): 401–29.

——. 2003. "Islamism, Revolution, and Civil Society." *Perspectives on Politics* 1 (2): 257–72.

Bianchi, Robert. 1989. *Unruly Corporatism: Associational Life in Twentieth-Century Egypt*. Oxford: Oxford University Press.

Bibars, Iman. 2001. *Victims and Heroines: Women, Welfare and the Egyptian State*. London: Zed Books.

Binder, Leonard. 1978. *In a Moment of Enthusiasm: Political Power and the Second Stratum in Egypt*. Chicago: University of Chicago Press.

Blaydes, Lisa. 2011. *Elections and Distributive Politics in Mubarak's Egypt*. Cambridge: Cambridge University Press.

Blaydes, Lisa, and Safinaz El Tarouty. 2010–11. "La concurrence interne au Parti National Démocrate Égyptien" [Internal competition in the National Democratic Party]. In *Fabrique des élections*, edited by Florian Kohstall and Frédéric Variel, 64–93. Cairo: Centre d'Études et de Documentation Économiques, Juridiques et Sociales.

Boas, Taylor Chase. 2014. "Pastor Paulo vs. Doctor Carlos: Professional Titles as Voting Heuristics in Brazil." *Journal of Politics in Latin America* 6 (2): 39–72.

Brady, Henry E., and David Collier. 2010. *Rethinking Social Inquiry: Diverse Tools, Shared Standards*. Lanham, MD: Rowman & Littlefield.

Braun, Robert. 2016. "Religious Minorities and Resistance to Genocide: The Collective Rescue of Jews in the Netherlands during the Holocaust." *American Political Science Review* 110 (1): 127–47.

Brooke, Steven. 2013. "Doctors and Brothers." *Middle East Report* 269:18–20.

——. 2017a. "Egypt." In *Rethinking Political Islam*, edited by Shadi Hamid and Will McCants, 17–31. Oxford: Oxford University Press.

——. 2017b. "From Medicine to Mobilization: Social Service Provision and the Islamist Political Advantage." *Perspectives on Politics* 15 (1): 42–61.

——. 2018. "Religious Infrastructure and Electoral Mobilization." Unpublished manuscript.

Brooke, Steven, and Neil Ketchley. 2018. "Social and Institutional Origins of Political Islam." *American Political Science Review* 112 (2): 376–94.

Brown, Nathan J. 2012. *When Victory Is Not an Option: Islamist Movements in Arab Politics*. Ithaca, NY: Cornell University Press.

Brownlee, Jason. 2007. *Authoritarianism in an Age of Democratization*. Cambridge: Cambridge University Press.

——. 2010a. "The Muslim Brothers: Egypt's Most Influential Pressure Group." *History Compass* 8 (5): 419–30.

——. 2010b. "Unrequited Moderation: Credible Commitments and State Repression in Egypt." *Studies in Comparative International Development*. 45: 468–89.

——. 2012. *Democracy Prevention: The Politics of the US-Egyptian Alliance*. Cambridge: Cambridge University Press.

Brownlee, Jason, and Joshua Stacher. 2011. "Change of Leader, Continuity of System: Nascent Liberalization in Post-Mubarak Egypt." *APSA-CD Newsletter* 9 (2): 4–9.

Brumberg, Daniel. 1992. "Survival Strategies vs. Democratic Bargains: The Politics of Economic Reform in Contemporary Egypt." In *The Politics of Economic Reform in the Middle East*, edited by Henri J. Barkey, 73–104. New York: St. Martin's.

Brusco, Valeria, Marcelo Nazareno, and Susan Carol Stokes. 2004. "Vote Buying in Argentina." *Latin American Research Review* 39 (2): 66–88.

Buckley, David. 2016. "Demanding the Divine? Explaining Cross-National Support for Clerical Control of Politics." *Comparative Political Studies* 49 (3): 357–90.

Buehler, Matt. 2015. "Continuity through Co-optation: Rural Politics and Regime Resilience in Morocco and Mauritania." *Mediterranean Politics* 20 (3): 364–85.

Butler, Daniel M., and Eleanor Neff Powell. 2014. "Understanding the Party Brand: Experimental Evidence on the Role of Valence." *Journal of Politics* 76 (2): 492–505.

Calvo, Ernesto, and Maria Victoria Murillo. 2004. "Who Delivers? Partisan Clients in the Argentine Electoral Market." *American Journal of Political Science* 48 (4): 742–57.

——. 2013. "When Parties Meet Voters: Assessing Political Linkages through Partisan Networks and Distributive Expectations in Argentina and Chile." *Comparative Political Studies* 46 (7): 851–82.

Cammett, Melani. 2011. "Partisan Activism and Access to Welfare in Lebanon." *Studies in Comparative International Development* 46 (1): 70–97.

——. 2014. *Compassionate Communalism: Welfare and Sectarianism in Lebanon*. Ithaca, NY: Cornell University Press.

Cammett, Melani, and Sukriti Issar. 2010. "Bricks and Mortar Clientelism: Sectarianism and the Logics of Welfare Allocation in Lebanon." *World Politics* 62 (3): 381–421.

Cammett, Melani, and Pauline Jones Luong. 2014. "Is There an Islamist Political Advantage?" *Annual Review of Political Science* 17:187–206.

Cammett, Melani, and Aytuğ Şaşmaz. 2017. "Political Context, Organizational Mission, and the Quality of Social Services: Insights from the Health Sector in Lebanon." *World Development* 98:120–32.

Campagna, Joel. 1996. "From Accommodation to Confrontation: The Muslim Brotherhood in the Mubarak Years." *Journal of International Affairs* 50 (1): 278–304.

Central Accounting Authority. 2015. *Dirasa 'an Tahlil Takalif al-Fasad Bi-l-Tatbiq 'Ala Ba'd al-Qata'at Fi Misr* [An analytical study of the cost of corruption and its application to some sectors in Egypt]. Cairo: Al-Jihaz al-Markazi li-l-Muhasabat.

Challand, Benoît. 2008. "A Nahda of Charitable Organizations? Health Service Provision and the Politics of Aid in Palestine." *International Journal of Middle East Studies* 40 (2): 227–47.

Chhibber, Pradeep K. 2014. *Religious Practice and Democracy in India*. Cambridge: Cambridge University Press.

Chiffoleau, Sylvia. 1990. "Le désengagement de l'état et les transformations du système de santé" [State disengagement and the transformation of health systems]. *Maghreb Machrek* 127:84–103.

Chiozza, Giacomo, and Hein E. Goemans. 2004. "International Conflict and the Tenure of Leaders: Is War Still Ex-Post Inefficient?" *American Journal of Political Science* 48 (3): 604–19.

Chubb, Judith. 1982. *Patronage, Power and Poverty in Southern Italy: A Tale of Two Cities*. Cambridge: Cambridge University Press.

Clark, Janine A. 1995. "Islamic Social Welfare Organizations in Cairo: Islamization from Below?" *Arab Studies Quarterly* 17 (4): 11–28.

——. 2004. *Islam, Charity, and Activism: Middle Class Networks and Social Welfare in Egypt, Jordan, and Yemen*. Bloomington: Indiana University Press.

Clark, Janine A., and Emanuela Dalmasso. 2015. "State Actor–Social Movement Coalitions and Policymaking under Authoritarianism: The Moroccan Party of Justice and Development in the Urban Municipality of Kenitra." *Middle East Law and Governance* 7 (2): 185–211.

Cooper, Mark. 1982. *The Transformation of Egypt*. Baltimore: Johns Hopkins University Press.

Corstange, Daniel. 2016. *The Price of a Vote in the Middle East: Ethnicity and Clientelism*. Cambridge: Cambridge University Press.

Cox, Gary W., and Mathew D. McCubbins. 1986. "Electoral Politics as a Redistributive Game." *Journal of Politics* 48 (2): 370–89.

Danish-Egyptian Dialogue Institute. 2012. *Parliamentary Elections in Egypt 2011/2012: An Anthropological Research Project*. Cairo: Danish-Egyptian Dialogue Institute.

Darra, Usama. 2011. *Min al-Ikhwan Ila Midan al-Tahrir* [From the Muslim Brotherhood to Tahrir Square]. Cairo: Dar al-Misri li-l-Nashr wa-l-Tawzi'.

Darrag, Amr. 2017. "Politics or Piety? Why the Muslim Brotherhood Engages in Social Service Provision." In *Rethinking Political Islam*, edited by Shadi Hamid and Will McCants, 218–30. Oxford: Oxford University Press.

Dasuqi, 'Abduh Mustafa, and al-Sayyid Ramadan al-'Abadi. 2013. *Al-Ikhwan al-Muslimun Fi Muhafazat Misr* [The Muslim Brotherhood in Egypt's governorates]. Cairo: Muassasat Iqra li-l-Nashr wa-l-Tawzi' wa-l-Tarjama.

Da'ud, Muhammad 'Abd al-'Aziz. 1992. *Al-Jam'iyyat al-Islamiyya Fi Misr Wa-Dawruha Fi Nashr al-Da'wa al-Islamiyya* [Islamic associations in Egypt and their role in spreading the Islamic call]. Cairo: Al-Zahra' li-l-'Alam al-'Arabi.

David, Paul A. 1985. "Clio and the Economics of Qwerty." *American Economic Review* 75 (2): 332–37.

Davis, Nancy J., and Robert V. Robinson. 2006. "The Egalitarian Face of Islamic Orthodoxy: Support for Islamic Law and Economic Justice in Seven Muslim-Majority Nations." *American Sociological Review* 71 (2): 167–90.

——. 2012. *Claiming Society for God: Religious Movements and Social Welfare in Egypt, Israel, Italy, and the United States*. Bloomington: Indiana University Press.

Diaz-Cayeros, Alberto, Beatriz Magaloni, and Barry R. Weingast. 2006. "Tragic Brilliance: Equilibrium Party Hegemony in Mexico." Unpublished manuscript.

Dixit, Avinash, and John Londregan. 1996. "The Determinants of Success of Special Interests in Redistributive Politics." *Journal of Politics* 58 (4): 1132–55.

Downs, Anthony. 1957. *An Economic Theory of Democracy*. New York: Harper & Row.

Druckman, James N., Donald P. Green, James H. Kuklinski, and Arthur Lupia. 2011. *Cambridge Handbook of Experimental Political Science*. Cambridge: Cambridge University Press.

"Egypt Provider Survey Report (Draft)." 1994–95. Department of Planning, Ministry of Health and Data for Decision Making. Cambridge, MA: Harvard School of Public Health.

Egypt: Service Provision Assessment Survey 2002. 2003. Cairo: Ministry of Health and Population, El-Zanaty Associates, and ORC Macro Joint Report.

Eligür, Banu. 2010. *The Mobilization of Political Islam in Turkey*. Cambridge: Cambridge University Press.

Elsayyad, May, and Shimaa Hanafy. 2014. "Voting Islamist or Voting Secular? An Empirical Analysis of Voting Outcomes in Egypt's 'Arab Spring.'" *Public Choice* 160 (1–2): 109–30.

Erle, Jakob Wichmann, Jakob Mathias, and Alexander Kjærum. 2016. *Egypt Electoral Constituencies: Socio-Economic Classification of Egypt's Party Electoral Constituencies*. Cairo: Danish-Egyptian Dialogue Institute.

Esposito, John L. 2003. Introduction to *Modernizing Islam*, edited by John L. Esposito and Francois Burgat, 1–16. New Brunswick, NJ: Rutgers University Press.

Farag, Mohammad Abd al-Salaam. 1986. *The Neglected Duty: The Creed of Sadat's Assassins and Islamic Resurgence in the Middle East*. Translation and introduction by Johannes J. G. Jansen. New York: Macmillan.

Fayed, Ammar. 2017. "Is the Crackdown on the Muslim Brotherhood Pushing the Group Towards Violence?" In *Rethinking Political Islam*, edited by Shadi Hamid and Will McCants, 244–61. Oxford: Oxford University Press.

Fearon, James D. 1997. "Signaling Foreign Policy Interests: Tying Hands versus Sinking Costs." *Journal of Conflict Resolution* 41 (1): 68–90.

Fenno, Richard F. 1978. *Homestyle: House Members in Their Districts*. New York: Little, Brown.

Ferris, Jesse. 2012. *Nasser's Gamble: How Intervention in Yemen Caused the Six-Day War and the Decline of Egyptian Power*. Princeton, NJ: Princeton University Press.

Filmer, Deon, and Lant H. Pritchett. 2001. "Estimating Wealth Effects without Expenditure Data, or Tears: An Application to Educational Enrollments in States of India." *Demography* 38 (1): 115–32.

Finan, Frederico, and Laura Schechter. 2012. "Vote-Buying and Reciprocity." *Econometrica* 80 (2): 863–81.

Fiske, Susan T., Amy J. C. Cuddy, and Peter Glick. 2007. "Universal Dimensions of Social Cognition: Warmth and Competence." *Trends in Cognitive Sciences* 11 (2): 77–83.

Fridkin, Kim L., and Patrick J. Kenney. 2011. "The Role of Candidate Traits in Campaigns." *Journal of Politics* 73 (1): 61–73.

Funk, Carolyn L. 1996. "The Impact of Scandal on Candidate Evaluations: An Experimental Test of the Role of Candidate Traits." *Political Behavior* 18 (1): 1–24.

Futuh, ʿAbd al-Munʿim Abu al-. 2012. *Shahid ʿAla Tarikh al-Haraka al-Islamiyya Fi Misr, 1970–1984* [Eyewitness to the history of the Islamic movement in Egypt, 1970–1984]. Cairo: Dar al-Shuruq.

Gabas, Amgad Khalil al-. 2005. *Al-Barlaman Wa-l-Jamʿiyya al-Ahliyya: Dirasa Hala Li-Mashruʿ Qanuni al-Jamʿiyya al-Ahliyya Raqmayn 153 Li-Sana 1999 Wa-84 Li-Sana 2002* [Parliament and civic associations: A case study of the legal project regarding the two laws governing civic organizations, No. 153 of 1999 and 84 of 2002]. Cairo: Markaz al-Ahram li-l-Dirasat al-Istratijiyya wa-l-Siyasiyya.

Gaines, Brian J., James H. Kuklinski, and Paul J. Quirk. 2007. "The Logic of the Survey Experiment Reexamined." *Political Analysis* 15 (1): 1–20.

Gallagher, Nancy Elizabeth. 1990. *Egypt's Other Wars: Epidemics and the Politics of Public Health*. Syracuse, NY: Syracuse University Press.

Gandhi, Jennifer. 2008. *Political Institutions under Dictatorship*. Cambridge: Cambridge University Press Cambridge.

Gandhi, Jennifer, and Ora John Reuter. 2008. "Opposition Coordination in Legislative Elections under Authoritarianism." Paper presented at the Annual Meeting of the American Political Science Association, Boston.

Gans-Morse, Jordan, Sebastian Mazzuca, and Simeon Nichter. 2014. "Varieties of Clientelism: Machine Politics during Elections." *American Journal of Political Science* 58 (2): 415–32.

Geddes, Barbara. 1999. "Authoritarian Breakdown: An Empirical Test of a Game Theoretic Argument." Paper presented at the Annual Meeting of the American Political Science Association, Atlanta.

——. 2005. "Why Parties and Elections in Authoritarian Regimes?" Paper presented at the Annual Meeting of the American Political Science Association, Washington, DC.

George, Alexander L., and Andrew Bennett. 2005. *Case Studies and Theory Development in the Social Sciences*. Cambridge, MA: MIT Press.

Gerber, Alan S., and Donald P. Green. 2000. "The Effects of Canvassing, Telephone Calls, and Direct Mail on Voter Turnout: A Field Experiment." *American Political Science Review* 94 (3): 653–63.

Gibson, Edward L. 1997. "The Populist Road to Market Reform: Policy and Electoral Coalitions in Mexico and Argentina." *World Politics* 49 (3): 339–70.

Ginsburg, Paul B., and Glenn T. Hammons. 1988. "Competition and the Quality of Care: The Importance of Information." *Inquiry* 25 (1): 108–15.

Goldstone, Jack A. 2003. "Introduction: Bridging Institutionalized and Noninstitutionalized Politics." In *States, Parties, and Social Movements*, edited by Jack A. Goldstone, 1–24. Cambridge: Cambridge University Press.

Greene, Kenneth F. 2007. *Why Dominant Parties Lose: Mexico's Democratization in Comparative Perspective*. Cambridge: Cambridge University Press.

——. 2010. "The Political Economy of Authoritarian Single-Party Dominance." *Comparative Political Studies* 43 (7): 807–34.

Grzymała-Busse, Anna. 2015. *Nations under God: How Churches Use Moral Authority to Influence Policy*. Princeton: Princeton University Press.

Habib, Muhammad. 2012. *Dhikrayat Dr. Muhammad Habib: 'An al-Hayat, al-Da'wa, al-Siyasa Wa-l-Fikr* [Memoirs of Dr. Muhammad Habib: Concerning life, preaching, politics, and thought]. Cairo: Dar al-Shuruq.

Habyarimana, James, Macartan Humphreys, Daniel N. Posner, and Jeremy M. Weinstein. 2007. "Why Does Ethnic Diversity Undermine Public Goods Provision?" *American Political Science Review* 101 (4): 709–25.

Haenni, Patrick. 2016. "The Reasons for the Muslim Brotherhood's Failure in Power." In *Egypt's Revolutions*, edited by Bernard Rougier and Stéphane Lacroix, 19–40. New York: Palgrave Macmillan.

Hakim, Tawfiq el-. (1937) 1989. *The Maze of Justice: Diary of a Country Prosecutor*. English version translated by Abba Eban. Austin: University of Texas Press.

Hale, Henry. 2007. "Correlates of Clientelism: Political Economy, Politicized Ethnicity, and Post-Communist Transition." In *Patrons, Clients and Policies: Patterns of Democratic Accountability and Political Competition*, edited by Herbert

Kitschelt and Steven I. Wilkinson, 227–50. Cambridge: Cambridge University Press.

Hamayotsu, Kikue. 2015. "Patronage, Welfare Provisions, and State-Society Relations: Lessons from Muslim-Dominant Regimes in Southeast Asia (Indonesia and Malaysia)." In *Religion and the Politics of Development*, edited by Philip Fountain, Robin Bush, and R. Michael Feener, 155–76. New York: Palgrave Macmillan.

Hamid, 'Abd al-Rauf al-, and Muhammad Sabir 'Arab. 2002. *Misr Fi al-Qarn al-'Ashrin: Mukhtarat Min Watha'iq al-Siyasiyya (al-Mujallad al-Thani)* [Egypt in the twentieth century: Selections from political documents (volume 2)]. Cairo: Dar al-Watha'iq al-Qawmiyya.

Hamid, Shadi. 2014. *Temptations of Power: Islamists and Illiberal Democracy in a New Middle East*. Oxford: Oxford University Press.

Hammad, Walid. 1997. "Islamists and Charitable Work in Jordan: The Muslim Brotherhood as a Model." In *Islamic Movements in Jordan*, edited by Hani Hourani and Jillian Schwedler, 169–94. Amman: Markaz al-Urdun al-Jadid.

Harmsen, Egbert. 2008. *Islam, Civil Society and Social Work: Muslim Voluntary Welfare Associations in Jordan between Patronage and Empowerment*. Amsterdam: Amsterdam University Press.

Harrigan, Jane, and Hamed El-Said. 2009. *Economic Liberalisation, Social Capital and Islamic Welfare Provision*. New York: Palgrave.

Harvey, David. 2006. *Spaces of Global Capitalism*. New York: Verso.

Hassan, Mazen. 2013. "Elections of the People's Assembly, Egypt 2011/12." *Electoral Studies* 32 (2): 370–74.

Haykal, Muhammad Hasanayn. 1983. *Autumn of Fury: The Assassination of Sadat*. New York: Random House.

Heydemann, Steven. 2004. *Networks of Privilege in the Middle East: The Politics of Economic Reform Revisited*. New York: Palgrave Macmillan.

Hibou, Béatrice. 2006. "Domination & Control in Tunisia: Economic Levers for the Exercise of Authoritarian Power." *Review of African Political Economy* 33 (108): 185–206.

Hicken, Allen. 2011. "Clientelism." *Annual Review of Political Science* 14:289–310.

Hicks, Raymond, and Dustin Tingley. 2011. "Causal Mediation Analysis." *Stata Journal* 11 (4): 605–19.

Hilal, 'Ali al-Din. 1987. *Intikhabat Majlis al-Sha'b 1984: Dirasa Wa-Tahlil* [The 1984 lower house elections: Study and analysis]. Cairo: Markaz al-Ahram li-l-Dirasat al-Istratijiyya wa-l-Siyasiyya.

Hinnebusch, Raymond. 1988. *Egyptian Politics under Sadat: The Post-Populist Development of an Authoritarian Modernizing State*. Boulder, CO: Lynne Rienner.

Hirschman, Albert O. 1970. *Exit, Voice, and Loyalty: Responses to Decline in Firms, Organizations, and States*. Cambridge, MA: Harvard University Press.

Hirst, David, and Irene Beeson. 1981. *Sadat*. New York: Faber and Faber.

Hishmat, Gamal. 2011. *Tazwir al-Irada: Jarimat al-Dawla Wa-Tajribat Na'ib* [Falsification of (the people's) will: The crimes of the state and a parliamentary deputy's experience]. Gharbiyya, Egypt: Dar al-Bashir li-l-Thaqafa wa-l-'Ulum.

Howard, Marc Morjé. 2003. *The Weakness of Civil Society in Post-Communist Europe*. Cambridge: Cambridge University Press.

Huber, Evelyne, Thomas Mustillo, and John D. Stephens. 2008. "Politics and Social Spending in Latin America." *Journal of Politics* 70 (2): 420–36.

Huddy, Leonie, and Nayda Terkildsen. 1993. "Gender Stereotypes and the Perception of Male and Female Candidates." *American Journal of Political Science* 37 (1): 119–47.

Huntington, Samuel P. 1968. *Political Order in Changing Societies*. New Haven, CT: Yale University Press.

Hwang, Julie Chernov. 2012. *Peaceful Islamist Mobilization in the Muslim World: What Went Right*. New York: Palgrave Macmillan.

Ibrahim, Saad Eddin. 1988. "Egypt's Islamic Activism in the 1980s." *Third World Quarterly* 10 (2): 632–57.

———. 1997. *An Assessment of Grass Roots Participation in the Development of Egypt*. Cairo: American University in Cairo Press.

———. 1998. *Egyptian Law 32 on Private Sector Organizations: A Critical Assessment*. Cairo: Center for Political and Strategic Studies.

Imai, Kosuke, Luke Keele, Dustin Tingley, and Teppei Yamamoto. 2011. "Unpacking the Black Box of Causality: Learning about Causal Mechanisms from Experimental and Observational Studies." *American Political Science Review* 105 (4): 765–89.

Imai, Kosuke, Luke Keele, and Teppei Yamamoto. 2010. "Identification, Inference and Sensitivity Analysis for Causal Mediation Effects." *Statistical Science* 25 (1): 51–71.

'Isa, Salih. 1977. "Al-Ikhwan al-Muslimun: Ma'sat al-Madi Wa-Mushkilat al-Mustaqbal [The Muslim Brotherhood: The tragedy of the past and problem of the future]." Introduction to the translated version of Richard Mitchell's *The Society of the Muslim Brothers*, 3–50. Cairo: Madbuli.

Ismail, Salwa. 2006. *Political Life in Cairo's New Quarters: Encountering the Everyday State*. Minneapolis: University of Minnesota Press.

Jain, Anita, Samiran Nundy, and Kamran Abbasi. 2014. "Corruption: Medicine's Dirty Open Secret." *British Medical Journal* 348:4184.

Jamal, Amaney A. 2009. *Barriers to Democracy: The Other Side of Social Capital in Palestine and the Arab World*. Princeton, NJ: Princeton University Press.

al-Jam'iyya, al-Shar'iyya. n.d. *Al-Jam'iyya al-Shar'iyya al-Ra'isiyya: al-Da'wa, al-'Amal al-Salih, al-Ighatha, al-Tanmiya* [Al-Jam'iyya al-Shar'iyya: Proselytizing, welfare work, relief efforts, and development]. Pamphlet.

Jann, Ben. 2014. "Plotting Regression Coefficients and Other Estimates in Stata." *Stata Journal* 14 (4): 708–37.

Kalyvas, Stathis N. 1996. *The Rise of Christian Democracy in Europe*. Ithaca, NY: Cornell University Press.

Kandil, Hazem. 2012. *Soldiers, Spies, and Statesmen: Egypt's Road to Revolt*. Verso Books.

———. 2014. *Inside the Brotherhood*. New York: John Wiley.

Kassem, Maye. 1999. *In the Guise of Democracy: Governance in Contemporary Egypt*. Reading, UK: Ithaca Press.

Kefaya Movement. 2006. *Corruption in Egypt: A Dark Cloud That Does Not Vanish*. http://big.assets.huffingtonpost.com/Kefayafasad.doc.

Kepel, Gilles. 2003. *Muslim Extremism in Egypt: The Prophet and Pharaoh*. Berkeley: University of California Press.

Ketchley, Neil. 2017. *Egypt in a Time of Revolution*. Cambridge: Cambridge University Press.

Kienle, Eberhard. 1998. "More Than a Response to Islamism: The Political Deliberalization of Egypt in the 1990s." *Middle East Journal* 52 (2): 219–35.

———. 2001. *A Grand Delusion: Democracy and Economic Reform in Egypt*. London: I.B. Tauris.

———. 2004. "Reconciling Privilege and Reform: Fiscal Policy in Egypt, 1991–2000." In *Networks of Privilege in the Middle East: The Politics of Economic Reform Revisited*, edited by Steven Heydemann, 281–96. New York: Palgrave.

King, Stephen Juan. 2009. *The New Authoritarianism in the Middle East and North Africa*. Bloomington: Indiana University Press.

Kitschelt, Herbert 1986. "Political Opportunity Structures and Political Protest: Anti-Nuclear Movements in Four Democracies." *British Journal of Political Science* 16 (1): 57–85.

——. 2000. "Linkages between Citizens and Politicians in Democratic Polities." *Comparative Political Studies* 33 (6–7): 845–79.

Kitschelt, Herbert, and Daniel M. Kselman. 2013. "Economic Development, Democratic Experience, and Political Parties' Linkage Strategies." *Comparative Political Studies* 46 (11): 1453–84.

Kitschelt, Herbert, and Steven I. Wilkinson. 2007a. "Citizen-Politician Linkages: An Introduction." In *Patrons, Clients and Policies: Patterns of Democratic Accountability and Political Competition*, edited by Herbert Kitschelt and Steven I. Wilkinson, 1–49. Cambridge: Cambridge University Press.

——, eds. 2007b. *Patrons, Clients and Policies: Patterns of Democratic Accountability and Political Competition*. Cambridge: Cambridge University Press.

Kocher, Matthew, and David Laitin. 2006. "On Tarrow's Space." *APSA-CP Newsletter* 16 (2): 8–18.

Kuran, Timur. "Now Out of Never: The Element of Surprise in the East European Revolution of 1989." *World Politics* 44 (1): 7-48.

Lacroix, Stéphane. 2012. *Sheikhs and Politicians: Inside the New Egyptian Salafism*. Washington, DC/ Doha: Brookings Doha Center Policy Briefing.

Lawson, Chappell, and Kenneth F. Greene. 2014. "Making Clientelism Work: How Norms of Reciprocity Increase Voter Compliance." *Comparative Politics* 47 (1): 61–85.

LeBas, Adrienne. 2011. *From Protest to Parties: Party-Building and Democratization in Africa*. Oxford: Oxford University Press.

Lenz, Gabriel S. 2009. "Learning and Opinion Change, Not Priming: Reconsidering the Priming Hypothesis." *American Journal of Political Science* 53 (4): 821–37.

Levitsky, Steven. 2003. *Transforming Labor-Based Parties in Latin America: Argentine Peronism in Comparative Perspective*. Cambridge: Cambridge University Press.

Levitsky, Steven, and Lucan A. Way. 2010. *Competitive Authoritarianism: Hybrid Regimes after the Cold War*. Cambridge: Cambridge University Press.

Lewis, Maureen. 2007. "Informal Payments and the Financing of Health Care in Developing and Transition Countries." *Health Affairs* 26 (4): 984–97.

Lindbeck, Assar, and Jörgen W. Weibull. 1987. "Balanced-Budget Redistribution as the Outcome of Political Competition." *Public Choice* 52 (3): 273–97.

Linz, Juan J. 1975. "Totalitarian and Authoritarian Regimes." In *Handbook of Political Science*. Vol. 3, *Macropolitical Theory*, edited by Nathan Polsby and Fred Greenstein, 175–411. Boston: Addison Wesley.

Lust, Ellen. 2009. "Competitive Clientelism in the Middle East." *Journal of Democracy* 20 (3): 122–35.

Lust-Okar, Ellen. 2005. *Structuring Conflict in the Arab World: Incumbents, Opponents, and Institutions*. Cambridge: Cambridge University Press.

Magaloni, Beatriz. 2006. *Voting for Autocracy: Hegemonic Party Survival and Its Demise in Mexico*. Cambridge: Cambridge University Press.

Maguire, Diarmuid. 1995. "Opposition Movements and Opposition Parties: Equal Partners or Dependent Relations in the Struggle for Power and Reform?" In *The Politics of Social Protest: Comparative Perspectives on States and Social Movements*, edited by J. Craig Jenkins and Bert Klandermans, 199–228. Minneapolis: University of Minnesota Press.

Mahdavi, Paasha. 2015. "Explaining the Oil Advantage: Effects of Natural Resource Wealth on Incumbent Reelection in Iran." *World Politics* 67 (2): 226–67.

el-Mahdi, Rabab. 2008. "'Ummal al-Mahalla: Intilaq Haraka 'Ummaliyya Jadida" [The Workers of Mahalla: The launch of a new worker's movement]. In *'Awdat al-Siyasa: al-Harakat al-Ihtijajiyya al-Jadida Fi Misr* [The return of politics: The new protest movements in Egypt], edited by Dina Shehata, 45–69. Cairo: Al-Ahram Center for Political and Strategic Studies.

Mahoney, James. 2000. "Path Dependence in Historical Sociology." *Theory and Society* 29 (4): 507–48.

Mahoney, James, and Kathleen Thelen. 2010. "A Theory of Gradual Institutional Change." In *Explaining Institutional Change: Ambiguity, Agency, and Power*, edited by James Mahoney and Kathleen Thelen, 1–37. Cambridge: Cambridge University Press.

Mainwaring, Scott. 2003. "Party Objectives in Authoritarian Regimes with Elections or Fragile Democracies: A Dual Game." In *Christian Democracy in Latin America: Electoral Competition and Regime Conflicts*, edited by Scott Mainwaring and Timothy Scully, 3–29. Stanford: Stanford University Press.

Majlis al-Sha'b. 1990. *Al-Qanun Raqm 206 Li-l-Sana 1990* [Law No. 206 for 1990]. Cairo: Al-Amiriyya.

Maligi, al-Sayyid 'Abd al-Sattar. 2009. *Tajribati Ma'a al-Ikhwan: Min al-Da'wa ila al-Tanzim al-Sirri* [My experience with the Muslim Brotherhood: From the Islamic call to the secret organization]. Cairo: Al-Zahra' li-l-'Alam al-'Arabi.

Malt, Ahmad al-. 1993. *Risalati Ila al-Shabab* [My message to the youth]. Tanta, Egypt: Dar al-Bashir al-Thaqafa wa-l-'Ulum al-Islamiyya.

——. 1998. "Dr. Ahmad al-Malt: Na'ib al-Murshid al-'Am Li-l-Ikhwan al-Muslimin" [Dr. Ahmad al-Malt: Deputy general guide of the Muslim Brotherhood]. In *Al-Haraka al-Islamiyya: Ru'ya Min al-Dakhil* [The Islamic movement: A view from the inside], edited by al-Sayyid Abu Da'ud, 127–36. Cairo: Dar al-Nasr li-l-Tiba'a al-Islamiyya.

Masoud, Tarek. 2008. "Why Islam Wins: Electoral Ecologies and Economies of Political Islam in Contemporary Egypt." PhD diss., Yale University.

——. 2014a. *Counting Islam: Religion, Class, and Elections in Egypt*. Cambridge: Cambridge University Press.

——. 2014b. "What's the Matter with Cairo? Religion, Class, and Elections after the Arab Spring." Unpublished manuscript.

McAdam, Doug. 1986. "Recruitment to High-Risk Activism: The Case of Freedom Summer." *American Journal of Sociology* 92 (1): 64–90.

McAdam, Doug, and Sidney Tarrow. 2010. "Ballots and Barricades: On the Reciprocal Relationship between Elections and Social Movements." *Perspectives on Politics* 8 (2): 529–42.

McDermott, Rose. 2011. "Internal and External Validity." In *The Cambridge Handbook of Experimental Political Science*, edited by James N. Drukman, Donald P. Green, James H. Kuklinski, and Arthur Lupia, 27–40. Cambridge: Cambridge University Press.

McGraw, Katherine M. 2003. "Political Impressions: Formation and Management." In *The Oxford Handbook of Political Psychology*, edited by David O. Sears, Leonie Huddy, and Robert Jervis, 394–432. Oxford: Oxford University Press.

McMann, Kelly M. 2006. *Economic Autonomy and Democracy: Hybrid Regimes in Russia and Kyrgyzstan*. Cambridge: Cambridge University Press.

Mecham, Quinn. 2014. "Islamist Parties as Strategic Actors: Electoral Participation and Its Consequences." In *Islamist Parties and Political Normalization in the Muslim World*, edited by Quinn Mecham and Julie Chernov Hwang, 17–39. Philadelphia: University of Pennsylvania Press.

——. 2017. *Institutional Origins of Islamist Political Mobilization*. Cambridge: Cambridge University Press.

Mecham, Quinn, and Julie Chernov Hwang. 2014a. "The Emergence and Development of Islamist Political Parties." In Mecham and Hwang, *Islamist Parties and Political Normalization*, 1–16.

——. 2014b. "The New Dynamism of Islamist Parties." In Mecham and Hwang, *Islamist Parties and Political Normalization*, 175–91.

Menza, Mohamed Fahmy. 2012. "Neoliberal Reform and Socio-Structural Reconfiguration in Cairo's Popular Quarters: The Rise of the Lesser Notables in Misr Al Qadima." *Mediterranean Politics* 17 (3): 322–39.

Menza, Mohamed Fahmy. 2013. *Patronage Politics in Egypt: The National Democratic Party and the Muslim Brotherhood in Cairo*. London: Routledge.

Michels, Robert. (1915) 1966. *Political Parties: A Sociological Study of the Oligarchical Tendencies of Modern Democracy*. Reprint, New York: Free Press. Citations refer to the 1966 edition.

Mitchell, Richard. 1987. "The Islamic Movement: Its Current Condition and Future Prospects." In *The Islamic Impulse*, edited by Barbara Freyer Stowasser, 75–86. Washington, DC: Taylor & Francis.

Mittermaier, Amira. 2014. "Beyond Compassion: Islamic Voluntarism in Egypt." *American Ethnologist* 41 (3): 518–31.

Momani, Bessma. 2005. *IMF-Egyptian Debt Negotiations*. Cairo: American University in Cairo Press.

Moore, Clement Henry. 1980. *Images of Development: Egyptian Engineers in Search of Industry*. Cambridge, MA: MIT Press.

Morsy, Soheir A. 1988. "Islamic Clinics in Egypt: The Cultural Elaboration of Biomedical Hegemony." *Medical Anthropology Quarterly* 2 (4): 355–69.

Moustafa, Tamir. 2007. *The Struggle for Constitutional Power: Law, Politics, and Economic Development in Egypt*. Cambridge: Cambridge University Press.

Mubarak, Hisham. 1995. *Al-Irhabiyun Qadimun! Dirasa Muqarana Bayn Mawqif al-Ikhwan al-Muslimin Wa Jamaʿat al-Jihad Min Qidayat al-ʿUnf (1928–1994)* [The terrorists are coming! Comparative study of the positions of the Muslim Brotherhood and the Jihad Organization on the issue of violence (1928–1994)]. Cairo: Markaz al-Mahrousa li-l-Nashr wa al-Khidmat al-Sahafiyya wa-l-Maʿlumat.

Mujani, Saiful, and R. William Liddle. 2009. "Muslim Indonesia's Secular Democracy." *Asian Survey* 49 (4): 575–90.

Munson, Ziad. 2001. "Islamic Mobilization: A Social Movement Theory Approach." *Sociological Quarterly* 42 (4): 487–510.

Mutz, Diana C. 2011. *Population-Based Survey Experiments*. Princeton: Princeton University Press.

Naggar, Ahmad El-Sayed el-. 2009. "Economic Policy: From State Control to Decay and Corruption." In *Egypt: Moment of Change*, edited by Rabab El-Mahdi and Philip Marfleet, 34–50. London: Zed Books.

Naguib, Sameh. 2009. "Islamism(s) Old and New." In Mahdi and Marfleet, *Egypt*, 103–19.

Nandakumar, A. K., Mukesh Chawla, and Maryam Khan. 2000. "Utilization of Outpatient Care in Egypt and Its Implications for the Role of Government in Health Care Provision." *World Development* 28 (1): 187–96.

Nasir, Gamal ʿAbd al-. 1954. "The Egyptian Revolution." *Foreign Affairs* 33 (2): 199–211.

Nasira, Hani. 2003. "Al-Jamʿiyyat al-Khayriyya Wa-l-Insaniyya al-Islamiyya Fi Misr: Dirasa Nazariyya Wa-Midaniyya" [Islamic charitable associations in Egypt: Theoretical and field study]. Paper presented at the Conference on Charitable and Civil Societies, Paris.

Nelson, Thomas E., and Donald R. Kinder. 1996. "Issue Frames and Group-Centrism in American Public Opinion." *Journal of Politics* 58 (4): 1055–78.

Nichter, Simeon. 2008. "Vote Buying or Turnout Buying? Machine Politics and the Secret Ballot." *American Political Science Review* 102 (1): 19–31.

O'Donnell, Guillermo, and Philippe C. Schmitter. 1986. *Transitions from Authoritarian Rule: Tentative Conclusions about Uncertain Democracies.* Baltimore: Johns Hopkins University Press.

Ottaway, Marina. 2003. *Democracy Challenged: The Rise of Semi-Authoritarianism.* Washington, DC: Carnegie Endowment for International Peace.

Ottaway, Marina, and Amr Hamzawy. 2007. "Fighting on Two Fronts: Secular Parties in the Arab World." Washington, DC: Carnegie Endowment for International Peace.

Ouda, Gihad, Negad El-Borai, and Hafez Abu Seʿada. 2001. *A Door onto the Desert: The Egyptian Parliamentary Elections of 2000, Course, Dilemmas, and Recommendations for the Future.* Cairo: The United Group/ Freidrich Neumann Foundation.

Pepinsky, Thomas B. 2009. *Economic Crises and the Breakdown of Authoritarian Regimes: Indonesia and Malaysia in Comparative Perspective.* Cambridge: Cambridge University Press.

——. 2014. "Political Islam and the Limits of the Indonesian Model." *Taiwan Journal of Democracy* 10 (1): 105–21.

Pepinsky, Thomas B., R. William Liddle, and Saiful Mujani. 2012. "Testing Islam's Political Advantage: Evidence from Indonesia." *American Journal of Political Science* 56 (3): 584–600.

Pierret, Thomas, and Kjetil Selvik. 2009. "Limits of 'Authoritarian Upgrading' in Syria: Private Welfare, Islamic Charities, and the Rise of the Zayd Movement." *International Journal of Middle East Studies* 41 (4): 595–614.

Pierson, Paul, and Theda Skocpol. 2002. "Historical Institutionalism in Contemporary Political Science." In *Political Science: The State of the Discipline*, edited by Ira Katznelson and Helen V. Milner, 693–721. New York: Norton.

Pioppi, Daniela. 2004. *From Religious Charity to the Welfare State and Back: The Case of Islamic Endowments (Waqfs) Revival in Egypt.* Florence, It.: Robert Schuman Centre for Advanced Studies, European University Institute.

Powell, Robert. 2006. "War as a Commitment Problem." *International Organization* 60 (1): 169–203.

Pratt, Nicola. 2005. "Hegemony and Counter-Hegemony in Egypt: Advocacy NGOs, Civil Society, and the State." In *NGOs and Governance in the Arab World*, edited by Sarah Ben Néfissa and Carlos Milani, 123–50. Cairo: American University in Cairo Press.

Przeworski, Adam. 1991. *Democracy and the Market: Political and Economic Reforms in Eastern Europe and Latin America.* Cambridge: Cambridge University Press.

Putnam, Robert D. 1994. *Making Democracy Work: Civic Traditions in Modern Italy.* Princeton: Princeton University Press.

Radi, Muhsin. 1990. *Al-Ikhwan al-Muslimun taht Qubbat al-Barlaman* [The Muslim Brotherhood under the dome of parliament]. Cairo: Dar al-Tawziʿ wa-l-Nashr al-Islamiyya.

Richards, Alan. 1991. "The Political Economy of Dilatory Reform: Egypt in the 1980s." *World Development* 19 (12): 1721–30.

Robinson, Glenn E. 1998. "Defensive Democratization in Jordan." *International Journal of Middle East Studies* 30 (3): 387–410.

Rock-Singer, Aaron. 2016. "Guiding the Pious to Practice: Islamic Magazines and Revival in Egypt, 1976–1981." PhD diss., Princeton University.

Rock-Singer, Aaron, and Steven Brooke. 2018. "We Read It for the Ads: *Al-Da'wa*, Commercial Advertising, and Social Change in al-Sadat's Egypt." Unpublished manuscript.

Rougier, Bernard, and Hala Bayoumi. 2016. "The Egyptian Vote in the 2011–2013 Sequence." In *Egypt's Revolutions*, edited by Bernard Rougier and Stéphane Lacroix, 139–59. New York: Palgrave Macmillan.

Rubin, Barry. 1990. *Islamic Fundamentalism in Egyptian Politics*. New York: Palgrave Macmillan.

Rustow, Dankwart A. 1970. "Transitions to Democracy: Toward a Dynamic Model." *Comparative Politics* 2 (3): 337–63.

Sadat, Anwar al-. 1974. October working paper. Cairo: Ministry of Information, State Information Service.

——. 1977. Address by President Anwar al-Sadat on Laying down the Foundation Stone of the St. Mark Hospital, October 11, 1977. Cairo: State Information Service.

——. 1978. "Address to the Conference of Private Institutions and Societies, May 9, 1978." In *Speeches and Interviews of President Muhammad Anwar al-Sadat*, 359–63. Cairo: State Information Service.

——. 1981. *In Search of Identity*. New York: Harper/Colophon Books.

Sahn, David E., and David Stifel. 2003. "Exploring Alternative Measures of Welfare in the Absence of Expenditure Data." *Review of Income and Wealth* 49 (4): 463–89.

Sami, Nasr al-Din 'Abd al-. 1991. "Al-Kharita al-Intikhabiyya" [The electoral map]. In *Intikhabat Majlis al-Sha'b 1990: Dirasa Wa-Tahlil* [People's Assembly elections 1990: Study and analysis], edited by 'Ali al-Din Hilal and Usama al-Ghazali Harb, 15–56. Cairo: Markaz al-Ahram li-l-Dirasat al-Istratijiyya wa-l-Siyasiyya.

Sayed, Nasr M. el-, Peter John Gomatos, Consuelo M. Beck-Sagué, Ursula Dietrich, Hagen Von Briesen, Saladin Osmanov, José Esparza, Ray R. Arthur, Mohammed H. Wahdan, and William R. Jarvis. 2000. "Epidemic Transmission of Human Immunodeficiency Virus in Renal Dialysis Centers in Egypt." *Journal of Infectious Diseases* 181 (1): 91–97.

Schady, Norbert R. 2000. "The Political Economy of Expenditures by the Peruvian Social Fund (FONCODES), 1991–1995." *American Political Science Review* 94 (2): 289–304.

Scheiner, Ethan. 2006. *Democracy without Competition in Japan: Opposition Failure in a One-Party Dominant State*. Cambridge: Cambridge University Press.

Schmitter, Philippe. 1979. "Still the Century of Corporatism?" In *Trends toward Corporatist Intermediation*, edited by Phillippe Schmitter and Gerhard Lehmbruch, 7–52. Thousand Oaks, CA: Sage.

Schwedler, Jillian. 2006. *Faith in Moderation: Islamist Parties in Jordan and Yemen*. Cambridge: Cambridge University Press.

Seddon, David. 1993. "Austerity Protests in Response to Economic Liberalization in the Middle East." In *Economic and Political Liberalisation in the Middle East*, edited by Tim Niblock and Emma Murphy, 88–113. London: I.B. Tauris.

Shadish, William R., Thomas D. Cook, and Donald Thomas Campbell. 2002. *Experimental and Quasi-Experimental Designs for Generalized Causal Inference*. Wadsworth Cengage.

Shammakh, 'Amir. 2011. *Al-Waqa'i' al-Ikhwaniyya: Rasad Tarikhi Li-Ahamm Ahdath Allati Marrat Biha Jam'iyyat al-Ikhwan al-Muslimin* [Ikhwan facts:

Documentary study of the most important events in the history of the Brotherhood]. Cairo: Dar al-Tawzi' wa-l-Nashr al-Islamiyya.

Shehata, Samer. 2008. "Inside an Egyptian Parliamentary Campaign." In *Political Participation in the Middle East*, edited by Ellen Lust-Okar and Saloua Zerhouni, 95–110. Boulder, CO: Lynne Rienner.

Shehata, Samer, and Joshua Stacher. 2006. "The Brotherhood Goes to Parliament." *Middle East Report* 36 (240): 32–39.

Shukr, 'Abd al-Ghaffar. 2006. "Al-Muqaddima" [Introduction]" In *Al-Jam'iyyat al-Ahliyya al-Islamiyya Fi Misr* [Islamic Civil Associations in Egypt], edited by 'Abd al-Ghaffar Shukr, 1–42. Cairo: Markaz al-Buhuth al-Arabiyya.

Shukri, Ghali. 1981. *Egypt: Portrait of a President, 1971–1981*. London: Zed Press.

Sidel, John T. 2014. "Economic Foundations of Subnational Authoritarianism: Insights and Evidence from Qualitative and Quantitative Research." *Democratization* 21 (1): 161–84.

Simmons, Beth A., and Daniel J. Hopkins. 2005. "The Constraining Power of International Treaties: Theory and Methods." *American Political Science Review* 99 (4): 623–31.

Simpser, Alberto. 2013. *Why Governments and Parties Manipulate Elections: Theory, Practice, and Implications*. Cambridge: Cambridge University Press.

Singer, Matthew, and Herbert Kitschelt. 2011. "'Do Everything' (DoE) Parties: When Can Politicians Combine Clientelistic and Programmatic Appeals?" Unpublished manuscript.

Singerman, Diane. 1996. *Avenues of Participation: Family, Politics, and Networks in Urban Quarters of Cairo*. Princeton, NJ: Princeton University Press.

Siyam, 'Imad. 2006. "Al-Haraka al-Islamiyya Wa-l-Jam'iyyat al-Ahliyya Fi Misr" [The Islamic movement and civic associations in Egypt]. In *Al-Jam'iyyat al-Ahliyya al-Islamiyya Fi Misr* [Islamic civil associations in Egypt], edited by 'Abd al-Ghaffar Shukr, 73–150. Cairo: Markaz al-Buhuth al-Arabiyya.

Skocpol, Theda. 1979. *States and Social Revolutions: A Comparative Analysis of France, Russia and China*. Cambridge: Cambridge University Press.

Skovgaard-Petersen, Jakob. 1997. *Defining Islam for the Egyptian State: Muftis and Fatwas of the Dar al-Ifta*. Leiden, Neth.: Brill.

Sniderman, Paul M., and James Piazza. 1995. *The Scar of Race*. Cambridge, MA: Harvard University Press.

Snyder, Richard. 2001. "Scaling Down: The Subnational Comparative Method." *Studies in Comparative International Development* 36 (1): 93–110.

Soliman, Samer. 2006. *Al-Musharaka al-Siyasiyya Fi Intikhabat al-Niyabiyya 2005: Al-'Awaiq Wa-l-Mutatallabat* [Political participation in the 2005 Egyptian parliament elections: Constraints and demands]. Cairo: Al-Jam'iyya al-Misriyya li-l-Nuhud bi-l-Musharaka al-Mujtamaiyya/ European Union.

——. 2011. *The Autumn of Dictatorship: Fiscal Crisis and Political Change in Egypt under Mubarak*. Stanford: Stanford University Press.

Spires, Anthony J. 2011. "Contingent Symbiosis and Civil Society in an Authoritarian State: Understanding the Survival of China's Grassroots NGOs." *American Journal of Sociology* 117 (1): 1–45.

Springborg, Robert. 1979. "Sayed Bey Marei and Political Clientelism in Egypt." *Comparative Political Studies* 12 (3): 259–88.

——. 1989. *Mubarak's Egypt: Fragmentation of the Political Order*. Boulder, CO: Westview Press.

Stacher, Joshua. 2004. "Parties Over: The Demise of Egypt's Opposition Parties." *British Journal of Middle Eastern Studies* 31 (2): 215–33.

——. 2006. "Damanhour by Hook and by Crook." *Middle East Report* 238:26–27.

———. 2012a. *Adaptable Autocrats: Regime Power in Egypt and Syria*. Stanford: Stanford University Press.

———. 2012b. "Egypt." In *Countries at the Crossroads 2011: An Analysis of Democratic Governance*, edited by Jake Dizard, Christopher Walker, and Vanessa Tucker, 199–218. Lanham, MD: Rowman & Littlefield.

Staniland, Paul. 2012. "Organizing Insurgency: Networks, Resources, and Rebellion in South Asia." *International Security* 37 (1): 142–77.

Stepan, Alfred C. 1988. *Rethinking Military Politics: Brazil and the Southern Cone*. Princeton: Princeton University Press.

Stokes, Donald E. 1963. "Spatial Models of Party Competition." *American Political Science Review* 57 (2): 368–77.

Stokes, Susan C. 2005. "Perverse Accountability: A Formal Model of Machine Politics with Evidence from Argentina." *American Political Science Review* 99 (3): 315–25.

Stokes, Susan C., Thad Dunning, Marcelo Nazareno, and Valeria Brusco. 2013. *Brokers, Voters, and Clientelism: The Puzzle of Distributive Politics*. Cambridge: Cambridge University Press.

Stork, Joe. 1989. "Political Aspects of Health." *Middle East Report* 161:4–10, 53.

Sullivan, Denis J. 1994. *Private Voluntary Organizations in Egypt: Islamic Development, Private Initiative, and State Control*. Gainesville: University Press of Florida.

Sullivan, Denis J., and Sana Abed-Kotob. 1999. *Islam in Contemporary Egypt: Civil Society vs. the State*. Boulder, CO: Lynne Rienner.

Svolik, Milan W. 2012. *The Politics of Authoritarian Rule*. Cambridge: Cambridge University Press.

Szwarcberg, Mariela. 2015. *Mobilizing Poor Voters: Machine Politics, Clientelism, and Social Networks in Argentina*. Cambridge: Cambridge University Press.

Tadros, Mariz. 2006. "State Welfare in Egypt since Adjustment: Hegemonic Control with a Minimalist Role." *Review of African Political Economy* 33 (108): 237–54.

———. 2011. "The Securitisation of Civil Society: A Case Study of NGOs–State Security Investigations (SSI) Relations in Egypt." *Conflict, Security & Development* 11 (1): 79–103.

———. 2012. *The Muslim Brotherhood in Contemporary Egypt: Democracy Redefined or Confined?* New York: Routledge.

Tahir, Ahmad Muhammad al-. 2006. *Jama'at Ansar al-Sunna al-Muhammadiyya: Nash'atuha, Ahdafuha, Manhajuha, Juhuduha* [The Ansar al-Sunna al-Muhammadiyya group: Their formation, goals, method, and efforts]. Cairo: Ansar al-Sunna.

Talhami, Ghada Hashem. 2001. "Whither the Social Network of Islam." *Muslim World* 91 (3–4): 311–24.

Tammam, Husam. 2009. "A Reading of the Media Performance of the Muslim Brotherhood in the 2005 Parliamentary Elections: A Case Study of the City of Alexandria." In *The Middle East in the Media*, edited by Arnim Heinemann, Olfa Lamloun, and Anne Françoise Weber, 195–210. London: Saqi.

———. 2012. *Al-Ikhwan al-Muslimun: Sanawat Ma Qabl al-Thawra* [The Muslim Brotherhood: the prerevolutionary years]. Cairo: Dar al-Shuruq.

Tarouty, Safinaz el-. 2015. *Businessmen, Clientelism, and Authoritarianism in Egypt*. New York: Palgrave Macmillan.

Tarrow, Sidney G. 2011. *Power in Movement: Social Movements and Contentious Politics*. Cambridge: Cambridge University Press.

Tezcür, Günes Murat. 2010. *The Paradox of Moderation: Muslim Reformers in Iran and Turkey*. Austin: University of Texas Press.

Thachil, Tariq. 2011. "Embedded Mobilization." *World Politics* 63 (3): 434–69.

——. 2014a. *Elite Parties, Poor Voters: How Social Services Win Votes in India*. Cambridge: Cambridge University Press.

——. 2014b. "Elite Parties and Poor Voters: Theory and Evidence from India." *American Political Science Review* 108 (2): 454–77.

Thelen, Kathleen, and Sven Steinmo. 1992. "Historical Institutionalism in Comparative Politics." In *Structuring Politics: Historical Institutionalism in Comparative Analysis*, edited by Sven Steinmo, Kathleen Thelen, and Frank Longstreth, 1–32. Cambridge: Cambridge University Press.

Trager, Eric. 2011. "The Unbreakable Muslim Brotherhood." *Foreign Affairs* 90 (5): 114–26.

——. 2016. *Arab Fall: How the Muslim Brotherhood Won and Lost Egypt in 891 Days*. Washington, DC: Georgetown University Press.

Tuğal, Cihan. 2013. "Contesting Benevolence: Market Orientations among Muslim Aid Providers in Egypt." *Qualitative Sociology* 36 (2): 141–59.

Van Cott, Donna Lee. 2005. *From Movements to Parties in Latin America: The Evolution of Ethnic Politics*. Cambridge: Cambridge University Press.

Van de Walle, Nicolas. 2006. "Tipping Games: When Do Opposition Parties Coalesce?" In *Electoral Authoritarianism: The Dynamics of Unfree Competition*, edited by Andreas Schedler, 77–94. Boulder, CO: Lynne Rienner

Van Evera, Stephen. 1997. *Guide to Methods for Students of Political Science*. Ithaca, NY: Cornell University Press.

Vandewalle, Dirk. 1992. "Ben Ali's New Era: Pluralism and Economic Privatization in Tunisia." In *The Politics of Economic Reform in the Middle East*, edited by Henri J. Barkey, 105–26. New York: St. Martin's.

Vannetzel, Marie. 2016. "Confronting the Transition to Legality." In *Egypt's Revolutions*, edited by Bernard Rougier and Stéphane Lacroix, 41–61. New York: Palgrave Macmillan.

Wallace, Jeremy. 2013. "Cities, Redistribution, and Authoritarian Regime Survival." *Journal of Politics* 75 (3): 632–45.

Walton, John K., and David Seddon. 2008. *Free Markets and Food Riots: The Politics of Global Adjustment*. New York: John Wiley.

Wang, Fang. 1994. "The Political Economy of Authoritarian Clientelism in Taiwan." In *Democracy, Clientelism, and Civil Society*, edited by Luis Roniger and Ayse Gunes-Ayata, 181–206. Boulder, CO: Lynne Rienner.

Warren, David H. 2017. "Cleansing the Nation of the 'Dogs of Hell': Ali Juma's Nationalist Legal Reasoning in Support of the 2013 Egyptian Coup and Its Bloody Aftermath." *International Journal of Middle East Studies* 49 (3): 457–77.

Waterbury, John. 1983. *The Egypt of Nasser and Sadat: The Political Economy of Two Regimes*. Princeton: Princeton University Press.

——. 1985. "The Soft State and the Open Door: Egypt's Experience with Economic Liberalization, 1974–1984." *Comparative Politics* 18 (1): 65–83.

Wegner, Eva, and Miquel Pellicer. 2009. "Islamist Moderation without Democratization: The Coming of Age of the Moroccan Party of Justice and Development?" *Democratization* 16 (1): 157–75.

Weitz-Shapiro, Rebecca. 2014. *Curbing Clientelism in Argentina: Politics, Poverty, and Social Policy*. Cambridge: Cambridge University Press.

Wickham, Carrie Rosefsky. 2002. *Mobilizing Islam: Religion, Activism and Political Change in Egypt*. New York: Columbia University Press.

Wiktorowicz, Quintan. 2000. "Civil Society as Social Control: State Power in Jordan." *Comparative Politics* 33 (1): 43–61.

——. 2001. *The Management of Islamic Activism: Salafis, the Muslim Brotherhood, and State Power in Jordan*. Albany: SUNY Press.

——. 2004. *Islamic Activism: A Social Movement Theory Approach*. Bloomington: Indiana University Press.

Wiktorowicz, Quintan, and Suha Taji-Farouki. 2000. "Islamic NGOs and Muslim Politics: A Case from Jordan." *Third World Quarterly* 21 (4): 685–99.

Wilson, Edward O. 1999. *Consilience: The Unity of Knowledge*. New York: Vintage.

Wood, Geof. 1997. "States without Citizens: The Problem of the Franchise State." In *NGOs, States and Donors: Too Close for Comfort*, edited by David Hulme and Michael Edwards, 79–82. New York: St. Martin's.

World Bank. 1991. *Egypt: Alleviating Poverty during Structural Adjustment*. Washington, DC: World Bank.

——. 1993. *The World Development Report 1993: Investing in Health*. Washington, DC: World Bank/Oxford University Press.

——. 2010. *Intensive Learning Implementation Completion and Results Report*. Washington, DC: Health Sector Reform Program Report.

Wyatt, Andrew. 2013. "Combining Clientelist and Programmatic Politics in Tamil Nadu, South India." *Commonwealth & Comparative Politics* 51 (1): 27–55.

Yadav, Stacey Philbrick. 2013. *Islamists and the State: Legitimacy and Institutions in Yemen and Lebanon*. London: IB Tauris.

Yip, Winnie C., and Aniceto Orbeta. 1999. "The Relative Importance of Price and Quality in Consumer Choice of Provider: The Case of Egypt." Working Paper No. 80, Harvard School of Public Health, Cambridge, MA.

Yunus, Muhammad. 2006. "Al-Qarn al-'Ashrin Wa-Juhud al-Harakat al-Da'awiyya Fi Misr" [The twentieth century and the efforts of the Da'wa Movements in Egypt]. PhD diss., University of Karachi.

Zaki, Moheb. 1995. *Civil Society and Democratization in Egypt, 1981–1994*. Cairo: Ibn Khaldun Center for Development Studies.

Zaki, Muhammad Shawqi. 1980. *Al-Ikhwan al-Muslimun Wa-l-Mujtama' al-Misri* [The Muslim Brotherhood and Egyptian society]. Cairo: Dar al-Tawzi' wa-l-Nashr al-Islamiyya.

Zartman, Ira William. 1990. "Opposition as Support of the State." In *The Arab State*, edited by Giacomo Luciani. New York: Routledge, 220–46.

Zawahiri, Ayman al-. 2001. *Fursan Taht Rayat al-Nabi* [Knights under the Prophet's banner]. Al-Furqan Media.

Zayd, Sana' Abu. 2006. *Qiyam Fi Suwar Li-l-Tabib* [Illustrated values of the doctor]. Cairo: Islamic Medical Association.

Zollner, Barbara. 2007. "Prison Talk: The Muslim Brotherhood's Internal Struggle during Gamal Abdel Nasser's Persecution, 1954 to 1971." *International Journal of Middle East Studies* 39 (3): 411–33.

Zubaida, Sami. 1992. "Islam, the State and Democracy: Contrasting Conceptions of Society in Egypt." *Middle East Report* 179:2–10.

Index

Names and terms beginning with al- or El are alphabetized under the main portion of the name (for instance, *al-Da'wa* will be found in the Ds). Page numbers with an italic *t* or *f* appended indicate tables or figures.

9 781501 730627